The American College of Switzerland Zoo

The American College of Switzerland Zoo

Revised Edition

James E. Henderson

Published by Tablo

Table of Contents

Prologue

I started this book one evening while I was taking a course about explosives for my current job. I was sitting in a Spartan dorm room with a glass of wine that I had just carried back from a nearby bar thinking about my son. It was the summer before his senior year in high school, and he had just started college-hunting trips. I began reminiscing about my years in college, especially one year I spent in a small school perched on the side of a mountain in Switzerland. For me, that year was very strange, almost surreal, compared to the life I had led before.

My father was an army colonel, which had made him the black sheep of an Ohio Quaker family. I grew up as an army brat and, before I entered high school, had lived in a dozen different homes, including a few on military bases, in several different states. In a way, the army was my life, too. The only friends I kept longer than a couple of years were army brats whose dads happened to get stationed on the same base.

That's not quite true. My relatives also played an important role in my life. We visited my Quaker grandparents at Christmas and on vacations. My cousins often came in for the holidays, and they were friends that I would keep for life. I can remember eavesdropping on several conversations between my father and his family about how he could justify working in the army despite having been raised to reject war. Voices were never raised, and the dialog included lots of quiet time for listening and attempting to understand each other. However, my impression was that while they listened and accepted, there was little agreement. In fact, my grandmother even stood in protest outside the biological warfare center in Fort Detrick when we were stationed there. Then again, her protesting did not affect the fact that she was nearby, and we picked her up at the line each evening and took her to dinner in Frederick, Maryland.

When I was old enough to start high school, dad found out that we would have to move twice over the next four years so he offered me a chance to attend Olney, a small Quaker boarding school in Ohio. It was the school that he, my grandparents, and many other relatives had attended. So, at fourteen, I went to Olney, and spent the next four years with several of my cousins learning about my Quaker roots.

I learned how my father and his parents had kept their cool during their talks as I grew up in this school run by a caring and nurturing staff and surrounded by peaceful rolling hills. Like many students, it took me a while to get used to sitting for an hour in silent meetings for worship, but over the years I found it provided time for inner reflection.

I liked this simple, peaceful life so well that I went to Earlham, a Quaker college in Indiana. The heavy trees and open green areas of the campus also appealed to my love of nature. However, this college took academics to a new level, and I found it difficult to maintain my grades while being involved with the rest of campus life. By spring term, I was on academic probation and spent all my waking hours on my studies.

Then, in 1966, as my sophomore year approached, my father was offered an assignment in Germany as a reward for his service and to keep him in the army after he was eligible for retirement. To me, it seemed like a great chance to escape my current predicament and to spend a year in Europe. This story begins then as I found myself transported to another continent and in a third reality.

Chapter One

Enter the Prince

At lunch on the second day of classes my new friend Jim Wilds and I were waiting for the food to be served as our buddy Gil walked in with the brown-eyed blonde of the Fab Four – four beautiful blondes that Wilds and I had spotted on our first day on this Alp. The three of us had yet to inspire the slightest interest from them or from the wealthy and arrogant but even lovelier goddesses who seemed to run the girls' dorm. It would be some time before we'd realize that we were in the wrong class and that "class" had nothing to do with history or French.

As we watched Gil, we wondered if his blonde hair and sharp profile had just broken the barrier. He said something to the brown-eyed blonde, and she smiled as she headed to join the other three. Wilds and I sat in silent amazement as Gil walked to our table.

"Have either of you heard about a prince coming today?" Gil asked.

"Do you know that girl?" I asked.

"Who, Dee-Dee? Yeah, she's in my French class," he responded.

I looked at Wilds and asked, "What are we doing wrong?"

Wilds smirked and said, "Maybe we should bleach our hair blonde. What's this about a prince?"

"I don't know. Dee-Dee was talking about how all the girls are getting dolled up for the arrival of the prince, today. I thought maybe one of you had heard something."

From behind me a strong feminine voice with an upstate New York or Vermont accent said, "Some prince is supposed to be comin' in at lunch today. The dorm is in a tizzy!"

I turned to see a slim girl with a very long light-brown ponytail looking at me. She had a square jaw and small, hazel eyes. On second thought, her eyes weren't small; she wasn't wearing the eye makeup that

I was getting used to seeing. In fact, she wasn't wearing any makeup, just a healthy tan and some recent sun on her cheeks. That face took me back to my Quaker boarding school.

"I'm Jim Henderson," I said and held out my hand.

"Kaeti Ecker, pleased to meet ya." She took my hand with amazing strength.

"What's this about a prince?" I asked.

"Don't know any more than that, but it looks like we're going to find out," she said as she looked over my shoulder.

As I turned toward the door, I noticed the out-rush of most of the girls in the room. We followed their lead as I introduced Kaeti to my friends. Kaeti was my height in her flats, and slim to the point of having almost no breasts, just a couple of little bumps under her blouse. She wore slacks that hugged her boy-like hips, and she walked with a lithe stride, pushing, cat-like, off her toes. Her walk reminded me of the gymnasts I had worked with.

"Are you into sports?" I asked as we walked.

"Just wait until there's snow up top and you'll get your answer."

"I guess you're a skier?"

"Love it! You?"

"I played JV soccer for my college last year and gymnastics!" I bragged.

"No, do you ski?"

"Ah, no, – but I can stand on a sled without killing myself."

"So not the same. You just wait!"

We stood at the balcony overlooking the entry foyer awaiting the prince. The Fab Four were properly arranged in the front, and the rich goddesses were toward the back near the steps up to the girls' dorm, where they could be seen but not appear overly impressed.

Wilds asked how to greet the prince. "Should we bow and curtsy?"

"I'm not curtsying!" Kaeti said.

"Don't look at me," I said. "I'm a Quaker. We got sent to prison in England for refusing to use the Royal 'You' with the King."

"Royal who?" Wilds asked.

I explained that in the 1600's commoners used "thee" and "thou" with each other and addressed only the King and royalty as "you." If you said "thee" to the King, you went to jail. Well, the Quakers felt everybody was equal and refused; therefore, they went to jail. Kaeti had a quizzical look on her face when I finished my explanation, but Wilds gave me a goggle-eyed expression that said he had just learned more than he needed to know.

A black limo pulled in front of the school. I wondered briefly how the driver had navigated the curvy narrow road from the valley up to our little village in that large car. Two men in black suits got out. Both looked powerfully built. One came in the front revolving door as the other waited by the car. They were either bodyguards, or the prince was way older than any of the other students. The one inside surveyed the gathered audience and signaled the other, who opened the door of the limo. A tall slim man in a suit got out and walked toward the door. He had collar-length black hair that appeared to hide his face; but as he walked in the door, the truth was revealed. He had very dark skin; our prince was definitely from somewhere in Africa. Everyone stood stunned. Wilds piped, "Wow!" and, without thinking, I said, "Outstanding!" Kaeti punched me in the arm with some force, and the three of us covered our mouths to keep from laughing outright. The effort brought tears to my eyes.

By the time I had cleared the tears, the prince was walking past us, nodding and heading for a specially prepared lunch at the President's table. I couldn't help but stare. His skin was very dark, and his heavy hair was sculpted straight down to his collar on the sides and back, and cut into square bangs over his eyes. His hair looked like Prince Valiant's in the funnies. (Actually, there used to be a TV show with an Indian prince who might be a better comparison, but that guy had beads in his hair.) Once he was in the light, I noticed that the prince was a very handsome guy with dark intense eyes set off by his high cheekbones. He was about six feet tall, lean, and... well, "regal" is the only word for his posture, stride, and manner. He was definitely a prince, only one with a very dark complexion.

While the Fab Four followed his movements with mouths slightly agape, the goddesses managed to keep their cool. I learned later that one girl had fainted from the shock. I felt sure that it was Nonni. I can't imagine her wealthy southern-princess brain being able to cope with an African prince. Likely the only Africans she knew worked in her home and lived on the bad side of Mobile or wherever she was from. For that matter, I don't remember any Blacks in public school in the 1950s. But boarding school and college held a mix of everyone. The Quakers had never known prejudice, and I learned that people were people in spite of skin color or religion. In fact, the Quakers, including several of my ancestors, played a major role in the Underground Railroad. One of my relatives even showed me a hidden room in her house that had been used by escaping slaves.

Wilds, Kaeti, and I rushed outside to burst out laughing and to compare notes on the reactions we had seen. When we broke up, I watched Kaeti's lithe stride as she went back into the building. Her hair was pretty and really caught the sunlight. It wasn't one color but ranged from blonde in places to light brown in others. You could tell that she left it natural. *Nice!* Wilds, noticing my focus, poked at my shoulder with his bony knuckles.

"Hey," I said, "she's female and she talked to us. Beside I kinda like tomboys. If nothing else she could be a good friend in the girls' dorm."

Before heading back inside to lunch, I quickly scanned the mountains across from us. I still couldn't believe that I was in a Swiss college tucked in a notch on the side of a mountain surrounded by these majestic Alps.

Chapter Two

Escaping Vietnam

How had I ended up in Switzerland in this school for the wealthy? Well, during the first term of my freshman year at Earlham College I had tried to do everything, except study, and I was still on academic probation by the end of the year. Then, as summer approached, my lieutenant colonel father received orders for Germany, and I decided to drop out of my college and take a year in school somewhere in Europe. So, at the beginning of that summer in 1966 I found myself on a ship with my parents, sister, and two miniature dachshunds crossing the Atlantic Ocean, learning survival German and international road signs. Our ship, the USNS General Patch, hit the tail of a hurricane; so I also learned how to slow dance on a heaving deck, walk stairs on the down side of the swells, and tie myself off when trying to feed and walk the dogs who were stuck together in a small kennel on the poop deck. I believe that I am using the correct term for that part of the ship, but for me and my sister, the term "poop" was quite literal.

We disembarked in Bremerhaven, and after a mad dash in a taxi from the ship to Customs, I jumped out of the cab and went searching for a bathroom. When I was directed to them, I stood staring at two bathroom signs marked *"Herren"* and *"Damen."* With a "her" in one and "dame" in the other, I wondered which one was the men's room. I thought that my survival German had saved me. I opened the door marked *Herren*, and I saw a cute girl, almost my age, standing at the sinks. Had I not noticed the urinals, I would have retreated immediately. Instead I stood there frozen until she turned, a cleaning cloth in hand, spotted my consternation, giggled, and politely walked out. It took a while to get used to the relative openness of Europeans about toilets, especially the coed toilets in southern Europe. If you men find it

sometimes difficult using the urinal with an overly curious man beside
you, try having an eighteen-year-old girl at the sink smiling and
nodding.

I don't remember much about the journey from Bremerhaven to
Landstuhl, which was to be our home for the next three years. The
autobahns were very similar to highway I-70, which had just been
finished across the farmland of Ohio from my boarding school, through
Columbus, where my favorite uncle and non-Quaker grandmother
lived, and to my college in Indiana. I don't remember the speed on the
autobahns being excessive, but dad was doing all the driving because I
had yet to get my international driver's license.

Our home in Landstuhl was in a converted German military post on
a hill across from a tumbled-down castle, but I didn't have time to get
settled in. A letter waiting for me when we arrived said that if I had not
yet been accepted at a college I needed to report to the nearest draft
board. Did I mention this was 1966, the middle of the Vietnam War? So
my immediate mission was to find a college somewhere in Europe that
taught in English and would accept me quickly and without question!

The Landstuhl newcomer's center said there were three colleges that
fit the bill: the American College of Paris, the University of Maryland
extension in Munich, and the American College of Switzerland. I began
my search using a Eurail pass that would allow me to transfer freely
between trains all across Europe for a month. I hopped on my first train
in Landstuhl and two transfers later I was at my first stop, the American
College of Paris. It had interesting, old buildings in the middle of the left
bank crush. I joined the summer students at a hootenanny and thought
that I could learn to like the school. But it would be very different from
the open, rolling hills of my boarding school or the heavy trees and
greens of my college. The school's admissions office cared little about
my transcripts but let me know the costs and sent me on my way.

Next stop was the University of Maryland extension in Munich.
This school was scary! Something out of a German prison camp story,
complete with stone walls and tiny roads surrounding it like a moat.
Admittedly, the fact that it was across the street from the world famous

Hoffbrau Haus bar had some appeal, but I hadn't learned to care much for beer. I don't remember even going to the admissions office. I just wanted to get far away from there. My next destination was Switzerland.

Perhaps I was more relaxed by the time I began riding the trains from Bavaria toward Lake Geneva because I started to meet people. Before that ride, my only communication had been to ask "where is the train for *.*" in French or German and letting someone point me in the right direction. I wasn't able to talk to anyone on the trains until I shared a cabin with a middle-aged German woman who taught Spanish. My school-learned Spanish flashed back to me, and we had a great time talking about Germany and my travels. She even gave me a short course in German by translating through Spanish. I thought it very odd that the Germans put their verbs at the end of their sentences, instead of after the subject, like in English and Spanish. I told her that I was - to Switzerland – going, – and she told me that I would – Switzerland – love!

When I got on the next train in Basel, Switzerland, every cabin on every car seemed full. I was afraid that I would have to stand until I heard what I thought was Spanish coming from a lively group in one car. I looked in the door, smiled tentatively, and said, *"Hola!"* The cabin was full with what appeared to be one large family: grandmother, two men and two women in their thirties, a teenage girl with long dark hair and a shy smile, and a couple of rowdy dark-haired young boys. They motioned me inside and wedged me in between the two boys. No sooner had I sat down than I was overcome with the smell of unwashed bodies, garlic, and sausage! My eyes watered; I couldn't get my breath, but I couldn't leave. I was afraid of hurting their feelings – so I stayed. The young boy on the side toward the window took a bite of a long dark sausage and passed it to me. I stared at it for a second. The car grew quiet, and I noticed everyone staring at me. The sausage smelled spicy, like a pepperoni pizza. My hunger took over, and before I knew it I was taking a large bite and passing it on. Everyone laughed, smiled, and went back to talking. A man across from me leaned forward with a bottle of wine. Along with him came the intense odor of sweat and garlic that almost knocked me down. However, several swigs later with more sausage, bread, cheese, and who knows what else, I joined the party! The air was still thick, but it no longer mattered. My end of the conversation was limited; my questions were met with polite nods. Their accent was so thick and they talked so rapidly that I could make out only a couple of words here and there.

As I got up to leave, I was hugged and kissed and sent away like a son going on vacation. As I stood outside the train I shouted *"adios"* back through the window as the train pulled out of the station. This was met with a chorus of *"ciao"* and *"arrivederche."* Only then did I realize that the swirl of language around me had been Italian. The words were similar, and the wine had become a universal translator. I was in Lausanne, Switzerland, and my next train would take me to Aigle. Aigle would be my last transfer station where I would catch the train to Leysin and the American College of Switzerland.

I sat quietly on the next train, drained from the party and the wine. I listened to the people speaking around me. I heard French and German with the soft Swiss accent I would later come to like. It was not that I understood a word they were saying, but by watching the people's expressions and body language, I could imagine that I knew what they were talking about. I was so fascinated by my fellow travelers that I sat quietly as I missed the Aigle station. Shortly after I must also have fallen asleep because the conductor rudely awakened me when he checked my ticket, started shouting in German, and pointing back the other way. He put me off in the dark at San Moritz. I knew San Moritz from my James Bond novellas. I had read them all and seen each movie several times. I bought a T-shirt from a local stand to prove that I had been there and sat in the dark waiting for the train back.

I discovered why I hadn't recognized Aigle as my transfer point when the train stopped in a small station that didn't have connections to other trains. When I tried to ask about the train to Leysin, the conductor just pushed me off his train and pointed down a dark street into the town where most of my fellow travelers seemed to be walking. I followed them for several blocks because they seemed to know where they were going and watched them get into a trolley with three or four cars.

Approaching an older man as he started to get into one car, I asked in German, *"Wo ist der Zug für Leysin?"* He looked at me confused so I tried French, *"Ah... le train pour Leysin?"* This time I pointed to a small card where I had written the city name since I wasn't sure how it was pronounced.

"Oui," he said. Actually it sounded more like 'Wa.' Then he let me get in the car ahead of him, but he didn't follow me in. Instead he turned and walked forward to another car.

The interior of my car was dimly lit. My fellow passengers included a group of older teens who may have been my age, but they were engaged in a private conversation. I sat in quiet desperation. I was so tired that I couldn't keep my eyes open, yet I would soon be arriving in a town that I didn't know, and I had no plans for finding a place to stay. I had an early meeting the next morning at the American College of Switzerland. Fatigue and worry seemed to overwhelm me. I briefly nodded off; and when I woke, I felt worse. It felt like my body was being pressed back into the wooden bench; my head kept bumping against the hard wooden surface. It was almost like my seat had reclined and I was lying on my back. In desperation, I began listening closely to the conversation of the group of teens. From my distorted perspective, they seemed to be perched high over me on their seats. Between the heads of two boys with their backs to me sat an attractive blonde girl, eighteen or nineteen years old, who was talking nonstop. Her three companions could only grunt and nod politely in response. She spoke so quickly that I couldn't make out separations between her words. Her language was nasal and melodic but unlike anything I had heard in the past couple of days. I was certain that it wasn't Spanish, German, French, or even Italian. Desperate for help, I forced myself up toward the group. My head seemed to weigh a ton.

"Do any of you speak English?" I asked.

"Wha'the'elldoya'thinkah'mspeakin'?" came the reply in a deep southern drawl.

That was my introduction to Nonni, a wealthy southern princess who was a sophomore at the Swiss college. I later discovered that she could fluently butcher French, as well as English, *"Co-mo-sa-va,* y'all?"

A few minutes of talking with the other students and I had a guide to and a recommendation for a local hotel that was just across the street from the college. When we came to the station, the guy who was to take me to the hotel had to help me out of my seat. It was only then that I realized that the trolley was sitting at the station at almost a forty-five-degree angle. Sometime during my trip, the trolley had changed into some kind of cog train on the side of the hill. Realizing that and standing fully upright, I felt reinvigorated as I was escorted toward the hotel. We walked down from the station along a dark street to a stairway that led down to the front of a dark building. He pointed toward the door and told me to knock, then turned and pointed to the front of a building with the sign "The American College of Switzerland," and I could just barely make out the word "ZOO" scratched in the paint on the bottom of the sign. I wasn't to understand the truth of that graffiti until much later. As my escort walked swiftly into the darkness to rejoin his friends, I went down the stairs.

The small light by the front door illuminated the sign "Hotel Primevère." That and a few lights visible on the upper levels were the only signs of life. I pushed a doorbell and quickly roused the owner. She didn't speak any English but let me know that she had a room for me and that the *petit déjeuner* (breakfast) was included. I suddenly realized that I was hungry. I hadn't eaten since leaving the party with my Italian family. I asked about food. Actually, I pointed with the cupped fingers of one hand toward my mouth and patted the other hand on my stomach. She shook her head and pointed to a sign on the wall that showed the hours of the various meals. The free *petit déjeuner* was next from 7:30 to 9:30 the following morning. She led me up a flight of stairs inside the building and showed me my room. There was a little sink in the room, but the toilet and baths were down the hall. There was no TV, not even a clock radio. The bed was too soft, the sheets too rough and stiff, and the blanket was a huge, heavy feather pillow. I wondered momentarily about my allergy to chicken feathers and fell asleep as if drugged.

I awoke to a bright light streaming through my curtains; I stared blearily at my watch resting on the side table. Both of the watch hands were together and straight up: twelve noon! My appointment was at 9 a.m., and, worse, I had missed the free breakfast!! I jumped into my clothes and stormed down the stairs. The owner was cleaning the floor in the lobby. I tried desperately to find out if I could still get breakfast, a roll or anything. She kept pointing to the sign that had the hours of the meals and to her wrist. I knew that I was late, but I pleaded! She finally pointed to my watch. I looked down and saw it read 6:40 a.m.

In a daze, I walked back to my room and sat on a stiff wooden chair by the bed for a few minutes collecting my thoughts, only then realizing that earlier, when my watch said 6:30, I had read it upside down. Having some time to wait and thinking it awfully bright for that early in the morning, I walked over to look through the wall of curtains that covered one side of my room. They hid a set of glass doors that led to a balcony.

The edges of my balcony were framed with gingerbread and flowers, but what they framed was what I was focused on. Hanging like a portrait inside the frame were the Swiss Alps! Shear, jagged peaks, some capped with white snow, some blackened as the sun rose behind them. Once I tore my eyes from the mountains, I walked onto the balcony and looked down on a small gingerbread village perched on the side of this mountain. Yes, I said "this mountain." During that trolley ride last night, I may have been tired, but the force pressing me into my seat was not so much fatigue as it was the effect of gravity as the cog train climbed the steep slopes from the valley below. The slopes were so steep that I could not see more than a glint of light, perhaps reflected off a river in the valley. The train had carried me to this beautiful little village of gingerbread houses and flowers perched on the side of a mountain. Nothing else mattered at this point but the thought that I had to go to college here!

Chapter Three

The Summer

The remainder of the summer was fantastic! I had my first German beer with my parents, in a restaurant next to the Landstuhl castle. This was a collapsed ruin of a castle said to be haunted that sat across the valley from our new home, the Landstuhl Army Medical Center. I was eighteen years old, soon to be nineteen; and in Ohio, I could drink 3.2 beer but I didn't like its bitter, watery taste. I would just as soon drink a root beer. However this German beer was another matter; Bellheimer Silber Pils seemed to flow smoothly down my throat. But more important was my dad's recognition that I was becoming a man. I had been away from home since I was fourteen; four years at a Quaker boarding school, Olney, in southeastern Ohio, and a year at a Quaker college, Earlham, in Indiana. My life was my own, but I still felt like a kid at home, wherever that home was.

My dad bought a beat-up Opel station wagon from a departing soldier, and my newly minted friend, Gary, a fellow army brat living on the Landstuhl base, and I camped on the French Rivera in hopes of finding beautiful women and nude beaches. Hopefully at the same time! As it turned out, in 1966, the French despised Americans. I guessed that it had something to do with our going to war in Vietnam after they gave up. On the beach in Marseilles, the only nude person we saw was one rotund, hairy guy with dirty clothes who stripped as he walked from the street to the Mediterranean. He wallowed for a short while in the shallow water, scrubbed sand in his armpits and between his butt cheeks, splashed off and walked back in the opposite direction while reclaiming and donning his filthy clothing.

We managed to spend time with a couple of girls our age after we claimed that Gary was from Canada and I from Mexico. I was not tall, five foot nine and a half in the right shoes. I was in good shape from playing JV soccer and doing gymnastics at my college. I also had a nice tan, dark curly hair, and spoke school-learned Spanish rapidly enough with a Mexican accent I had picked up from one of my soccer buddies. I easily confused the young, raven-haired, dark skinned beauty who claimed to know some Spanish, and we rapidly retreated to English and hand signs. It all worked well until later in the afternoon when we started to go to a movie. That was when the German Opel with the big green USA military plates gave us away, and the girls rapidly retreated. The next day three guys on scooters tried to run us down while we were crossing the road to the beach. One scooter hit Gary's ankle, spraining his Achilles tendon. We left soon after to head home. I drove all the way back north with Gary's wrapped ankle propped up on the dash.

Back in Germany, sometimes with my parents and sometimes with Gary, I finished the summer by going to various wine and beer fests across the Rhineland Pfaltz. Each little city had a festival for baked fish, or pretzels, or whatever, and we hit all of them – drinking, singing, and peeing with the best of them! Although the drinking was fun, the resulting vomiting and massive headaches, and my father's quiet, patient voice quickly taught me moderation.

The American girls on the neighboring bases were also fun. There were stolen moments at the teen club dances, and necking in the back seat of the Opel; nothing serious, just fun. I even had a run-in with twins at the swimming pool, or *swimbad*; both had shoulder-length light brown hair that curled up at the end. They were attractive in a cute Gidget way. I followed my usual pattern of choosing the more thoughtful, less rowdy one, Kathy. Besides, at the pool, she said I had the strongest back she had ever seen and thought that I looked like some country singer. I hoped the singer was someone she liked because I had no clue who he was. Four years at my boarding school with WWVA Wheeling West Virginia as the only reliable radio station and I had no desire to hear any more country music or keep up with their stars.

Kathy and I got very close that month, or was it only three weeks? One night, we got extremely close, and if it hadn't been for a Quaker teaching flashing through my overheated brain, which I had compressed down to, "if you want to marry a virgin, you should be a virgin," I might have lost it. Somehow in the heat of that night, that thought came to me, and we slowly cooled down. Soon after that, the relationship also cooled down. Teenage summer relationships, especially between army brats, tend to break pretty cleanly. Besides it was nearly time to go to my newfound college high in the Alps.

I drove my family south through Germany in our burgundy Buick station wagon. My dad and I were in the front and my sister, Millie, and mom in back. The Autobahn traffic was amazing. With our V-6, I was cruising at eighty mph and being continually passed by a white or a black Mercedes flashing its lights and flying by at one hundred plus. At first, passing trucks was a challenge. They went about seventy mph, so I needed to pass them, but pulling into the passing lane was taking my family's lives into my hands. A Mercedes did not slow down for anyone! As an example, south of Heidelberg we saw a series of accidents on the opposite lanes that extended at least ten kilometers, called K's. The beginning was a pile of at least five cars, and from there back at the crest of each hill another half dozen or so cars were folded into each other. After a while I settled into a routine of passing trucks in the open spots between the Mercedes. In order to perfect the timing, I found myself looking in the rear-view mirror more than I looked ahead. Eventually I felt like a medium speed cog in the machine that is Autobahn traffic. It was challenging but fun!

At first Switzerland was a bit disappointing. The land was wide and flat as we traveled south from Basel and the only visible mountains caused the distant horizon on our left to appear jagged. Then, as was our habit in Germany, we started stopping at castles. You know, before Germany my only experience with castles were the castle at Disneyland, and those in Disney cartoons. In Switzerland, when we visited the Château de Chillon, perched on the side of Lake Geneva, which I would soon know as Lac Léman, images of knights and damsels in distress flashed through my mind. But these were the ghosts of real people, not the fairy tale heroes or Disney cartoon characters of my youth. This castle was dirty and old. The shields and swords on the walls were real and may have been used by some real knight. It even had dungeons and ancient toilets, or rather, holes in the wall that emptied into the lake. It was intimidating to realize how old this land was. These castles had been built before Columbus discovered America. Hell, I had stayed in hotels that were built in the 1300s! The Château de Chillon marked the beginning of the trip up the mountain.

Chapter Four

The Magic Mountain

On the journey up, we passed by one more castle in Aigle, the Château d'Aigle. It appeared to be in very good shape with turrets at each corner and tiny window slots high up on the walls. We stopped at a gas station, and dad walked in to ask about it. Dad's German was rusty, and when he came back, he said that he was told it wasn't a castle. It was a prison. He said that didn't make sense but he hadn't had the energy to argue the point in German. It turned out to be a castle used as a prison. What a frightening experience it must have been to be locked up in that massive stone edifice with the tiny slit windows.

Dad drove as we started on the windy road that left Aigle and headed up the side of the mountain. The road was so narrow that two cars could just pass, and there was no centerline dividing the lanes. Our station wagon felt like it took up more than half the pavement. I was glad that dad was driving. Each of us prayed that we would not meet a truck or a bus coming the other way. We quickly climbed out of the valley. I looked down out my window to the right as the stream below fell from ten feet to fifty. There were no guardrails; only occasional stone posts.

As the stream dropped another fifty feet, we saw our first car – or rather heard it. A shrill two-tone alpine car-horn screamed, then tires squealed as the nose of some small black sedan came sliding around the rock face ahead of us. The car sailed by, just barely fitting between us and the rock face; and then with another burst of shrill horn, it rounded the next turn. Just as the car passed, the right side of our car dropped off the pavement onto the small gravel shoulder that marked the edge of the earth, the only thing between us and the stream below. Dad quickly got us back onto the pavement and around the corner. My eyes flashed back and forth between my dad who appeared frozen to the steering wheel and the shear drop. I could hear my sister crying in the back seat. As the next car screamed past, we realized that we were in for a long ride. All the drivers on this mountain drove as if they were in some Alpine rally.

We picked up the habit of slowly approaching each blind turn, then honking our horn and listening for return horns. The road rose another hundred feet, then five hundred. I stopped watching when the mountainside became a sheer granite wall that extended up into the clouds above and down to the fog that had hidden the stream. The road couldn't be carved into the wall; instead it was supported by large pillars set into the granite face below. I had seen similar roads in the Rockies, but this structure had a concrete roof above it. Dad speculated that the roof was to keep rocks from landing on the road. The road was wider inside this structure, and at that moment God smiled on us because that is where we met the truck. We passed each other slowly, measuring rearview mirrors and door handles to be sure we wouldn't loose anything. At least the truck driver wasn't one of the rally drivers we had met before.

After a while, the valley actually appeared to start coming up to meet us, and we seemed to meet fewer cars. Perhaps we were just growing more accustomed to the shrill interruptions. The road was relatively level when we reached the turn to Leysin. We drove over a couple of rolling hills and saw the village in a little notch on the side of the mountain. Gingerbread-decorated houses and larger buildings were dotting the flat area, and the buildings spread up the slope of the mountain toward a shear escarpment that guarded the peaks above.

Leysin is two distinct villages; the lower where the college is, which includes a flat area and cow pastures, and the upper, which has the grand hotel, the bank, and many of the businesses. The two villages are divided by an area that is too steep to build on but has a dramatic staircase built into the face of the mountain. Since most of the buildings are built on the side of the mountain, all of the living space faces the mountains across the valley. The European practice of not numbering the ground floor in a building had not made any sense to me before Leysin. Here, the bottom floor was below ground level on the back, or uphill side; therefore, it might as well be the basement. In fact, in the steeper areas the first two to three floors of each building had no windows on the back because they were below ground level.

The views from each building were of the Alps. Across the valley was the peaked wall of the Chamossaire. This edifice would become a constant backdrop to all the events of the coming year. To the south were the jagged peaks of les Dents du Midi. These multiple, eternal peaks seemed to change minute by minute as the sun moved across the sky, week by week as the snow flowed down from their summits, and month by month as the earth's orbit changed its angle relative to the sun. In the north up the valley, the steep flat pyramid-like side of the Eiger was just visible. Many climbers had lost their lives on that shear rock face.

The clouds also constantly changed the view. Often in the morning they would fill the valleys below the village and make the peaks appear to be floating volcanic islands. Later they would be sail wispily above us, making white paintbrush strokes on the intensely blue sky. Occasionally a small cloud would get hooked on the top of one of the peaks and would stay there like some jaunty white beret. The clouds would often come up from the valley as the sun hit them, climb the sides of the mountains, cross the little flat area in the lower village, and invade a hotel or dorm room through an open balcony door. Their cold chill would haunt your room until the interior heat warmed them and turned them invisible.

The sounds that carried to the rooms were not the shrill horns of the cars negotiating the winding road below. They were sounds of cows calling for attention, or the ringing of the bells that hung from their necks. Occasionally you would hear the call of a Cuckoo among the trees, although, try as I might, I never saw one and would often wonder if some Swiss youth was playing a great trick on the students and tourists.

We stayed at the Hotel Primevère, where I had stayed when I first discovered Leysin. It was directly across the street and down hill from the college. We parked in back and walked up the back side from the parking below. Each balcony had colorful gingerbread cutouts on the corners and across the top, and each railing had a window box of beautiful flowers. The owners had also planted flower gardens in the small open area below their hotel. Mom and my sister were thrilled! I knew they would be. Just the sight was enough to make them forget the terror of the trip up the mountain.

The owners were friendly. I only remembered meeting the wife during my last stay, but both she and her husband seemed to remember me, and they welcomed me back. It turned out that he was the chef for the evening meals and had a fair grasp of English. He said that we had talked about the journey up on the cog train. I didn't remember him; but once I had seen this beautiful village my only focus had been getting accepted to the college.

In the hallway coming back from the bathroom to my room, I met the first ACS student, near the stairs. Donna was almost my height with blonde hair that was a little poofed at the sides and curled near her shoulders. Her eyes were strikingly blue, and her smile was infectious. She was round where girls should be and very friendly. Things were definitely looking up!

Mom found the second student. She came down the stairs from her room with a tall, lean, deeply tanned, bleached blonde football star. He must have been a real sweet-talker because mom was prancing like a schoolgirl. Mike Stallone was his name. That he was muscular was evident, even in his shirt; he had a chest that Donna would have been jealous of. Well, maybe not Donna, but half the girls in my stateside college. And his broad shoulders and powerful arms – they weren't really big, like a weight lifter, just sharply defined. My years of gymnastics had never provided a look like that! With me Mike was more reserved. There was a hint of danger in his stance, and something in his eyes that said, "I am here, keep your distance." His eyes were heavy-lidded and drooped to the side of his face. On a less carved and intimidating face, they might have given him the appearance of a sad puppy, but he was definitely a Doberman. He talked out of the side of his mouth in a slightly mumbled accent that had to come from Jersey or Philly, but you weren't invited to ask. At mom's request, he offered to show me around the school. Personally, I would have rather had Donna for an escort.

School wouldn't start for a couple of days. I had to register for classes, get a room assigned, find a bank, and my family wanted to explore the area. Stallone, as I started calling him because Mike just didn't seem adequate, was helpful. He took us on the long switchback road to the upper village, where I opened my **Swiss bank account**. If only my boarding school buddies could see me now! Stallone disappeared when we were in the bank, and we found our own way back down to the school. This involved a long daring trek down the flight of stairs built into the mountainside. I started to count but lost track after 150, and we weren't half way down. The stairs wound down behind the college's main building.

The main building was more utilitarian than many in the town. It had once been a hospital when this area was know as "The Magic Mountain" and tuberculosis patients came from all over the world to be cured by the sunlight and the clean mountain air. The patients' rooms, complete with balconies on the southeast side of the building, had become the girls' dorm. The lower floors also housed single teachers. The vertical monolith that made up the rest of the building held the classrooms, the dining area, and offices.

From the main building, someone pointed out the sophomore dorm. It was down a steep hill across the street from the school, perhaps a block east, a block south, and a block down, if blocks had anything to do with this village. The most direct route was a tiny trail no bigger than a cowpath that started at an opening in the fence across the street from the school just past or up the road from the Hotel Primevère. The trail wandered diagonally across and steeply down a grass-covered slope to the front of the dorm. The dorm, like every other building, was built into the mountainside. From this perspective I could imagine being able to step out a backside window on the European second floor to the grassy slope behind the dorm.

But we weren't ready to head to the dorm yet. Instead, my family zigzagged our way down the roads through the lower village. Where the upper village had several businesses and larger stores, the lower one had small shops, churches, bars, and restaurants. The Patisserie Parisienne, a pastry and bread shop, was the first stop. We had almond croissants, small warm buns with a cross of frosting on top, which Millie called "hot cross buns," and hot tea in clear glasses held in metal frames with a metal cup handle to keep the glass from burning your hand. Then we went past Le Nord, a large bar with foosball tables, called *zim-zim* in French Switzerland, and pinball machines. Le Nord would become a regular hangout. Then there were cheese and wine stores and a butcher. Like German villages, groceries were bought one day at a time from many different stores, all of which were within walking distance of the homes.

The small alleys that spread from the main switchback road held the homes. They were smaller than the hotels, and many were on the flatter area so they did not look out over the buildings across from them at the mountains. But most had upper balconies where the family could view the mountains on one side or the other along the alley. The ends of these alleys led to pastures dominated by other homes. These pastures beckoned, but they were fenced and experience in the farmland of Ohio had taught me to be wary of crossing people's property. More than one friend had told stories of having a load of rock salt shot at him by some irate farmer afraid of loosing a single apple from his trees. I had no experience with the Swiss but had no desire to upset anyone. Besides, the mountains beyond the pasture were what truly drew my eye, and walking across one pasture would get me no closer than I already was.

We got up close and personal the next day. But before we did my folks had a surprise for me. Dad had learned that one of the sergeants from Landstuhl had dropped off his son that day and left. Mom was a little concerned about his being abandoned so quickly, so she had taken him under her wing. I met my third ACS student. Dick was a little shorter than me with straight light brown hair that hung in his eyes, a stocky build, and a round face. He had a big smile, eyes that seemed to flash with more than a hint of deviltry, and a boastful attitude that seemed to make him larger that life, or so he thought. I had seen his type before. As a freshman he was either going to fit in as the prankster, or he was going to be quickly ostracized. Alan at boarding school had been in trouble from the day he arrived, but Squeaky at Earlham had been adopted as the mascot of the football players on our hall. The five of us drove up the valley from Leysin toward Gstaad. Dad said that the Kennedys had a place in Gstaad because it was so intensely beautiful. He wanted to see what was so special about the town.

On the way, we spotted the Diablerets ski lift and decided to go up. As we stood waiting for the lift, I stared at the shear rock face that the cables ascended. I couldn't get a handle on its size. There were trees at its base, but they looked more like bushes in comparison to its enormous height. The lift itself, called a teleferic, had two cars; one was about halfway up when I first saw it, and the other about half way down. As the one descended, its size grew. By the time it settled into its stall, it was the size of a small Winnebago. We got in with a dozen or so other tourists. Then the attendant got in, and the car started to move.

We left the security of base pylons and began the ascent. The next pylons were several thousand feet above us on the top of the cliff. Should the cable snap anywhere in between; we were dead! Dick seemed to brazen it out by talking about roller coaster rides he had been on in the states as we watched the cliff towering in front of us. When we looked back at the mountain peaks rising around us and stared down at the shrinking lift housing below us, we all got quiet, even Dick. Around the lift housing were scattered green bushes that we had last seen as full-sized trees, and those little bushes were disappearing as we watched them. As we approached the top of the cliff, the car appeared to speed toward the shear rock wall and then slow slightly before jumping up and clearing the top edge. At this point, the lift housing was a toy Monopoly house, and the trees were a vague dark green smudge around it. We finally relaxed as the teleferic rumbled over the rollers of the cliff-top pylon, sending us sailing across the upper fields.

This lift was only the first of two. The second took us between a lower peak and an upper snow-covered peak. The view from the second lift was unbelievable, rock and snow-covered mountains in all directions! Once out of the lift, we walked through the snow on the very top of the world. The air was thin and cold, and we immediately wished that we had brought warmer clothes. Millie grabbed a snowball and pitched it at me. I dodged, and it hit Dick. The next thing I knew, we were in a pitched battle on top of the world. At this point, Millie seemed to be throwing more snowballs at Dick than me, so I ducked back into the relative warmth of the upper lift housing. I watched as dad took some pictures, and we quickly returned to the teleferic for the ride back down. Millie was shivering in the lift as we started to descend. Dick offered his jacket. Hmmm... None of my business, I guess.

As we passed from the upper peak, I thought about the snow and of learning to ski. This area wasn't too steep and might be fun, but what if I got lost and went too close to the precipice? I'd end up like that Bond villain in "On her Majesties Secret Service," falling and spinning forever.

As we got into the second lift, the attendant was joined by a maintenance man who opened a hatch on the top of the car and climbed up onto the roof. My first thought was that we would be stuck there while he checked some of the bolts, but the lift started to move with him on top. We all stood fascinated as he crawled up the armature holding the car and sat next to the cables. I hadn't realized that there was more than one cable. His job seemed to be inspecting and occasionally painting some red grease on the cable, and he was still there as we fell off the cliff-top pylon and watched the earth drop beneath us. He sat up top the entire ride down. I kept checking through the open hatch to be sure that he hadn't fallen off, but he just sat there focused on his job. I silently bet that he was one of the rally drivers that we had met on the road to Leysin. I even thought for a second that I might have the nerve to change places with him, but a look down from inside our steel and glass car quickly dispelled that fantasy. Millie and Dick seemed to be in quiet conversation on the other end of the teleferic.

I took over the driving from there to Gstaad. It didn't really impress me, just another pretty village with larger homes surrounded by giant mountains; and if we saw anyone famous, we didn't recognize them. Besides I was already in love with my little Swiss village and had yet to fully explore it. I couldn't wait to get back.

Chapter Five

The Sophomore Dorm and the Satyrs

My dad and Stallone helped move my clothes into the sophomore dorm, which was a converted hotel almost identical to, although a little more Spartan than, the one we had stayed in. My room was on the top floor, two doors down from Stallone. The room was huge with two beds, two desks, and a sink. As he left, Stallone shot me a crooked smile and told me that my roommate was called "Tiny."

While I was unpacking, my roommate came in. Tiny, he was not! He ducked as he came through the doorway. He stood six foot five, in his low-cut white tennies. That was large in the States, but in Europe he was a giant! European doorframes didn't accommodate him. Tiny was everything that I wished I had been: tall, sandy hair, with a boyish face and manner. He was also well proportioned, not skinny with long, gangly legs like most really tall guys. His body looked normal, just large! His giant smile and laugh was a little goofy, but he seemed like a great person to have as a roommate. His size would also be helpful if that edge I saw on Stallone ever became focused on me.

After meeting my family, Tiny told me that his brother was also at the school, but he had no desire to room with him. I understood what he meant when I thought back to my sister invading my space at boarding school. He also said that his dad was a U.S. Senator. In a couple of hours, we were fast on the path to becoming good buddies.

Next door, on the side opposite from Stallone, in a small room tucked in the eve of the roof lived a strange scarecrow of a guy. Jim Wilds, who would become my best friend at ACS, was the son of an engineer for Caterpillar, and he called Glasgow, Scotland, his "home." He was severely thin with sloped shoulders, a nose that was a little large for his face, and ears that stuck out through his straight brown hair.

His hair was so limp that it stayed in place for only a few minutes after he combed it, even with hair lotion. I would later find that you could tell how much beer Jim had drunk by how much hair was in his eyes. Once I could no longer see his eyes, it was time to carry him back to the dorm. At ninety-six pounds, wet, he wasn't hard to carry – except for his unusually sharp elbows that would occasionally catch me in the ribs. Another thing Stallone seemed to revel in was throwing drunks over one of his powerful shoulders and bouncing them back to the dorm. I feel compelled to add, "God help the person who tossed his chips!" But, in reality, just the thought of possibly puking on Stallone's back sobered you up enough to make it to the dorm – or in a truly desperate situation, to scream to be let down, which, in this case, involved being tossed down, a bone-jarring, head-thumping experience. On his plus side, Wilds was always upbeat, always seemed to be in the right place when something strange was happening, and had an unfailing memory for every sordid detail.

Over the course of the next couple of days, I would meet many of the dorm residents, some memorable, some not. I met Gil at my first dinner at school, and we were allies in the first few minutes. He was a fellow military brat, in his case Air Force, and his home currently was Wiesbaden Air Force Base near Frankfurt, not forty K's from mine. Gil was a little taller than me, with pale skin and almost white blonde hair that he brushed high off his strong, honest, blue-eyed, Boy Scout face. We shared many of the same life lessons traveling around the world with our parents. We both tended to make friends quickly but somewhat superficially so that the next move wouldn't be as hard.

In the room between mine and Stallone's, Tiny introduced me to Jolie and Cliff. Both were in their second year, and both were wealthy. Jolie was the adopted son of Al Jolson, "The Jazz Singer." He had brown hair with deep-set blue gray eyes setting off his masculine, quasi-Richard Burton face. When I first walked into his room, he had a cigarette in one hand and a beer bottle in the other. He set the beer down momentarily to shake my hand. That was one of the few times I saw Jolie without a beer or a wine bottle or a mixed drink. In fact, if Jolie wasn't an alcoholic before he came to Leysin, he became one on the Magic Mountain.

Where Jolie was ruggedly handsome, Cliff was ruggedly not! He had muddy, rusty brown hair that didn't look natural, but I am not sure why anyone would choose that color hair. If it hadn't stayed that impossible color the whole school year, I would have sworn that it was a bleach job gone orange. He had some pock marks and a permanent shadow of a beard that ran down his neck, which made him look older than he was. Both guys had an aloof air about them; although compared to Jolie's cool resolve, Cliff was just plain stuck up.

In Stallone's room I met Spyder. At first I thought his nickname came from the long thin arms and legs that spouted from his torso. His greased black hair, black turtleneck, and tight black jeans only seemed to enhance that image. However, I found that he had earned his name rock climbing the many cliffs around the area. Spyder had a large pointy nose and dark eyes that gave his thin face an intense look, and he never looked relaxed, even when he was drunk.

On the floor below I ran into Willie Perone and Baby John. What a pair they made! Willie gave the impression of coming from money, some rich Italian-American family, or perhaps *The Family*. He was tall, thin with a bush of brown, kinky hair crowning his head, and a pubic-hair mustache. During the year he sprouted a matching goatee. I guess I shouldn't judge because I couldn't even grow a mustache. If fact, the only reason I shaved was to hide the fact that, at nineteen, I could only grow peach fuzz. Willie, too, looked older that I suspect he was, as if he had already lived a long, and not always easy, life.

Baby John, on the other hand, looked youthful and bright! He was done up in the dazzling Mod clothes of Piccadilly Circus fame: striped bell-bottoms and a flowered shirt, Beetle boots and a sash for a belt. His light brown hair was bowl-cut from just over his eyes, around the sides just covering his ears, and down onto his high shirt collar in the back. Through the year his hair would grow to his shoulders, and his bangs would be tucked behind one ear. Small rectangular glasses that partially hid his blue eyes were perched on his hawk-like nose. He was playing an acoustic guitar when I came in – and it was rare to see him without it. When wandering campus or the village he also carried a knitted bag over his shoulder that he insisted was his "bean-bag" and not a purse. I would soon find that Willie and Baby John shared my love for a good philosophical debate on any given topic, made all the better with a glass of wine or bottle of beer.

Also on that floor were the Arabs. I use the term loosely. I am not sure which Middle Eastern countries they came from. Imad and Ibrahim were both stocky and dusky-skinned with dark hair and eyes. One had longer hair and wore glasses. The other had piercing black eyes and a broad smile. I am not sure which was which because I didn't get to know them well, even after befriending Imad's brother, Issa. You know, I am not sure that Issa even lived in the dorm. I don't remember visiting his room. I suspect that he may have had an "official" room in the dorm but had rented a place in the village.

Willie introduced me to Issa one evening in the upper village with his wife Maha. They had unbelievable wealth. Issa's father was a sheik or nobleman of some family in Lebanon, and his wife was the daughter of another. Their union was intended to cement relations between the two families. Issa was also stocky and dark, and he had a quiet power about him that I had not seen in his brother or his roommate. Whether that quiet power was natural or something he had learned from his father, you knew at a glance that he would be a leader of something when he got out into the world. He made a point of saying that his name is the Arabic version of Jesus. Issa's wife, on the other hand, was just quiet. She was short and plump. That probably isn't fair. She was attractive, but more full-figured than my teenage standards. Issa made a point of showing off her wedding ring. It had a square cut diamond in the middle the size of the nail on my pointer finger. Around the outside supporting the center stone were at least twelve or sixteen impossibly long, thin, rectangular-cut diamonds. Issa explained that the long, thin cut of each of these stones made them more valuable than the center stone. An easy guestimate was that she was wearing a 911S Porsche Targa, my dream car, on her hand.

That reminds me. Issa had one of the few cars owned by students at the college. It was a new, four-seat, MGB MkII, with synchromesh in all four gears, that could tear up the road off the mountain! Other than that, Robert's classic Matchless motorcycle was the only other set of wheels. Robert, a stocky, dark-haired, unassuming guy with thick-rimmed glasses had a kind of Clark Kent thing going. While he was always friendly and helpful, he had a hidden power about him, not unlike his motorcycle, that got him respect, even from Stallone. I guess I should mention the Turk's Porsche. The Turk, a strange, greasy, dark, bushy-haired guy, who, Wilds had heard, had announced he was gay, said that he had blown the transmission out of his Porsche somewhere in Italy on the road to school. He also said that his dad was going to replace it, but I never saw it, and I never had the desire to ask him about it. Gays were not people that I cared much for, especially after my freshman college roommate got drunk and crawled naked into bed with me. A brief wrestling match ensued that ended with me threatening to kill him as I held him out the second story window. I know – not very Quakerly – but I was the son of a Quaker colonel, you figure it out!

During an early group bull session in Stallone's room, I met Bernd and Roark. They were two second-year students and already legendary studs! Wilds had told me about Bernd. Rumor was that last year he had started through the alphabet having sex with each of the coeds until the girls recognized his pattern in the K's. He then waited a few weeks and started back from the end of the alphabet and got to the S's before the year ended. If Bernd was attractive to the opposite sex, I didn't see why. He was tall, a little over six feet, and gangly with slightly stooped shoulders and short-cropped brown hair. His head was too small for his body, and his nose too big, but his large blue eyes gave him a boyish look that, taken alone, might have been considered cute. He was, however, athletic. He was instructor, captain, and the best skier on the racing team, and taught several other PE classes; in fact, he had just taken over the mountain climbing class. It seems that the school's former sports director--the mountain climber, John Harlin--had not survived the prior winter. While making the celebrated first direct ascent of the

Eiger's north face, his rope broke and he fell 4,000 feet. Five teammates continued the final 2,000 feet to the summit and named the climb *The John Harlin Route*. I heard that it was now considered the most famous, if dangerous, climb in the Alps. Anyway, perhaps athletics was Bernd's ticket to the girls' dorm.

Roark, on the other hand, was a handsome Swede: light brown curly hair, chiseled features, and sparkling green eyes. To hell with the girls, women swooned over this guy! He was rumored to make his tuition as a gigolo on the French and Italian Riveras each summer, and I had no doubt that he did. Roark had little desire for the girls at the school, other than the occasional, exceptionally difficult challenge. His dates came from the villages – the tourists, college staff, or wandering wives – and from surrounding towns. Women would ride the cog train or brave the winding road to visit Roark.

The bull session also included Jolie, with a cigarette and beer of course, Cliff, and Tiny. Someone had brought a case of beer, which was illegal in the dorm, but who knew! While the discussion started out about trying to find a way to make alcohol legal in the dorm, it soon reverted to how to get into as many coeds' pants as possible during the upcoming year. I drank a beer but stayed out of the conversation. I didn't figure that being a Quaker virgin would play well in this crowd. The local Swiss beer, called Feldschlösschen, was a little more bitter than German beer but not bad, especially after the second one. We were drinking it warm, but even in the local bars it was never served cooler than a wine cellar.

Chapter Six

Princesses and Goddesses

Other than Nonni, the nonstop-talking, southern bell I had met on my first trip up the mountain to visit ACS, and Donna, the cute, well-rounded blonde at the hotel, I had yet to meet many coeds at school. The first meeting occurred after Wilds and I climbed the cowpath from the dorm and walked through the rotating door on the front of the school. As we entered we saw the Fab Four standing regally on the balcony overhead. Both of us stood there with mouths open and eyes bulging, looking at the four slim, mini-skirted girls who looked like actresses standing on the set of a James Bond movie. All four had long, straight blonde hair, although each had a different tone as if the studio's hairdresseser had selected their colors so no two were alike. Then the makeup artist had outdone herself highlighting their eyes. My Quaker relatives would have been shocked, but on these princesses the makeup perfectly enhanced the size and shape of their blue eyes. Actually one had brown eyes, but for me a blonde with brown eyes was an even bigger turn-on! My very first girlfriend in second grade had that combination. Years later I learned that her mother had bleached her hair, but that didn't change the effect that combination had on me now.

Each of the Fab Four had matching shoes and purses that complemented their outfits and wore dangling earrings and expensive but not showy jewelry. But what caught my attention, after their long blond hair and longer legs, were their pert breasts, slim hips, and even slimmer waists. *Ouch!* I started rethinking the sanity of my current life-decision while imagining each of them naked! It shook me to my Quaker roots. Other than in movies, the shortest skirts I'd seen were an inch or two above the knee, and dangling earrings were forbidden at boarding school. The principal had explained that they drove men to distraction. Well I was distracted, but it had little to do with the earrings!

Of note, the haughty attitude of two of these princesses led them to disaster. I never learned their names because within the first month, they were caught shoplifting in one of the local cities and expelled from Switzerland. Only Dee-Dee, the brown-eyed one, and Lenore made it through the year. While these princesses were surely Stallone's, or Bernd's targets, therefore out of my league, their image would haunt my fantasies for several years.

One other thing was flashing through my mind while I stared at the Fab Four. I had had many relationships in high school; in fact, as a senior with multiple sports' letters, I was in demand. But freshman year in college was hard! I was low man on the totem pole, looked even younger than my age, and even playing on the JV soccer team hadn't raised me to a level that brought any female attention. I was hoping to stage a comeback during my sophomore year, but with Stallone and the legendary studs in the men's dorm, these princesses in the girls', I was worried that I was way out of my league!

The Fab Four were not the only beautiful girls I saw that day. In fact, after the princesses came the goddesses: blonde Andrea with her lash-veiled, bedroom eyes, Pat with her long auburn hair, Gretchen and Nancy with their long dark brown hair, and Carol with her short cowl of black hair that glinted red in the sun were equally beautiful and even more unassailable. Each one had a mature poise that made the Fab Four seem almost childlike in comparison.

And not all of the girls were gorgeous; some were exotic! Tiny Tyng had her long dark hair, dark skin, almond-shaped eyes, and small round breasts. Spanish Miriam had even longer black hair, almost black eyes, and the erect posture of a flamenco dancer. Irish Colleen had shoulder-length raven black hair that framed her ivory skin and intensified her green eyes. It was several months before I realized she was from the U.S. Penny from the Virgin Islands had skin darkened and hair bleached by the intense sun of the islands and a body that had to look fantastic in a bathing suit.

These girls were so extraordinary that my nineteen-year-old brain couldn't see past the exterior. Nor was I invited to join any conversation where I might have learned more about them. For now, they were only colors and shapes – incredible shapes...

Then from the exotic to the truly strange, there was Alice. Her real name was Susan, but everyone knew her as Alice, as in "Alice in Wonderland." Alice was a tiny blonde, four-foot eight-inches tall, who wore baby doll clothes, walked in tiny Mary Jane shoes, carried a tiny purse, and took tiny steps through her own tiny world. At first sight, she and the long-haired Mod Baby John collided like opposite poles of magnets brought too close together and were not parted again for the entire school year.

There were a few good all-American girls like Donna from the hotel. Jana had very long dark brown hair, enormous brown eyes, and a smile for everyone. Paula, with her short brown hair, had almond eyes and dusky skin that could have come from some foreign land, and she seemed to make friends with everyone. Sam with shoulder-length brown hair and haunted eyes had a way of finding all the parties. These and many other first-year girls were bright, enthusiastic, and ready to start the school year. The second-year girls, like slim, bubbly Tita with her short blonde hair that never seemed to hold a given shape and slimmer, athletic Kaeti with her long straight light brown ponytail that fell almost to her waist, were more reserved. Both were wary of getting too close to the guys. Likely due to living through the previous year's mating season – but I will get to that later...

I forgot to mention the college's twins: Judy and Sally. They were both lovely all-American blondes with gorgeous bodies that no one ever got near. The biggest studs tried and failed. They lived with their parents somewhere on the mountain and were seen only in class and for short periods at the special occasions. I got to know Judy a little because she was a member of the Searcher's club, a kind of select debate / discussion club that met in the evenings for several weeks in the dead of winter and talked about life, birth, death, infinity, and whatever else happened to pop up. Judy was Magna Cum Laude at graduation with her 4.0 GPA. Sally was seen so infrequently that she may have dropped out.

The thing that was evident about the students at this school was that they were from money, perhaps even Wealth. They were the kids of the Jet Set, with parents who had multiple homes and traveled the world. Some had the money and power to be appointed as officials at the European embassies, others thought nothing of flying their sons or daughters to a school in Europe for a year or two, and still others were wealthy Europeans and Middle-Easterners who wanted their sons or daughters to learn American ways on an Alp in Switzerland. The few military brats, like me, who happened to be living with their parents in Europe and, therefore, found this college economically practical, were the minority.

Chapter Seven

The Zoo and Its Keepers

At first the academic side of the college seemed pretty normal, but I soon began to wonder about my classes and the staff. Rumor was that the school was registered as a business in Switzerland. My first thought was that its classes were structured around the U.S. criteria, and may not have met Swiss standards. However, I soon found out that the college wasn't accredited in the U.S. I phoned my parents when I learned this, and they contacted my stateside college, which agreed to accept my courses when I returned provided they offered something similar. Did I mention that ACS was a junior college and only had a two-year curriculum?

And then there was the staff and faculty... The staff was local and apparently pretty shrewd businessmen. I only got to know a couple.

President Arnold was a short, mustached gentleman with a big belly. So big, in fact, that the underground school paper was titled "The Gut." This rotund gentleman gave the appearance of a classic figurehead, and I didn't get to know him well. That is until he started teaching judo. Only then did I get a clue of The Gut's hidden power.

I did, however, get to know the academic dean quite well, unfortunately. Dean Zagier was a very short rat-faced man. The joke around school was that he was so short that he had to look up to Alice. The truth was he wasn't much taller. Dean Zagier had a massive inferiority complex that manifest itself as overbearing megalomania with the Napoleonic twist of occasionally tucking his right hand into his vest. When I had first visited the school and fallen in love with the mountain, he had paraded me around the school extolling its virtues when all I wanted to do was get signed up. His description of the library was so effuse that I was astounded when he walked me into the large coat closet that held the school's three hundred or so books. My boarding school library was a little larger, and Earlham's library was a three-story building. He didn't understand when I asked how one would research a paper but suggested that the Montreux library had several dozen books in English that I could use to supplement my research. What did that mean? I would have to get off the mountain and go twenty K's around Lac Léman only to find thirty-six or forty-eight more books on a variety of topics!

I was concerned because I was going to have to make good grades that year, and, at Earlham, good grades required a lot of study and research. My freshman grades weren't good; I was on academic probation. I had played soccer, been in the model UN, helped build the freshman homecoming float, and done a dozen other things instead of studying last year, so I was determined to make up for that on this mountain. Plus, the draft board was on my ass; if I didn't get my grades in shape, I would be in a fight to get my conscientious objector status, and, with a colonel in the army for a father, that might be a tough fight. If unsuccessful, I'd be on the next plane to Vietnam.

The dean was also my English teacher. His class was so basic that I was worried that it wouldn't be accepted for credit back at Earlham. He was teaching us how to organize and write an analytical paper, a course I had taken in high school and was an ability that was required to pass freshman English. I dropped out of his class at the end of the fall quarter. This was a difficult move given that he was the academic dean. The upshot was I got to take a few more interesting courses.

The teachers were an odd assortment of characters, but just think about what might motivate a person to teach in an unaccredited junior college perched on an Alp. There were skiers, players, refugees, and, possibly, a hidden bodyguard or two. After all, there were a lot of rich kids, but only the prince had his own visible protection.

After dropping out of English, I took political philosophy with Mr. Connolly, a tall, good-looking man who appeared to have been born on skis. In class, he had a tendency to wax philosophical. If fact, his classes were very enjoyable when we could lead him into some tangent of life in the seventeenth, eighteenth, or nineteenth centuries that dealt with the idiosyncrasies of historic personalities and had little to do with politics.

Basic French was taught by Madame Bailet, a very attractive older woman with blonde hair, an inviting smile, and a very sexy walk. I paid close attention in French class. She was married to Monsieur Bailet, also a French teacher, who was as handsome as she was beautiful. What a couple! Wilds caught the rumor that the two of them took separate vacations. It seems Madame Bailet would go to Paris to take a few lovers, and Monsieur Bailet would stay in Leysin and educate a few willing coeds. I fanaticized about their reversing their vacation plans. Another rumor was that she had entertained Roark on more than one occasion.

My history teacher, Mr. Coates, was a chain smoker. He would light one cigarette from the last to be sure he had a lit one at all times. He waved his cigarettes when he lectured and rarely took a puff. It was also notable that his hands were so steady he could hold an ash that was three-fourths the length of the cigarette! Mr. Coates was a drinker and had promised more than one student an "A" if the student could outdrink him. I suspect that history was the only "A" that Jolie ever got in college. I got my grades the old-fashioned way: I worked for them... when I wasn't skiing or drinking.

Mr. Van Vuuren, my art teacher, had been a South African commando in a previous life. I saw him launch himself six feet into the air and hang horizontally, then kick down at an imagined opponent's head in an attempt to knock it from its shoulders. He would land lightly facing the opponent and launch back up in the opposite direction. Stallone had seen the same performance and gave a grunt that I interpreted as an acknowledgement of superior firepower. When I told Willie about the demonstration, he said that Van Vuuren's fellow commando worked in Geneva as a bouncer in a large nightclub. Willie said this guy wore an oversized suit to make him appear smaller and was pushed around the club in a wheel chair by a body builder. When trouble started, the commando launched up from the wheel chair seven or eight feet into the air. The body builder was there just to steady the wheel chair.

Mr. Van Vuuren was an artist and enjoyed his craft. He encouraged and expanded my painting skills while cluing me into the fact that most painters don't get rich. Art was for enjoyment, but successful careers were few and far between. Baby John excelled in painting. Alice was also in art class, and her works were quite creative and pretty, but, where Baby John and I were working on three- by five-foot canvases, Alice's efforts were, as one might expect, tiny!

I audited Madame Linden's French living class. Basic French was taking me to a level that I could use to communicate, but Madame Linden taught us about fine wines and dining. It was fun, and she told great stories! She was born in Russia and had been a wealthy actress who escaped the Bolshevik revolution by going over the border to Poland. She was in Poland when the Germans overran it, so she slipped through Germany into France. In Paris, a bomb had destroyed her dressing room, and she gave up the stage. She later moved to and stayed in Switzerland.

The exceptions to the general state of the teachers were our two PhDs: Dr. O'Brian and Dr. Zagier. Dr. O'Brien was excited by his specialty, international relations. He was a focused, thoughtful lecturer who could bring out the best in a student who was willing to listen, and I listened. In fact, because of him, I changed my major to political science and my career focus. Eight months in his classes and I wanted to become a foreign-relations specialist for an international firm. In addition to his international relations course, I also audited his course on the European Economic Community. My ability to keep up with class was aided by the fact that either Imad or Ibrahim had dropped out and given me his books. As a result of the course, I became a supporter of the European Union. Well... I had an EU sticker on my car when I returned to the States! Also, the only research paper I put together at ACS was on my predictions of the future of the European state and its competition with the U.S. economy. I was even able to find several books for my research in Dr. O'Brien's library.

Dr. Zagier was Dean Zagier's wife. You know, I believe that it was in Dr. Zagier's psychology class that I learned that the dean's mannerisms were symptomatic of a massive inferiority complex. The good doctor also happened to be a full head taller than the dean and an excellent, knowledgeable, experienced professor. In addition, she was a practicing psychologist in Montreux or Lausanne. I got straight A's in her class in the winter quarter before she decided to commit herself to a mental hospital. Her husband, the dean, took over, and he sat in class day after day reading from the text, unable to answer anything not covered in the book. I made all A's on his tests but got a C as my spring quarter grade. My complaints fell on deaf ears, as he was the academic dean.

ACS was a college, I guess, although the classes didn't approach the academic rigors of my stateside college and, in fact, often reminded me of in-depth high-school courses. Most of the tests were multiple guess and right out of the book. Essay tests involved spouting back the teacher's words. Other than in political philosophy and in psychology with Dr. Zagier, no one expected you to think during tests. I wrote only one paper, and it was limited because of the lack of research material on the subject in the library. Other than a desire to make good enough grades to raise my GPA and avoid the draft, I can't say that I cared much about my studies. Therefore, I will just bullet typical school days before, after, and during ski season to get that over with!

School Life – Fall and Spring (before and after the ski season)

9:00 a.m. to 4:30 p.m. classes in the main

4:30 p.m. to 6:00 p.m. Sports and occasional homework

6:00 p.m. to 7:00 p.m. Dinner

7:00 p.m. to 8:00 p.m. – have a beer at Le Nord and a game of *zim-zim* (foosball)

8:00 p.m. to 11:00 p.m. – finish homework – when finished have another beer

School Life – The Ski Season

9:00 a.m. to 4:30 p.m. classes in the main

4:30 p.m. to 6:00 p.m. SKI!

6:00 p.m. to 7:00 p.m. Dinner

7:00 p.m. to 8:00 p.m. – have a beer at Le Nord and a game of *zim-zim*

8:00 p.m. to 11:00 p.m. – homework – when finished have another beer

Chapter Eight

An Audience with the Prince

About a week into the school year I hopped down the stairs to visit Willie and was stopped by the sight of a man in a suit at the other end of the hallway. The sight was so unusual that I stood staring at him for a while. I recognized him as one of the prince's bodyguards, and he appeared to be posted outside the end room. After a moment, he motioned me over. I moved hesitantly forward wondering what he wanted and stopped a few feet in front of him. He nodded his head slightly with his dark eyes focused on mine, and in a heavy, harsh accent, he said, "You may go in."

Calling on the prince hadn't even occurred to me. *What the hell!* I thought, although I managed only a meek "Ah... okay..." The bodyguard knocked, waited for a response from inside that I couldn't quite make out, and opened the door for me to enter.

As the door swung open, the first thing that I saw was a deep red carpet hiding the wooden floors. As I walked onto its luxurious pile, I wondered how clean my shoes were. I thought about taking them off when I turned to find the African prince sitting on a chair in front of a rather large desk. He looked over his right shoulder at me, his head tilted slightly to the left with a curious smile on his lips. His long black hair framed his high cheekbones and ended at the line of his strong chin. "Come in and join me!" he said with an excellent British accent while he held up his left hand and opened his fingers, exposing the lighter colored skin on his palm. "You are my first visitor."

"Wow, you have a nice room, here!" I said lamely.

"I am glad that you like it. Sit."

I grabbed a wooden chair by the wall and moved it toward the prince, who had swiveled in his chair to face me. *Okay, so he also has some kind of fancy office chair. After all, he is a prince,* I thought.

I had no idea what to say, so I sat there drowning in the silence.

"I am Prince Paul –" it went on forever and ended with "– Makonnen of Ethiopia. Call me Paul," he said and held out his right hand.

I grabbed his hand to shake it, but he caught my hand and held it lightly between his forefingers and his thumb. I hoped that I hadn't messed up the proper protocol, but the bodyguard got me into this so I really wasn't prepared. I told him my name and that I currently lived in Germany but that I was an Army brat so I had lived in a lot of places and had no real place to call home. I mentioned that the longest I had lived in one place was the four years at my boarding school in Ohio.

"Boarding school?" he said. "I was in a boarding school in Scotland, called Gordonstoun. Have you heard of it?"

"No."

"My cabin was much larger there, but I had to share it with a roommate, Prince Charles of England." The name sounded familiar, but there were a lot of royalty called Charles in English history. We talked a bit about our past roommates. It seems that Prince Charles had large ears and was the butt of some nasty teasing because of it. Prince Paul didn't approve of the teasing but couldn't help much because they were always making fun of his accent.

"Your English accent is definitely better than mine!" I said with a smile.

"Yes, well that was a number of years ago. Besides, you speak American quite well," he joked back.

"Thanks!" and we both laughed.

We then compared experiences on boarding school for a while. While his seemed more rigorous academically, we both agreed that the schools tried to schedule every minute of your life so you didn't get into any trouble. Also, both tried to keep you isolated from the local towns. It was interesting that I seemed to have had more fun on my campus with social events and local outings while Prince Paul had weekend trips to Buckingham Palace and other places throughout Europe and the U.S. He had access to the Ethiopian embassy airplanes. That seemed amazing! When I left, I asked if I could come back with some friends, and he said that he would enjoy meeting other of his classmates.

Man, I was exploding with the story as I left Prince Paul's room. Yes, I said Prince Paul. In spite of my ancestor's reluctance to show deference to royalty, I never learned to call him Paul. Although, I will admit that Prince Paul became more of a dual name in my head, like Billy-Bob or Marsha Ann, than a sign of true deference to his noble birth. Anyway, I couldn't wait to tell someone. Willie wasn't in his room, so I bounded back upstairs to Wilds. I threw open his door without knocking, spotted Wilds, and the words started tumbling out of my mouth: "Prince Paul's downstairs..., Red carpet..., Buckingham Palace..., boarding school..."

I am not sure what Wilds was doing when I barged in, but he was sitting on the bed with his back to me and sounded a little embarrassed when he said, "Geez, Jim, knock first! Prince Paul is in our dorm? I thought that he'd have a chalet somewhere at the very least!"

Whatever it was that he had been doing, he rebounded quickly, and we were soon making plans for finding Gil and going back. I headed down to the second floor to find Gil while Wilds started searching in his secret stash in the wallboards. We were in luck, Gil was in his room, and when the two of us came back up Wilds met us on the third floor by the stairs. He had pulled on a baggy jacket that hung on him like an XXL shirt on a wire coat hanger, and he walked sheepishly behind us as we approached the guard. The guard gave what appeared to be a grim smile and nod in recognition and opened the door without knocking. As we shuffled onto the thick carpeting, something glass under Wilds' shirt clinked, and the guard gave him an alert, questioning look. To which Wilds only smiled, bowed, and backed into the room, closing the door behind us.

I am not sure that the prince was expecting me to return this quickly, but he took it in stride. Then, when Wilds pulled four beers out from inside pockets under his jacket, he grinned and held out a hand for one. A prince with a weird haircut or not, if we had anything to do with it, he would soon be just one of the guys. There weren't enough chairs for all of us so Wilds planted himself on the carpet. I then slid off my chair and followed him to the floor. Watching us, amused, the prince joined us on his push carpet. Finally, Gil grudgingly slid off his chair as well.

As we sat together on the carpet, we talked about a lot of things, but Prince Paul's life was the real story. For one thing, it turned out that the Prince Charles he had mentioned was the crown prince of England and they were buddies. In fact, his trips to Buckingham Palace were not touristy walks around the outside. He had slept in the palace and played through the halls with the other prince. Also, Prince Paul explained that he was a prince because he was Emperor Haile Selassie's grandson. His distant ancestors were King Solomon and the Queen of Sheba. Unbelievable! He admitted that he was only second to the crown in Ethiopia. It seems that his uncle was the crown prince. But Paul had been crown prince for a while when his uncle attempted an assassination of Emperor Haile Selassie and fell from favor. Once the uncle regained favor, he was reinstated, and Prince Paul moved back to second place again. None of us had the nerve to ask Prince Paul what a person had to do to regain favor after an assassination attempt.

During that first bull session, even sitting on the carpet, Prince Paul had a special poise and a grace that set him apart. Soon after, many other students were vying for his attention, and we saw less and less of him. And it wasn't long before our dorm mates perverted him and brought him down to our level. In fact, once he cut his Prince Valiant hairdo, he was often mistaken for one of the guys at Le Nord. Also, I suspect that being the prince's first visitors gave the three of us a little extra recognition. While he didn't often seek out any of us, he didn't ignore us, like many of the upper crust.

Prince Paul also had one very interesting habit at school. Once the coeds were used to his skin tone, he was giving a ring and getting engaged almost monthly. He must have brought a box of engagement rings in all sizes from Ethiopia. It was definitely a way to bed a willing young female, who, for her part, could tell her grandchildren of the time she was engaged to a prince and that she had the ring to prove it!

However, I suspect the story would omit or edit his complexion and the name of his kingdom.

Chapter Nine

The Fondue Party

I guess at this point I should say a little about the preseason nightlife on the mountain. For the sophomore guys and some more adventurous coeds, Le Nord was pretty much it. It was a good sized bar with one Swiss Franc beer (about twenty-five cents for a half litre). The center of attention was the foosball, or *zim-zim*, table. There were pinball machines and tables where people could meet and talk, but the focus of the room was *zim-zim* and beer. There were other bars but none as close to our dorm.

There were other entertainments to be had at Le Nord. The beer bottles had a gasketed white ceramic top mounted on a wire clip. There were several ways of opening the bottles, but the most fascinating and difficult involved a bit of slight-of-hand. It looked like you struck the ceramic top with the side of your pointer finger, causing the top to pop out. In reality, you hit the side of the wire clip with your thumb, unhooking it before your finger struck the top. It took a lot of practice to perfect and involved accepting some finger bruises before you got it right. Then again, if you didn't know the trick and tried to really do it – especially drunk – you could do some damage to your finger! I imagine that you could break it – although the worst I saw was Dick, the sergeant's son from my army base. He managed to crack the top of the bottle and cut his finger as he smacked the top out of the bottle with brute force. Did I mention that ice was at a premium on the mountain? When I went to the bartender for ice for Dick's finger I got the standard two sugar cube size pieces that went into their warm cokes. Wrapped in a cocktail napkin, they did little to relieve the swelling on Dick's finger.

Cokes – the other beverage – were tiny! I hadn't seen a Coke this small since elementary school – and they cost the same as a half-litre of beer – and they were super sweet, warm and nasty with the two tiny ice cubes rapidly melting inside. It didn't take a genius to figure out that – beer was the drink at Le Nord! Oh, other entertainments included coaster flipping, coaster puncturing, ahh… salt shaker balancing; lets see, there had to be other fun things to do…– maybe not!

Around the village there was supposed to be a bowling alley, although I didn't find it for some time, many other more distant bars and restaurants, a movie theatre – although the movies, even the American ones were dubbed in French with German subtitles. When we went to movies we snuck beers in and sat in the balcony making rude noises since most of us had no clue what was going on. More than once a kid snuck in some of the dinner soup or gravy and pretended to barf off the balcony on the unsuspecting viewers below. My input to the revelry was a little subtler. I brought in a small but loud European cap pistol to a James Bond movie I had seen a half dozen times in the States. I waited until Bond had looked around his hotel room unsuccessfully attempting to find an intruder. Then as he lowered his gun to return it to his holster, I fired! The audience jumped as one! That moment captured the rumor mill for almost an entire day. Have I mentioned that preseason weekday nightlife was pretty boring?

The weekends were a little better. There were a couple of places, like the Messange restaurant and nightclub just up the street from the main, that had jukeboxes and dancing. Have I mentioned that the college girls brave enough to leave the dorm after dark walked by me like I didn't exist? So, in order to dance, and I loved dancing! – I needed to find someone at the Messange who spoke enough English to understand what I was asking.

While trying to find dance partners, I got to know the Messange's owner, Herr Dietrick, a German. I ordered a German beer one night and he brought it down personally to meet the buyer. I suspect that he had hoped to find a fellow German and may have been a little disappointed at first, but we struck up a good friendship after I expressed my love for his country's beer. Over the year I even gave him some English lessons. Well, he had a good vocabulary, but he kept putting the verb at the end of his sentences, like they do in German. I helped him practice the English placement. In turn, I got a few complementary German beers. A fair trade! Anyway, back to nightlife, there were more than occasional parties...

As a matter of fact, the second Saturday of the semester, the school decided to start the year off right with an introduction to the mountain and to Swiss foods and beverages. They reserved a famous Swiss Fondue restaurant called "L'Horizon" for a cheese fondue fest and gave the students directions for finding it. We hiked for miles up the switchbacks to and through the upper village, then out a dirt path that ran south along the mountain face. Wilds, Gil, and I strode along the long dirt path following several girls and scanning the distant peaks and the nearby pastures. Actually, calling the downhill slope "a pasture" was generous because grass was just barely clinging to its side. There were a couple of cow paths cutting across it, but the slope had to be greater than forty-five degrees. And when you included the drop from where the path had been built up on the side of the slope, the pasture had the appearance of a grass-covered cliff with a stand of trees in the distance that just hid the valley below.

The cow paths on the steep slope reminded me of a story my dad had told about a joke he played on my mom when they were dating. They were driving from her home in Columbus to meet his parents in Salem. The ride took them through a particularly hilly part of Ohio with lots of farms. When mom pointed out some cows on the steep slope of a nearby hill, dad, having been raised on the farm and just graduated as a veterinarian, took on a scholarly air and told her that the cows in this part of the State were breed for the hills. They had been developed with two legs on one side shorter than the other to help them walk on the hills. According to dad, they drove in silence for several miles until mom turned with a questioning look on her face and asked, "What happens when they turn around?" That memory stuck me as funny just then, and I tried to explain and expand on it with my friends saying that in Switzerland they could develop cows with two small legs on the side to hold them away from the slope. I expounded with, "The cows won't even have to lean over to eat; they could simply turn their heads to the side." Wilds and Gil just stared down the slope and looked at me as if I had lost my chips. Admittedly there weren't any cows on that particular slope, and the guys may not have recognized the small dirt trails as cow paths.

We rounded a turn and saw the restaurant. It was single-story building with a large sloping roof. Tables had been set up outside on a level area. I wondered how a tourist would even find the place. There were no signs, and parking, such as there may have been, was a good half-mile down the path. We gathered around the tables containing baskets overflowing with bread chunks as bowls of molten cheese were set on sterno-heated food warmers. Then, as the waitresses went around taking drink requests, Willie told everyone at our table that you had to drink wine, beer, or hot tea and that cold soda was not an option. He explained that the molten cheese tended to cool and harden to a ball in your stomach, but alcohol and hot beverages would help keep it liquid. He didn't have to twist my arm. The school was paying, and the waitresses were already bringing out bottles of Yvorne, a local Swiss wine. *I can't imagine any stateside college buying the booze. Unreal!*

After we had had massive quantities of the molten cheese-soaked bread and the requisite glasses of wine, the party got started. Several of us left the tables clutching almost full wine bottles. Stallone, Cliff, Spyder, and a few others had chased down a cow and were trying to ride it. I stayed out of it because I had done my cow riding in boarding school, and they are not horses; they are just too bony to be a comfortable ride. Besides a cow can get pissed and chase you off the pasture, which, in this area could mean off a cliff. Then someone got the bright idea of trying to knock the cow down. Cliff bounced of its side several times before a running shoulder block from Stallone knocked the cow to its knees. They took turns sitting on the cow while Bernd took trophy pictures of their success.

I ran into Dick, the sergeant's son from Landstuhl, at the party. He was hanging around with a group of freshman guys and seemed to be the center of attention. It looked like he would be okay. He said the freshman dorm was a dump in the lower village, quite a hike uphill to the main building. He offered to give me a tour later, but he was a little boastful for my taste. Besides if it was below our dorm, it was a very long hike! I quickly rejoined Wilds and Gil.

Stallone had brought a football, and the level area became the playing field. When the game turned coed, I joined in. There was plenty of throwing, running, blocking, and tackling, but I doubt anyone knew or cared about the score. Late in the merriment, Dee Dee, the brown-eyed one of the fab... ahh... two grabbed the football and ran past me. I caught her around the waist, and we crashed to the ground. Unfortunately, I landed on her leg, spraining her ankle, so she christened me her official "beast of burden." I carried her piggyback from place to place watching the dwindling revelry. Soon it was time for the long hike back to the school. Showing off, I helped Dee Dee up onto my shoulders and handed her our wine bottle. Sam, the cute all-American partier, decided to join our group as we staggered down the dirt path toward the upper village. Sam, like Wilds, had hair that fell into her face when she was drunk, and at this point, except for her feet and lovely breasts, you couldn't tell which way she was facing.

As we walked, Sam started saying how fun it would be to roll down the pasture on our side. I strongly suggested it would not be a good idea because she wouldn't stop rolling before she hit Aigle, four thousand feet below. She laughed, threw her hair out of her eyes, took a swig from her wine bottle, and tucked her arm under my arm and Dee Dee's leg.

The walk along the path began to take on a surrealistic edge as my alcohol and exhaustion started to show. It seemed to stretch on forever, and I was viewing it in small fragments as my eyes closed and opened every few steps. Suddenly, I was brought to my senses as Dee Dee clonked me on the head with the wine bottle. As my eyes opened, I saw Sam was starting to lean over to roll down the green cliff. Without loosing Dee Dee, I grabbed Sam and pulled her up and along the path. As we walked further down the path, I once again lapsed into darkness. Then a thump on the head, and my eyes would pop open in time to see

Sam dancing on the edge of oblivion or squatting on the side looking down, and it would start over again.

It seemed like I had walked for days, and it was dark before we got to the main building. I fought my way up the stairs carrying the one girl and dragging the other to the entrance of the girls' dorm. As I set Dee Dee down, she gave me a quick peck of gratitude on the cheek. Then, not to be outdone, Sam laid a big, sloppy, wet one on my lips. Her breath smelled like vinegar, but she was a cute drunk! Arm in arm, Sam and Dee Dee helped each other up the steps into the dorm.

I staggered and slid my way back down the path to our dorm, then up the elevator to my room. Tiny hadn't returned yet. I peed forever, brushed my teeth, and slid into bed. My stomach was roiling as I lay on my back in the darkness. Had I had enough wine to keep the cheese from solidifying? Was my bed rocking? Then it happened; my bed rose from the floor and flipped upside-down on the ceiling with me clinging to the mattress! OH SHIT! I turned my head to the side to look at the floor, ceiling, or whatever, and the bed righted itself! That was it! The floor was down, and I was sprinting across it toward the bathroom. I made it just in the knick of time. All of that wine and bread and cheese came shooting out of my mouth! Again and again it came until I only had dry heaves left. When those ceased, I just sat on the floor in my misery hugging the porcelain bowl. It felt cool against my flaming cheeks. After a while I staggered back to my room. Tiny had returned and was sprawled fully dressed across his bed. I didn't try to wake him. I just brushed my teeth again and lowered myself carefully onto the bed worried that I might soon be hanging from the ceiling. Later, I was awakened as Tiny went running out the door, no doubt on a mission similar to my earlier one.

Chapter Ten

Hell House

The evening before the student council elections, Willie, who was running for president, held a knockdown drag-out party in the lower village. He had rented a room and sprung for several kegs of beer. There was music and dancing at first. Then, as the evening wore on, someone started a gross-out contest. I would put Willie at the top of the list because of the results, but the event appeared to be spontaneous. First a burping contest, then underarm farts, and one really loud, nasty fart! Wilds had just taken a slug of beer when the butt report occurred and his initial convulsion of laughter sent two streams of beer out his nostrils! This act, whether intentional or not, gave him an early lead in the contest. Then, they were off to the races! The whole thing was kind of a whirlwind of twisted faces, odd sounds, and various exposed body parts: several moons, one trouser snake, and a set of gazongas that were more glorious than gross. Admittedly, I don't remember looking at the owner's face, just some long blonde hair falling on each side of the globes, but she definitely got my vote! Then, before whoever it was could get her bra back on, Tiny grabbed her, threw her on his shoulders, and nuzzled his large nose and chin into her panties. This brought squeals of shock and delight from the victim and many of the female observers and loud guffaws from the guys. Tiny had jumped into the lead!

At this point, things seemed to slow down, so I found Dee Dee, who was chuckling nearby, and started talking with her. After all, I had carried her down the mountain on my shoulders. Because I was talking to her, I missed seeing the action retreat to one corner of the room, but shortly thereafter groans and cries of "Gross," "Holy Shit" and "Yuck" seemed to come from that corner. This lasted for a while, and I didn't have a clue what was going on until Wilds came squirting out of the group and running in my direction. "He ate shit!" he yelled, "He ate shit!"

When he calmed down I got the story. One of the truly drunk contestants decided that he could win the contest by taking a dump in one of the flowerpots around the room. The crowd had circled him and goaded him on until they saw that he was really doing it, then they sat there in curious amazement. However, after this putrid performance, Willie had stuck a finger into the pot and come out with a small dark brown fragment that he popped into his mouth with great relish, accompanied by an disgusting wretch.

Now I suppose that someone could get drunk enough to eat shit. Someone could even be highly motivated enough to do it for a desired result. But knowing Willie, I doubted both. He drank a lot but seemed to keep it under control, and he wasn't stupid enough to chance whatever parasites or germs were in those feces. I suspect that he had somehow set this whole thing up and had a chunk of softened and shaped dark Swiss chocolate hidden in his palm when he reached into that pot. This, along with the drunken crowd, set the stage for one of the most amazing victories of all times at a gross-out party. Whatever the truth of the event, the results were in, and Willie had not only won the contest but was elected student council president the next day.

After Wilds finished telling his "gross" story, I turned to find that Dee Dee had left me standing once again! This time I didn't even get a peck on the cheek. Not that Wilds' story would have stimulated any such reaction. Therefore, Wilds and I found our way back to the dorm on our own, as usual.

By the afternoon following the election, Willie had moved into a room by himself – one of the benes of being president. I didn't mind having a roommate, but it would be cool to have my own room.

Shortly after that I was in Le Nord and overheard a group of people, including our new president, talking about forming a fraternity in the sophomore dorm. My first instinct was that Willie was pulling Bob's chain. Bob was a pudgy-faced, slicked-haired sophomore with the personality of a born-and-bred politician (you know, that tattooed "trust me" smile with a "vacancy" sign on the forehead). He was one of the losers from the student council campaign. Willie wasn't saying much, but I couldn't quite believe that Bob had come up with the idea on his own, and the idea seemed doomed to failure if only because of the lack of focus in the sophomore dorm.

I mentioned the conversation to Wilds and my feelings that the idea was doomed when I ran into him later, and he agreed, although he said that he always wanted to be a frat guy and added, "I didn't stand a chance in a real fraternity. But no respectable Greek organization would bother with us."

"Speak for yourself!" I said, jokingly.

"I meant our tiny college."

A strange thing happened that weekend: Stallone, Jolie, and Bernd were sitting in Le Nord talking with Bob and praising his idea of a fraternity. None of this made sense until I mentioned it to my roommate, Tiny. "It's all part of the plan," he said. "Bob runs the dorm, keeps the records, pays the bills, and answers to the school administration while we get booze and girls in our frat house!" BRILLIANT! Willie strikes again!

With the studs' support, a constitution was quickly drafted and offered to the administration for review. The organizers got around the Greek problem by declaring "The Association" a non-Greek sophomore fraternity. With the administration's buy-in, the stage was set for yet another party, of course! This was to be a formal signing party with the school president, the Gut, the student council president, Willie, and all the sophomores and dates.

Dates... I only knew a couple of girls, and Dee Dee was avoiding me. Well, I'm not sure that she ever even looked at me as more than a beast of burden. And Sam... well, I wasn't sure about her after her sloshing drunk lets-roll-down-the-hill, routine. Besides, she had been drunk enough that she might not even remember me. Walking into the main building worried that I might end up the only one at the party without a date, I ran into Kaeti coming out.

"You look lost in thought," she said, catching me by surprise.

"It's just that – wait! – ah… we… the Association, are having a formal dinner to mark the signing of…" I stammered.

"Sure, sounds like fun! When?"

"Great! Ah… Saturday – Did I mention it was formal?" *I have a date! Shear blind luck!*

The signing party was fun – good food and wine! Roark played his guitar. *Is there anything that guy can't do?!* Kaeti looked great in her long light-blue dress, although her heels made her a good inch taller than me. Her long hair looked silky as it glowed gold in the candlelight and set off her hazel eyes in a bewitching combination. Tiny came with Pam, a round-faced young lady with shoulder-length red hair and a hefty chest! *More than a mouthful is a waste,* I thought. – *Well, Tiny has a pretty big mouth! Pam makes Kaeti look like a boy – no, that isn't fair; Kaeti looks beautiful and feminine tonight.* With the formal signing of the constitution, we now had control of our frat house. The evening quickly wound down, and a perfunctory kiss at the girls' dorm steps let me know that Kaeti was just a friend. At the same time, I owed her a big favor. She had saved me from the certain embarrassment of not being able to find a date to the party.

The Association wasted no time in assigning priorities: Girls, booze, and party, PARTY, **PARTY!** Bob did take time to "hire" the janitor who already worked at the building and to get a sign made changing the dorm's name from Florimont, or flowery mountain, hardly the name for a masculine fraternity, to Helvatia House. Helvatia had something to do with the early Swiss people and really appealed to the administration – but "Hell House" had a better ring among the frat brothers. (Willie, again? Maybe…) Yes, Wilds and I were frat brothers, hard to believe! A scarecrow and a short Quaker!

Not a week passed before our inaugural party, a Purple Passion party! The paint wasn't dry on our sign! Jolie and Stallone went to work on the drink, Purple Passion. It was supposed to be a mixture of grape juice, gin, and white lightning. Unfortunately, Switzerland was not known for white lightning, so vodka was substituted. The formula was one gallon of grape juice for every half-gallon of gin and half-gallon of vodka. In theory, one could taste the gin but not the vodka; therefore, the drink tasted a little strong but not strong enough to be deadly. In reality, the stuff was deadly! To add to the effect, apples and oranges were cut up and floated in the mixture hours before the party. The hope was that the fruit would ferment and add to the alcohol. It didn't work, but the fruit added color and caused an unexpected effect for those of us who were trying to stay sober. Gallons of the deadly drink were mixed together in a trashcan with a plastic liner.

Sometime the week before, I had run into Sam at school, and she had thanked me for my help on the way back from the Fondue party. Great timing! I mentioned the party, and she said she would love to go! I had a date! That evening, I met Sam at the main building. She looked very cute, but her heels brought her up to my height when she stood straight. Fortunately for me, she did that rarely. Her outfit didn't look practical for the shortcut to our frat house, so we walked back and forth through the streets of the village.

The party was in our house parlor. The parlor was on the second, well, European first, floor, and should have been the center of dorm life; but that tended to be Le Nord, so the parlor had been converted into a workout room of sorts. Stallone had supplied a basic set of weights and handgrips. Someone else had contributed a Bullwoerker, a strange contraption sold on TV and in the back of "Popular Science" magazine. You could do a half-dozen exercises with it, but it got boring quickly. Stallone had shown me some exercises designed to beef up my upper arms and a sit-up designed to destroy my spine, and I had shown him how to do the headstand-handstand pushups that I used to strengthen my arms for gymnastics. Anyway, the exercise equipment was all hidden away and the room aired out to get it ready for the party. That, music, and a trash can full of purple passions was all the party preparations we did!

As we entered the parlor the party was just getting started. I handed Sam a drink and warned her about the booze, but she tipped her head back, drained the glass, and went to get a second. To my surprise, Kaeti showed up with Tiny. They seemed an odd couple, but they were both great people and Tiny was certainly taller than she was – so they should hit it off. Funny, after the signing party I thought he was into well-endowed women. Given our budding friendship, I did take Kaeti aside and warned her about the booze. I thought about saying something about Tiny, but had the feeling that Kaeti could take care of herself. She appeared to heed my warning about the purple passions by nursing one glass while eating the fruit.

Then Willie showed up with Kayanna. All thoughts of Tiny and Kaeti flew out of my mind. Willie came in quietly and cautiously, as usual, measuring each person with his eyes. Then Kayanna came in slightly behind him; her head was lowered with her long silky blonde hair shadowing her pretty face. Her shoulders were held forward as if to camouflage the beauty of her rather full chest. Had she been a true princess or a goddess, she would have thrust her chest forward and let the world know the gifts that had been bestowed on her. She was nervous and feeling out of place in this already bawdy room. But the differences between Willie and Kayanna were greater than the physical – beauty and the beast thing. By now I knew Willie as sharp minded, focused, more that a little torqued, but very worldly-wise. Kayanna, on the other hand, was a babe in the woods! Her personality could be seen if you ever got a look into her wide-eyed, innocent blue eyes. Actually wide-eyed and innocent would be the definition for all of Kayanna. Her father was an ambassador, if not the ambassador, to France, and she lived in Paris, but her very demeanor shouted that she had lived a sheltered life. Seeing the two together was definitely strange. Kayanna crowded closer to Willie as they disappeared in the room.

It was still early in the evening when I started getting a buzz. I was a little surprised by this because I had managed to nurse two glasses of punch while eating a bunch of the purple apples. They were great! I lost track of Sam for a while and ran into Kaeti while looking for her. "Hey, kiddo, you should have warned me about the fruit," Kaeti said. "I'm high, and I am still on my first cup!"

"Wow! I was wondering how I got so buzzed! Hey, have you seen my date?"

"Sam? She's over there by the punch."

"Again, oh no!"

I turned and saw Sam leaning against the wall by the punch trashcan with one blue eye just visible where her hair parted – and the eye appeared to be wavering back and forth. Then, as I started to walk toward her, the eye disappeared behind her hair, and she slid bonelessly down the wall into a seated position on the floor. I ran over and caught her before she fell over onto her side. She awoke at my touch with a look of total terror! She covered her mouth with one hand, grabbed my shoulder with the needle-like fingers of her other, and dragged herself to her feet. She then looked about crazed, and bolted out the door into the hallway. Sensing her urgency, I ran with her and guided her to the toilet. There I sat holding her hair out of her face and rubbing her back as she puked it all back up! From date to caregiver in half an hour, Great!

When she finished, without giving my presence a second thought, she turned, hiked up her skirt, dropped her panties, sat down and took a leak. When the liquid stopped, she stood, threw her arms around my neck, panties still at her ankles, and leaned into me for a kiss. In other circumstances she might have been inviting, but her recent performance, disheveled appearance, and unbelievable breath drove any thought of romance from my mind. I held her close, but a kiss was out of the question! Even when her hands were roving up and down my back and grabbing my butt, I was frantically trying to think of a way to take her back to her dorm. She gave up quickly and almost tripped when she started to walk out of the bathroom. I bent down to help her with her panties (something I had never done before with anyone out of diapers), and we moved out. She started back toward the parlor, but I convinced her that the party was over, and we headed toward the elevator.

On the walk back, we meandered as I tried to guide her through the streets and she tried to play hide and seek in the shadows from the street lights. I suspected that she was trying to find a place to make out – and if

I'd had a gallon of mouthwash, I might have been tempted. Then again, she was so far gone that she didn't know what she was doing or who she was doing it with, so I guess that I wasn't that tempted. I managed to escape a vomit-breath kiss at the stairs, but I could tell that Sam took offense at my escape. Oh well, another winning night! I should have gone with my first impression of Sam. What was her problem? She was nice looking. I suspected, with a little self-confidence, she could have been drop-dead gorgeous!

When I returned to Hell House, I surprised Tiny and Kaeti in our room. As I walked in, Kaeti dashed across the room with emotions flying across her face; first embarrassment, then a little anger as she looked back a Tiny, and then relief. Meanwhile Tiny was trying to levitate his six and a half-foot body off his bed.

"Geez, sorry!" I said as I started to back out.

"No, no please stay!" Kaeti said. "We were just –" Her eyes flashed around the room and alighted on Tiny's big red skis. "– looking at Tiny's skis!"

She then scanned the room and saw mine. I had almost forgotten they were there. "Are those yours in the corner?"

Quick thinking, I thought. "Yes, I got them at the PX before I came to school."

Tiny had sat up and was looking frustrated. Kaeti walked over and separated my skis, then began flexing one like an archer testing a bow.

"Harts, huh, really flexible. They should be great in deep powder! Tiny's Red Stars are really stiff. He needs that, given his size, but they won't be as easy to turn."

Kaeti then reached to the top of the ski and measured me with her eyes. "Hey, kiddo, how tall are you?"

"Five foot, nine and a half," I exaggerated... well, I didn't add "in shoes..."

"Huh, a little taller than me. Who measured these for you?"

"The guy at the PX, why?"

"Come here and reach for the top of your skis."

I complied. That put me a little close to Kaeti; in fact I could feel warmth radiating from her. I reached up and could just curl the tips of my fingers over the end of the skis.

"These are a little long for you, even if you were an experienced skier, and you aren't, right?"

"Is that bad?" At this point, Tiny set his elbows on his knees, supported his head between his large hands, and sighed.

"They'll be harder to turn. The flexibility will help." She hesitated for a minute. "The good news is they'll be a lot more stable at high speed."

"Okay, I guess…" Tiny shot me an evil eye from the bed. "I guess I'll go visit Wilds."

"That's okay! We were just leaving," Kaeti said, leveling an intense stare at Tiny. He got up with a sigh and they left.

Tiny returned about a half hour later when I was in bed. "Great timing Henderson!"

"Don't look at me! We'll have to work up some kind of signal. Hang a hat or something from the doorknob." A grunt was Tiny's only response.

To my surprise Gil started dating Sam shortly after that party. Maybe my stories of pantiless-fondling in the bathroom pricked his interest, so to speak, or maybe he felt she needed a father figure – fat chance! Anyway, they began to hit it off, and Sam started to get her act together. That was really good to see – but then I began wishing I had been able to effect the same change in her to my advantage… Anyway, Gil explained her to me. It seems that her parents had just told her that she was adopted. Instead of feeling love for those who took her in and raised her, she felt lied to by them all these years. She felt unloved by her adopted parents and rejected by her real parents. In fact, she felt that no one could possibly love her. Geez, with that explanation, maybe I didn't envy Gil. He was taking on a big burden. He was obviously enjoying himself because Sam could be seen leaving his room at all hours, but this relationship wasn't likely to last forever, and a rejection could just prove to Sam how unlovable she really was. That could be her last straw! Gil and I talked about that, and he knew the dangers but said that he was really getting to like Sam.

After a couple of dates, I started having a little more luck. Maybe confidence was my problem, too. One weekend night that didn't have a party most of us were hanging out at Le Nord drinking beer and playing *zim-zim*. After my team was beat and I pulled away from the table, I noticed Jana, a freshman with long brown hair and large brown eyes, sitting with some friends and looking my way. Actually there were half a dozen guys around the game, but she might have been looking at me. I picked up my beer, walked over, and asked if I could pull up a seat. Beer, the great confidence builder! I started talking with the group but stayed focused on Jana. At first she was a little shyer than the others, but I managed to get through to her. She was from upstate California, somewhere in the mountains by a big lake. She loved the mountains and skiing. Once the ice was broken, we talked for quite a while. She even stayed with me when her friends headed back up to the dorm.

I escorted Jana back to the dorm and joined the legion of couples saying goodnight on the steps. The kiss was brief; but as she turned the corner on the stairs, she pulled her long brown hair over her left shoulder and looked back with her lovely, sparkling brown eyes and smiled. That held a hint of promise, didn't it?

I was thinking about asking her out the next weekend when, from behind me, I heard an accented voice say, "Don' push eet, Stallone!" *Don't push it, Stallone! Someone has a death wish! What was that accent, Spanish?* As I turned to see who had said that, I found myself walking backwards up the stairs toward the girls' dorm. Stallone was just a few feet from me. His hands were clenched near his waist, his head was cocked forward and down to the right, and his total focus was on some Hispanic freshman, Lopez, I think. "Loco" might have been a better name at that moment. The only thing I knew about Loco was he had braces. Girls get braces, not guys, and girls have their brace work done before college. Maybe it was a jet set thing. Anyway, Loco hopped up onto the balls of his feet, brought his fists to his chest and began bouncing in front of Stallone. His long black hair made him look a little taller than Stallone, but he wasn't as muscular.

I backed up another step, totally focused on the two. Stallone hadn't moved. Loco bounced forward a bit, and then it happened. I saw Stallone standing with his fists at his waist. He tightened his torso, let out a sharp, whooping exhale, which was accompanied by a snapping noise that sounded like a fist contacting flesh as the fists disappeared and reappeared on either side of his face. I was focused on Stallone, confused by the snapping sound and by losing track of his fists, until I realized that Lopez had stopped bouncing. My eyes flashed to his face. His eyes were white, his left knee, followed by his right, were bending in slow motion. He dropped to his knees, and then fell slowly forward, ending as his head made a loud popping sound against the floor. His arms made no attempt to arrest his fall. His face was turned toward me; and as I stared, I noticed a trickle of blood run across his lower lip and fall onto the floor. I hadn't seen the punch! I was watching! I don't think I blinked or looked away, but I hadn't seen the punch! I guessed that explained the snapping noise, but his fists didn't go there.

To me, everything moved in slow motion after that. Stallone, joined by several guys, walked out. Lopez started to come around. A couple of freshmen helped him to his feet. The side of his face was red, but the blood that was running down his chin and falling onto his white shirt was coming from inside his mouth. Someone mentioned that his braces probably cut the inside of his cheek. I just stood there partway up the stairs into the girls' dorm with my right hand clenched on the railing.

Once I got my wits back, I headed toward our frat house and Wilds. Did I have a story! I found Wilds in his room.

"You won't believe this!" I said.

"Stallone decked Lopez," he interrupted.

"How…?"

"Cliff's been telling everyone."

"Wilds, you wouldn't believe his hands. I didn't see them move!"

"Golden Gloves."

"What?"

"Cliff said he was Golden Gloves champ in Philadelphia."

"What's Golden Gloves?"

"Don't know, maybe it's basic training for inner city thugs!"

"Whoa, quiet! Your sense of humor is going to get us both killed!"

"Then maybe it's like Little League for boxers! They didn't have it in my hometown."

"But Wilds, his hands..." and I went on to tell the story as best I could describe it.

Stallone was a God after that, a powerful, vengeful God! Freshmen and sophomores alike showed him deference. No one showed him less than total respect. Well, almost no one. Actually, I heard that the next day Cliff started joking around and telling Stallone "Look out, I know karate!" That ended a little less violently. Stallone pantsed him and held him up by his ankles while Bernd ran, got his camera and took pictures. I didn't see that episode, but I saw the photo when it was developed, and a severely edited version of it ended up in the yearbook.

To say the next party was a dud would be an understatement, but a few of us had a great time. It was Wilds' birthday, and he bought a keg and took it to his room. He invited all his frat brothers for a Saturday afternoon bash! Only Gil and I showed up. The three of us sat alone for a time trying to figure out how to tap the keg. It was a large wooden keg with wood plugs and a metal beer spigot that needed to be driven into one of the plugs, and we didn't have a hammer or a clue how to do it!

I ran down to the parlor, reminded several people in there about the party, and borrowed a steel weight from Stallone's barbells. Back in his room Wilds decided to do the honors and slammed the spigot with the weight into the plug. It didn't seat, and beer started shooting out of the hole in the end of the keg. At first we tried jamming the spigot in, but it wouldn't stay; then we gave up and started drinking the beer as it geysered from the keg.

Soon we were ankle deep in the beer that covered Wilds' floor and seeped under the doors onto his balcony. Gil had sealed the door to the hall with Wilds' towel. We began scooping up beer off the floor with mugs, drinking it, and then throwing mug-loads at each other. Wilds slipped while running from Gil, fell face-first into the pool, and slid over to the balcony doors. Then seeing the beer seeping under the doors, Wilds got the idea of opening them, which he immediately followed up on. The beer flowed out of the room, across the balcony, and over the side. Now, Switzerland is known for its spectacular waterfalls, but this may have been the country's first beer falls as it cascaded majestically from the fourth floor onto the parlor balcony and off to the ground below. There may only have been three of us at Wilds' birthday – but a great time was had by all! I will add that Wilds' room never smelled the same again. That stale beer had soaked into everything! Only the cold of winter offered any relief from the odor.

Chapter Eleven

Fall Sports

Our college and the American high school had lost their sports director when John Harlin had fallen from the Eiger, so students were encouraged to fill in the void. With students as the instructors, most sports before ski season were a joke. Although it was one place where money didn't really matter, except possibly what kind of equipment you had. Stallone had managed to wangle the position of basketball coach. I didn't do basketball, too short, but the guys seemed to enjoy what were basically pickup scrimmages. Also Kaeti said that Stallone was a very good coach for the girls. He was a focused instructor and held the girls to very high standards. Somehow I got the feeling that Kaeti wasn't telling the whole story. I heard from Gil that illegal use of hands took on new meaning when coach Stallone joined in on the girls' scrimmages! Not that he saw anyone complaining.

I had a brief – very brief – moment as soccer coach. Actually, I found a field complete with goals in my wanderings in the lower, flatter part of the village, and I took the trains to Montreux to buy a soccer ball with my own money. I talked with Stallone about it, and he said he had always wanted to try goalie. So one day after school we gathered several other willing participants and headed to the field. At first I showed off, juggling the ball with my feet, knees, and head; then I kicked it back and forth with the other guys while Stallone lined in the goal. One or two shots from the others, which Stallone fielded easily; then it was my turn. I picked my favorite spot-shot; the outside right corner of the box to the top left corner of the goal. I dribbled to the right and drove a hooking shot toward the goal with the outside of my right foot. Stallone made an amazing dive and almost got to the ball, but it dropped just past his hands, through the upper corner, and bounced down the hill behind him. He fell on his side and rolled to his feet. "Nice!" he said, but as he turned to retrieve the ball we noticed that it had started bouncing higher and further down the slope behind the goal. "Oh geez!" he shouted as we both started running after it. Stallone was maybe ten strides down the slope and I was barely off the field when the ball landed on a large rock and bounded behind a thin row of trees out of sight. Stallone stopped, but I raced to the trees and jumped onto a large boulder to see over the edge. The field beyond was very steep, and the ball was nowhere in sight. No wonder I hadn't seen the locals playing soccer here! Stallone and I talked briefly about getting nets, but I admitted that the shot was a little lucky and that I didn't always hit the goal. Therefore, we would have to net that whole end of the field. So much for soccer on an Alp! I hoped that some lucky valley kid enjoyed my new ball.

One sport that was not a joke was mountain climbing. Bernd was the instructor since the actual instructor had been killed in a fall. We had ropes and a carabineer or two but not much else. Bernd claimed that free climb is the only way to climb. As he delicately put it, "Artificial climbing with pitons and such was for pussies." On the other hand, it could be that all the climbing equipment had been owned by the former sports director. Anyway, I borrowed climbing boots that had a steel shank that kept the sole from bending. They were tough to walk in, but they allowed me to set my toe on a ½ inch wide ledge on a rock face and have a relatively sturdy platform to stand on while I moved my hands. Spider free-climbed to the top and set up a belay, or safety rope, for us amateurs. Bernd taught us to keep three points of contact at all times: two hands and a foot while you moved the other foot, or two feet and a hand while you moved the other hand. We took a relatively easy way up and were rewarded with a rappel down.

I guess that I need to explain that statement because rappelling is scary as crap when you first try it and Bernd was old school when it came to rappelling. You wrap the rope around your body; first between your legs, then up the left side to the front, over your left shoulder, around your back, and under your right arm to your right hand. It is a twisted configuration, but it seems to work. The friction of the rope as it runs across your body slows your descent. However, it gets a little warm in the crotch if you descend too quickly. Needless to say, I took to wearing lederhosen, or German leather shorts, after my first class. A full thickness of cowhide, rather than jeans, to protect the family jewels seemed eminently practical. The scariest part of rappelling is lowering your body backwards over the top edge of a cliff and trying to stand horizontally on the cliff face with the ground forty feet below. Logically, you knew that the belay rope would catch you if you messed up, but leaning over backwards on a cliff face was frightening. I was sure my gymnastics helped me some, but my basic distrust of someone else holding my life in his hands, to say nothing of the real climbing instructor's recent crash and burn, scared me to death! I made it over the edge – but it wasn't pretty. The gloves were too large for my hands, and the little finger of the left glove actually got caught between the rope and the cliff edge. As I jerked it out, I rotated slightly and almost fell sideways into the rock face. Then, when I started to reach out with my right hand to push away from the rock, I loosened my grip on the rappelling rope and slid a few feet before the belay caught me up. Once I was on the rock face and standing horizontally it was great fun walking and bouncing down the cliff face! Although the bouncing part was when it got warm…

Nancy had followed Bernd to the class. She was a tall blonde, five-foot ten, definitely well put together but a skyscraper, as far as I was concerned. She was only a little shorter that Bernd. Nancy had her hair tied up in two ponytails and wore a long- sleeve flowered blouse and very tight three-quarter length, rolled up jeans that gave her a Daisy Mae look. Like the rest of us, she was scared shitless before rappelling the first time. But watching her face turn red with excitement and fear as she went over the edge, and then looking down on her long legs and lovely body as she stood horizontally beneath us with her two blond ponytails flipping to each side her as she shook her head and laughed with delight made many of the male observers, including me, quite warm in another way. Rappelling was cool, once my initial fear was conquered; the weightless drop down the cliff made a fatiguing climb up worth the effort.

After the first week, we graduated to vertical climbs and overhangs. That was not fun! Some of the moves involved reaching up behind my head to a handhold that I couldn't see. Such moves were inevitable failures, and I dropped several feet through space until the belay rope pinched my waist and swung me into the rock face. Hands, shoulders, knees, and hips took a beating, but we kept trying. Also jamming and twisting our fingers into a crack to form some sort of living piton began to take a toll on the skin on our fingers and knuckles, but Bernd taught us some unique taping patterns to provide some protection. However, I am not sure which hurt more, tearing a scab off in a crack or pulling it off with the tape after the lesson was finished. Ouch, damn, it hurts just thinking about it!

One day Spyder put on a demonstration. It was unreal watching him creep up the cliff face and under the overhang. He even hung by his left hand for an instant, feet dangling, while he swung his right hand up to a higher handhold hidden from him on the upper face. He then jammed his feet back against a seemingly smooth surface under the face for traction for his next move. Now, this was amazing, but, for me, it wasn't his most unreal feat. One day, Gil was stuck on the overhang unsure of the location of his next handhold when, after calling instructions up, Spyder scrambled up the face without a belay. He intended to show Gil where the next handhold was; but about eight feet up, he missed his next handhold and fell. Below him were a series of boulders and scree that had broken from the cliff over the years. He came down feet first with his hands pointed down and his head well forward measuring his landing spot. He only lacked a tail from looking like a falling cat. Like his feet had eyes, they picked the flat areas of two of the larger boulders for the initial landing spot, and he pranced backwards over the boulders and out of the scree without putting a hand down. It was totally amazing! His nickname was well earned.

At dinner on Sunday of the following weekend, Gil came to our table with another story about Spyder. A group had left early in the morning for what Spyder called a hike and a picnic on the Chamossaire across from our mountain. Several couples went, including Gil and Sam, and Spyder and Carole with her cowl of black hair. They were an item now. In fact, Carole had just cut the bangs of her cowl to a point in the middle, which enhanced the intensity of her beautiful dark eyes. When Spyder and Carole walked together dressed in black, they could easily be mistaken for comic book superheroes.

Anyway, the couples had borrowed a car to drive to the far side of the valley, where they began their hike. They followed a stream until they reached a waterfall. There they picnicked. After a while, Spyder encouraged them to climb a fairly steep rock face beside the falls. The girls decided to watch from below while the guys showed off. Spyder led, then Gil, and the others were to follow. Gil was about fifteen feet up with Spyder another ten feet above him when a rock came falling past his right shoulder. "Hey, warn me!" Gil yelled, but as he looked up he saw Spyder's boots fly over his head. From his perch he looked down and saw Spyder falling the next fifteen feet in eerie silence to the slope of the hill. Spyder landed on his back, bounced over a bush, and came to rest on his side in a small level area. Carole ran over, screaming his name, while Gil scrambled down the cliff. When he got there, the others were standing in a ring around Spyder. Only Sam was standing to one side, crying. Gil pushed inside the group and saw Spyder unconscious with some blood coming from his mouth and more from under one cuff of his black turtleneck. Gil panicked! No one was doing anything! He grabbed the wrist that wasn't bleeding to feel for a pulse, but Spyder started to groan and move. Carole then swooped down, grabbed Spyder, and cradled him into her breasts. This brought a small, crooked smile from Spyder, who then pretended to nuzzle in. Seeing that, Gil went to comfort Sam.

Gil and the guys had to carry Spyder back down the hill, and they took him to the doctor in Leysin. Gil had just come from the doctor's office to tell us what had happened. All he knew was that Spyder had no broken bones. He had some bruised ribs, lots of scrapes and bruises, and he had bitten the tip of his tongue. An over twenty-five-foot fall onto his back with only bruises; a spider he truly is!

One fall sport was taught by the school's staff. The president asked if there was interest in Judo, and several of us responded. The first day of class, a coed group showed up. We had been given heavy off-white outfits, called Judo-gis and matching belts to tie around them. Gil helped Wilds and me put the outfits on in our rooms. The shoulders and upper half of the jacket were made of coarse, heavy-woven material, and the collar and front opening were bordered with a thick band of material that rivaled the sturdy belt that was to be tied around the waist. Gil explained that the material has to be heavy so it won't be torn during the grappling. Wilds said that he didn't care much for the use of the term "grappling." Gil also showed us how to tie the belt so we didn't look like fools. You have to run the belt twice around your body and tie it with a fancy kind of square knot.

The first day of class, the Gut, in his gi complete with a black belt, asked if anyone had taken Judo before, and like a fool, I mentioned that my dad had taught me some Judo as self-defense when I was twelve. In reality, my father had taught me only a couple of throws and how to fall. After the fact, I realized that several of the second-year students, like Gil, had taken this course last year but were smart enough to keep quiet. Therefore, I became his first demonstration dummy.

At first, he was kind to me as he demonstrated the starting position with his right hand grabbing the heavy belt-like material on the opening my Judo-gi near my chest, and his other hand holding the elbow of my right arm which, in turn, was grabbing his gi. We pushed and shoved each other for a while demonstrating the need to stay loose and move with the other's force and not to resist it, although his 250 pounds of force definitely had more effect than my 137 pounds. Next step was landing after a throw. The president, all 250 pounds of him, did a swift shoulder-roll through the air landing and rolling quietly across his back, ending with a resounding thump of his arm on the mat. Given my gymnastics, I had no problem with that and started showing Wilds and a couple of others how to perfect a shoulder roll.

Then, the Gut called me up for the next demonstration. "Do you know how to do a hip throw?" he asked.

"Sure" I said, grinning and looking crosswise at Wilds.

"Show us!"

As I reached for Wilds' gi, the Gut said, "No, with me!"

My jaw dropped as my eyes scanned his rotund physique and I wondered, even as short as I was, if I could get below his center of gravity. I closed my mouth, took a deep breath, moved forward, and grabbed his gi and elbow. I pushed him back and then pulled him toward me. As he rocked back upright, I stepped around behind him, as dad had taught me, and attempted to roll him over my hip. He fell back, but he didn't roll over my hip. Instead he landed on my tripping leg and tried to crush my hip and leg into the floor beneath the mat. Although I was in some pain, once he rolled off me, I got up, bounced around to shake it off, and he offered to demonstrate. He caught my gi and, without much fanfare, I saw the wall and several light fixtures before crashing into the mat. My arm did manage a resounding slap on the mat, but I suspect that was more the result of centrifugal force than of any conscious effort on my part. I returned quickly to my feet; a pain in my head had replaced the ache in my hip, but I didn't show it. There is something inside me that won't allow me to admit pain, especially in a room with coeds.

The Gut looked at me and held his hand out beckoning me to try again. I did. This time I got lower and moved quicker, placing my hip below his and levering it up as I pulled. All 250 pounds rolled quickly across my back and landed with a resounding smack of his arm on the mat. I suspected that he had helped me, like my dad had when I was twelve; but the surrounding students applauded, and the President shot me a quick nod of respect from the floor.

As he picked himself from the floor and began to straighten his gi, I saw something I hadn't expected. The coat of the gi had fallen open under his black belt, and with his pants tied below his great belly, I got a full view of its enormity. But it was the smaller bulges running down the belly that caught my attention. Now I am proud of my tiny six-pack, the result of thousands, if not hundreds of thousands of sit ups, but his gut had knots of muscle the size of my fist starting as the stomach emerged from his ribcage and moving down to just above his groin. The last set was longer and narrower than the others, and they made up a fourth set of muscles. The Gut had an eight-pack! I hadn't known that was possible! I stared at his stomach, mouth open, until he was fully up and his gi straightened. We bowed; he smiled and moved on to choose another dummy.

When I joined Wilds, I asked, "Did you see that?"

"Yeah, but I'm betting he helped."

"No fooling! No, did you see his gut?" I whispered.

"Hard to miss."

"No! I mean did you see his eight-pack!" I said a little too loud.

"More like a whole keg!" blurted Wilds.

The Gut had heard and looked around at that, and several students chuckled as he took Wilds for his next dummy.

After class, sweaty and bruised, Wilds and I walked down to our frat house. I told him what I had seen, but he didn't believe me. I asked several other students, and they just asked how badly I had hit my head. Well, I am pretty sure what I saw; and by the way he tossed Tiny and the larger guys around, I suspected that there was more than met the eye with our President Arnold. Oh, and that was Wilds' final judo class.

Chapter Twelve

A Walk in the Park

One Sunday, Tiny and I started talking about hiking to the top of the mountain. Wilds didn't sound too enthusiastic about it until Tiny mentioned taking the telecabine to the top of the Berneuse and hiking up from there. On route to the lift we stopped by the main building. Bernd and Nancy were talking outside, and at the mention of the adventure Nancy's eyes sparked to life. Given Nancy's enthusiasm, Bernd didn't need any convincing to join the hike, but he ran off to pick up something in town and promised to meet us at the lift. Tiny ran inside and came out arm-in-arm with the almond-eyed Paula. Neither of the girls seemed dressed for a long hike, but I wasn't complaining. We waited a few more minutes but spotted no one else so we started walking up to the lift. Bernd joined us as we approached the steps, and instead of the climbing gear I had expected, he was carrying a bag with several litre bottles of beer. I was beginning to wonder if this was going to be a hike or an excuse for a party as we boarded the telecabine.

As the lift started, everyone grabbed a beer but me. It was early afternoon, and I wasn't in the mood, plus I wanted to see what was ahead of us before I drank any alcohol. The lift held the six of us as we crossed the upper fields and headed for the escarpment. The view behind us was unbelievable, as we could see farther down the valley toward les Dents du Midi, but I was focused on the ground beneath us. These would be ski slopes, and they were steep. Would I ever master them? Then we rose over the cliff. The drop didn't even compare to the Diablerets in height, being only a couple of hundred feet, but it would be equally deadly for the errant skier. Bernd pointed toward the north and said there were openings in the cliff where the ski trails passed between the rocks. On the top of the cliff, the steep slopes leading to the edge held huge stainless steel barriers. Each consisted of four Xs held together with a massive central shaft. Bernd explained that they were used to prevent avalanches and that they would be buried under the snow in the winter. He also said that only the experts ski this area. Looking at the rocky area now, I couldn't imagine anyone skiing on it. In fact, the only apparent path to that area took you along the edge of the cliff, and part way down that path a skier would have to thread his way through a narrow cleft in a large upright spire of stone. Walking that route would be frightening, but sliding on snow! You'd have to be insane!

Getting out of the telecabine and walking onto the slope revealed a large bowl on the top of the mountain with a pond and a couple of cowsheds in the bottom, and a huge sharply pointed peak on the other side. Bernd explained that most of the skiing was done in this bowl. The side we were on was the north face, which got less sun; therefore, the snow was colder, which made it better for some reason. The opposite side was called the Chaux de Mont. It was steeper and more challenging to ski, but it got more sun. Apparently that was where most of the broken legs occurred. I didn't need to know that! The sharp peak was called the Tour D'Ai. To me, climbing that was the goal.

While we were still looking at the peak, there was a sudden deafening roar of jet engines from behind us and a shadow raced over us. We ducked and looked up when a second roar pierced our already ringing ears. We turned as a military jet skimmed up the side of the mountain alongside the lift housing, arced a few feet over our heads, and disappeared behind the Chaux de Mont. "What the hell!" I shouted.

Bernd regained his composure first and explained, "That's the Swiss Air Force. They live here and know every inch of these mountains, valleys, and every up and down draft! They practice here a lot."

It looked like he had something else to say, but the two jets had curled around a peak to our north and soared through the valley level with the villages below.

"WOW!" Wilds exclaimed!

"They fly like… like falcons," I added. "Can you imagine a dogfight between those guys and invaders?"

Bernd said, "I think that's the point."

The hike into the bowl was pleasant. The grass was spongy and a little slick. Nancy and Paula definitely did not have the right shoes, but Bernd and Tiny enjoyed catching them when they slipped. On the way, Wilds asked how I knew about falcons, and I talked about raising a Red Tail Hawk at boarding school, teaching it to fly and about joining a falconry club in Maryland and watching them fly their Peregrines. Then I told him about my senior "grady paper" on falconry and the fact that falcons can maneuver so fast that they are used to hunt other birds. Wilds was once again wishing he hadn't asked, but toasted my lecture several times with his beer.

As we reached the bottom of the bowl, we noticed that the pond was very clear and cold but not very deep. The sheds were larger than they had appeared from the lift and were massively constructed. Bernd said that they too would disappear under the winter snow. When exploring a cleft in a large rock, we found that some snow was still there. It had the appearance of a great white whale littered with small stones. There was just enough room to walk around it and gouge off handfuls of snow. Nancy threw the first missile at Bernd, and the war was on! Hiding between the rocks and running around the end of the whale, snowballs flew! I got Tiny, and he quickly retaliated. Wilds got creamed between Nancy and Bernd. This didn't last too long because the snow was mostly slush and full of pebbles so one or two hits on the skin, especially the face, were enough to make you cry "uncle."

The cliffs at the bottom of the Tour D'Ai also had caves, which I explored briefly, but I was ready for the ascent up the peak. Unfortunately, I was the only one ready to go on. Tiny and Paula had disappeared into one cave, and Bernd and Nancy were headed for another, while Wilds seemed to be happy with his beer and a large rock. I yelled to Bernd and asked how bad the climb was from here.

He called back, "It's a walk in the park! There's a clear path and metal rails in the steeper areas." So I started off on my own.

The path led between the rocks and the caves with some large boulders to climb and hop between. Then I was on a steep field similar to the one on the way to the fondue party. I began broad strides up the slope but found myself out of breath before I took twenty steps. It had to be the altitude and the reduced oxygen up here. After I caught my breath and started climbing again, I concentrated on taking long full, slow breaths, like I was on a long distance run. It was strange to have to control my breathing just to walk. Even with total focus I found myself running out of wind and resting every hundred feet or so. The field ended in another series of boulders. Bernd was right about metal bars. They were attached to the stones so you could pull yourself over steeper sections. The next section of field was not as steep, and the vegetation was dying out, leaving dirt and stone. I was getting used to taking deep breaths and seemed to be climbing more easily when I climbed a third set of boulders and rounded a large rock outcropping. On the other side I was startled by a narrow crossing with shear drops on either side that lead across to the upper part of the Tour D'Ai. I braced myself against the rock face and silently cursed Bernd. The walk up was bad enough, but I had never seen a crossing like this in any park. The vertical drop to the Chaux de Mont on the left was only seven to eight hundred feet and that was beyond frightening, but the drop to the right was thousands of feet off the mountain. There was a metal bar attached on the left between the rock faces on either end of the crossing but it was severely bent. I imagined a hiker falling sideways and hanging on for dear life as the bar bent. Then again it might have been Swiss teens swinging on the bar for the fun of it, or perhaps a climber tied off his rope on the bar and rappelled down the side. Whatever the reason, the bar was too far to the side and below knee level, and was not going to provide any security for the walk across.

I was frozen to the rock face for several minutes while I examined the crossing. It was several feet wide, but less than a foot was flat near the center while each side curved rapidly to the edge. I began to psych myself up – I could do this! I had walked across fallen logs much smaller than this! Hell, the girl's balance beam was much, much smaller – and hadn't I once tried tightrope walking. Geez, better not think about that! That wasn't the greatest ending. I focused on the far side, held my arms out like a tightrope walker, and strode out. The world spun clockwise and began tilting! I half-hopped, half-fell backwards to the rocks behind me. What had just happened? I had purposely not had any beer! Was it the altitude?

Again, clinging to the rocks, I began controlling my breathing. Then I started slower, first one step, then the next. I spotted it! The ground below on the right appeared to be moving faster than that on the left. My brain was trying to understand what my eyes were seeing. The land wasn't moving; I was, but the land on the right was so much further below than that on the left that it appeared to race by me with each step. The spinning was an illusion caused by the different perspective. Again, focusing on the far side, I took two more steps. The world spun, but my path stayed straight and level. I was in the middle now, and four quick steps took me to the other side. I hung there hugging the rock on that side for a long time. I had made it!

I searched the path up from there with my eyes. It appeared very narrow and circled to the right on the edge of the fall off the mountain. This was really somebody's twisted idea of a walk in the park. I'm going to kill Bernd! The slope beside the path wasn't vertical, but I found myself walking sideways with both hands clinging to its rocky surface. Almost invisible, wiry vegetation occasionally tangled in my fingers. I looked back at the crossing and realized that I would soon have to return. *Would I have the nerve? Would I get stuck up here like a cat up a tree? No, that isn't an option. Tiny might wonder why I wasn't in bed when he got up tomorrow, Wilds might wonder why I wasn't in class, but I doubt that I'd be rescued tonight – and imagine the disgrace of having to be carried off the mountain! The fall might be better. Whoa, that is a stupid thing to think! I made it here; I'll make it back,* I thought as I continued my sideways crawl up the path.

As I neared the top, the slope to the side flattened, and I began to feel silly crab walking along the landscape. I stood and peered over the shoulder. I was finally on the top! It was fairly flat and surprisingly small but big enough for me to feel myself on solid ground again. My confidence soared! *The world is at my feet! I made it while the others are still hiding in their caves! Hell, I should have brought a flag or something.* Maybe, I thought, *I'll leave my tee shirt on a stick – yeah sure! The nearest vegetation that could produce anything the size of a stick was probably back by the cowsheds.*

I turned slowly around and surveyed Switzerland to the west, north, and east, and Italy to the south. I could see Lac Léman and, perhaps, France beyond it. I was on top of the world! Examining the little patch of earth that was the top, I spotted a square stone that marked the highest point. It didn't look like much, but it was a symbol. I lay down on my back and rested my head on the stone. From this position, all I could see was brilliant blue sky and the sun. In my imagination I floated in a great blue sphere, the sun warming me while the wind cooled me. *Could this be what heaven is like?*

I must have stayed like that for quite a while because I noticed the sun moving slowly over me causing the shadows on my face to change. It started getting darker and colder. I began feeling alone and a little depressed by the thought that I would have to brave that crossing again, when I felt something compelling me to look down to my right side. There on the ground between my side and my elbow was a tiny white flower, smaller than a violet. Its five perfect, tiny petals were in the sun and faced the sky like I had been doing. I wondered that it could survive up here and was grateful that I hadn't crushed it as I lay down because it was now my companion. I had the warm feeling that God had just sent me a sign. I slid over to keep the flower in the sun while sheltering it from the wind with my arm, and we lay there together until my shadow grew quite long. I knew it was time to leave. It would get dark soon.

As I stood, I noticed that the Chaux de Mont was already deep in shadow. The path around the side seemed wider and I could walk upright. Clouds below had concealed the depth of the valley on the left, making it not appear as frightening. Then I came to the crossing. Perhaps it was the combination of the shadowed Chaux de Mont and the clouds or perhaps it was the feeling that God was near me, but I crossed it easily – a walk in the park...

I was cautious when I descended the first series of boulders, but I covered the upper field in a quick stride. I scrambled down the second set of boulders and onto the steep field. Then confidence or foolhardiness took over as I began bounding down the slope. I pounced up and out from the springy grass and landed with both feet together only to spring up and out again like some crazed, two-legged mountain goat. I quickly crossed the field and rounded the break in the rocks where I had left the others. It was dark down here, and I wasn't surprised that Wilds' rock had long been abandoned. I didn't bother looking in the caves because I was sure they were empty. It was surprisingly cold down here, and a colder breath was coming out of those caves. There was a wispy ghost-like vapor coming from the rocks where we had spotted the white whale. The shadow of the Chaux de Mont had covered the slope up to the telecabine, and I began to worry about it shutting down before I got there. The ski trail to the village was somewhere to my left, but I would hate to have to try to find my way down in the dark with the cliffs out there.

I began running up the slope toward the lift housing. It was steeper and further than I remembered walking down. As I came around the shoulder of a large rock, I saw that the lights were still on so I slowed my pace. If the operators were surprised when I walked in, they didn't show it. They barely acknowledged me and quickly closed me into the telecabine for the trip down.

The village was dark when I strode back toward the school. It wasn't that late, but I had missed dinner. It was about 7 p.m. when I walked into Le Nord. Willie and Jolie were tossing back a couple of beers, and I went over to get my own. It went down cool and clear. I hadn't realized how thirsty I was. I had a second before I asked about food. They had snacks here, but Willie said he knew a better place just down the road. I berated Bernd during our walk, but Willie reminded me that Bernd was a mountain climber and, to him, that probably was a walk in the park.

He also cleared up another thing for me about Bernd. "How did Bernd manage to sleep his way through the girls' dorm last year?" I asked.

"Bernd? No, that was Scott. He isn't here this year. He went through the alphabet to the M's and started at the back, but he hit Candy, a tall, gorgeous blond, and got hooked. If it were me, I would have started there! Some guys have all the luck!" Willie replied. Envy? Willie seemed to be so confident that this comment caught me by surprise. But that wasn't the last time he would surprise me.

Willie took me in the back door of a restaurant, and as we walked past the kitchen, he waved and shouted a greeting in Italian to several of the cooks and waiters. The place had long tables, like in the German beer tents at the festivals, and we pulled up a couple of chairs near the kitchen. On future visits I went through the front door and learned its name was the Chasseur. He ordered bifsteak-au-poivre, pomme frites, and a bottle of wine. As we waited I told Willie of my climb and the feeling of being on the top of the earth and being surrounded by the sky.

"Makes you feel closer to God," he added.

I know that my eyes almost popped out of my head. Had he been reading my thoughts? His comment came totally out of the blue, but something similar was running through my mind at that very second. I know that I wouldn't have mentioned it for fear of being teased, but I hadn't expected that kind of comment from him.

Soon I was telling him about the flower and of other strange things that had happened to me earlier, like a bird that seemed to lead me back to boarding school when I got lost my freshman year. I told him that I was a Quaker, and we were off to the theological races. When the steaks arrived, I realized how famished I was. They were delicious! Thin pieces of beef with peppercorns pounded into them. The pomme frites were the best french fries that I had ever tasted. They were super-thin and just the perfect balance between crisp on the outside and soft inside. The only thing missing was ketchup. Between the beer, the wine, and the meal, I have no clue what we talked about; but it was past midnight when we returned to Hell House, and it was back to class the next day.

Tiny grunted recognition and turned over when I came in and brushed my teeth. As I put my head on the pillow, I quickly relived the fear and the glory of that climb before falling into a deep sleep. Then I dreamed about flying over the mountains in that clear blue sky and diving into the valleys only to soar back up – until my alarm started ringing in my head! God, that was a short night! Sorry, God!

Chapter Thirteen

Freshman Dorm

One afternoon after class I ran into Dick, the sergeant's son, on my way out the front door. Funny how I had hardly seen the freshmen guys after school. I figured that they must have their own hangouts in the lower part of the village. Dick insisted that I go to the freshman dorm. Plus, he offered to buy me a beer. *What the hell...* We wandered past the Chasseur restaurant, the soccer slope... hard to call it a field – and into a cross street that I didn't know existed. The building was in bad need of a paint job but had lots of nice balconies. However, it was set sideways in a flatter part of the mountain, not facing the Chamossaire peaks like the buildings near our frat house. The upper floors of the dorm might have a view of les Dents du Midi down the valley, but the view from Dick's room on the first floor was the parking lot. My gut feeling was that the location left the freshman isolated from the rest of the school. I was glad that I wasn't a freshman, but I didn't say that to Dick.

I got my beer at a small bar down near their dorm. Dick seemed to be buying beers for anyone who showed up. I managed to slip into the conversation something that I thought he needed to hear. "These guys are rich; they probably don't give a crap who is buying beers." My comment didn't seem to affect Dick. Maybe he just didn't want to hear it. As I left, I realized that I hadn't noticed the devilish twinkle in his eyes that I had seen when we first arrived, but I had my own problems and wasn't ready to take on someone else's. A choice I would regret later – although much later.

I never returned to the freshman dorm. It rapidly gained a reputation for harboring troublemakers. Someone was tossing Molotov cocktails off the balconies onto the parking lot; not that there were any cars there... One night in Le Nord, Dick described the gasoline-filled beer bottles leaving short-lived flaming pools at various spots on the parking lot. He claimed that he wasn't part of that, but his eyes told a different story. If he wasn't doing it, he certainly wasn't complaining either. Also, there were rumors of more theft in the lower part of the village, which, some said, was caused by the freshman.

I heard about the worst episode when my roommate, Tiny, came storming in our room one afternoon. "Shit! Shit! SHIT!" he shouted as he prowled around the room.

"What's wrong?"

"My brother's been accused of stealing, and the police took him to prison! Shit! I need to find a car! I have to go see him!"

"I'll help. Do you know what happened?"

According to Tiny his brother had been with a group of freshman guys at a bar when a local hooker got her purse stolen. His brother was the only one they arrested. He didn't know why. It was a shock to me that they even had hookers in town, but I stayed with Tiny.

"Issa has a car. Let's check with Willie. He may know how to find him."

Issa's MGB MkII may have been designed to hold four passengers, but they didn't have Tiny in mind when they made that claim. With the passenger seat all the way back resting against the back seat, Tiny's knees were still in his face. I was wedged in the back behind Issa, who was no small guy, with my feet pinned under his seat as we raced down the mountain. Issa had a strong arm on the wheel and shifted well as we squealed down the mountain. Tiny said his brother was in the Château d'Aigle, the castle with the turrets at each corner and tiny window slots at the bottom of our mountain.

It was near dark as we left Leysin and pitch black as we arrived in the valley. The castle was dark and forbidding as we stood in a field beside it. No light showed through any of the slits. There didn't seem to be any office, and no one challenged us as we walked around the outside yelling up at each slit hoping for a return shout from Tiny's brother. We didn't hear or see a thing. It was curious that there were no sentries, but the stone edifice didn't seem to offer any avenue of escape. God, I'd hate to be Tiny's brother! This was inhumane!

As the next few weeks passed we learned that American citizens had no rights in Switzerland. Basically, they could put you in prison and throw away the key! Luckily, Tiny's dad had political pull and got a Swiss lawyer involved. After almost a month his brother was exiled from Switzerland never to return. Given the loss of two of the Fab-four, that seemed to be the Swiss solution to troubled foreigners. At least Tiny's brother was out of that castle prison...

As the year progressed, the freshman guys started coming further up into the village and joining the rest of us, but there was still a stigma on their dorm.

Chapter Fourteen

Parents' Visit

One Friday in late September, my parents and Millie surprised me by showing up at the school. They said that they had left a note for me with whoever answered the phone, but I hadn't received it. Dad had bought a white travel trailer in the Netherlands and had managed to pull it up the narrow twisty road from the valley. That took guts! The trailer was tinier than anything I had ever seen before. It supposedly slept three, but the two beds doubled as tables so they had to be made up each night. There was a small food prep area and a bathroom/closet, but the three occupants could not stand up at the same time in the remaining floor space.

As luck would have it, that Saturday the local farmers decided to bring the cows down from the upper pastures and through the village. Mom and Millie were wandering and window-shopping; and upon hearing the sounds of the cowbells, mom was certain that one of the local churches was practicing bell ringing. She ran excitedly up the narrow cobblestone road to find out which church it was in. Millie followed at a moderate dignified pace. As mom rounded a sharp switchback she ended up in front of the whole herd! Shocked by the appearance of so many cows she froze in place in the middle of the road. As Millie rounded the turn she too was shocked; but seeing her mother's peril, she ran forward, grabbed her, and pulled her into a narrow opening between two buildings. There was no back exit from the opening as the mountain slope climbed a good story and a half between the buildings so they were stuck. What was beautiful music from a distance was loud cacophony to anyone wedged in the narrow opening as the cows passed. What seemed like an hour later, the two exited their nook with ringing ears and waved politely at the passing boys driving the herd.

As my luck would have it, that night was a Sadie Hawkins party, and no girl had asked me so I felt duty-bound to invite my family. Crap! Well, the good news was that Kaeti was one of the organizers so she pulled us in and set us up at a great table. I also got to introduce my two other friends: Wilds and Gil. We had a choice of beer or Coke to drink. Dad asked for a beer; both mom and Millie wanted coke. Kaeti grabbed the cokes as I went for the beer. This was my first official school party with beer, so I didn't know what to expect. They were filling up 1½-litre stainless steel pitchers with beer (almost a half gallon!). I walked back with the two pitchers, one for dad and one for me, and clonked them down on the table. The whole family sat open-mouthed staring at the pitchers until mom piped up and said cheerily, "I guess I'll have to help your father with his!" Now mom is not a drinker. In fact, one glass of wine will have her dancing on tables – seriously, the following spring during the German festival, Fasching, she fell off a chair on her way to the table and almost fractured her hip – but that's another story…

This night, sharing dad's beer got embarrassing. Remember, I am almost not fitting in at all at this school, and now my mother is up dancing and wiggling in ways that mothers should never wiggle in public! I was ready to climb under the table, but she kept insisting that I dance with her. Geez! I was so happy when they decided to head back to their trailer that I almost carried mom out of the room! On the way back to the trailer, Millie asked about Dick. I hadn't seen him at the party, and I wasn't about to introduce her to the freshman dorm. I'm not sure what she saw in the guy.

They left Sunday to return home. I helped dad hitch up the trailer, wished them a safe trip down the mountain, and did a little jig when they disappeared around the corner. I hadn't realized how lucky I had been in the States to have my college almost two days drive from home.

Chapter Fifteen

The Mating Season

I wasn't part of the mating season, and I'm not sure that I understood what happened. My guess is that it had something to do with a relatively small number of wealthy sophomore guys and a few tall, good-looking freshmen using alcohol, popularity, gifts, and any other means at their disposal to get a rather large number of girls into any number of positions in an infinite number of secluded places. I saw only the rather sickening effects of the season as post-coital depression came close to reducing the population of the girls' dorm.

To blame it all on the studs is too simplistic. Pursuing women is the basic nature of college guys. The girls should have been able to handle the pursuit except for several factors unique to this college. First, the girls in the college outnumbered the guys almost two to one. In the village, it was worse with the American high school that averaged about three girls to one guy and several English and German girls' finishing schools. Second, there were an unusual number of extremely striking girls and only a few high-profile guys. Third, female popularity was tied to having a major stud on your arm. And fourth, the girls came from wealthy and important families where popularity was the norm, whether it was purchased or bequeathed as a mantle of their power. As the daughters of the rich and powerful, they had been worshipped and courted as the heirs apparent.

As the sharks circled for the kill, they picked on the weak and innocent first. They had the least defenses. In fact these girls' only defenses were to stick together and stay sober, or to snag guys that they could control through looks, or sexual favors, or both. The problem with sticking together and staying sober was that they didn't appear popular. Since these girls had learned that popularity meant standing out like their parents, it was difficult to move to the shadows or into the herd for protection. As for looks... Well, I've already described the princesses and the goddesses. Several were able to tame a man with looks alone. Those ever so slightly less beautiful would flaunt what virtues they had, seeking suitable companions to worship them as they had been worshipped in the past, and they were met by the studs. One glorious dance in the arms of a major catch – then a few drinks, a little necking, and the girls were given a choice: have sex with them or watch them move on.

Again, I don't know but I suspect that many of the innocent were virgins and, like me, saving it for marriage. But they were now torn between virginity and popularity. A few drinks, a threatened walkout, and they jumped in the sack to hold their man. The shitty thing about it is that the studs' plans did not include long-term relationships. Their motive was to score with as many as possible. Therefore, sex did not guarantee a relationship; in fact, it almost guaranteed an end to it.

While Gil had a good thing going with Sam, Wilds and I were out of the loop. I guess his skinniness and my lack of height and, perhaps, our parents' lack of power and wealth put us out of the contest. We couldn't supply enough status to make a girl "popular." In any case, we were sitting at breakfast when the first results of the mating season appeared. I don't want to reveal her name, let's call her Jackie. Jackie was a really cute, thin, animated, freshman girl with short black hair and large red lips, kind of a Shirley MacLaine in *Irma La Douce*. She came into the dining room with large white gauze bandages wrapped around her wrists. Donna, at the other end of the table, whispered that Jackie had slit her wrists last night and was taken to the doctor.

Have I mentioned the school's doctor yet? He had a bizarre sense of humor! The college's only legitimate reason for missing class was to get a doctor's excuse. But a trip for a girl to the school's doctor, even with a mere headache, meant stripping naked for a full physical examination. After being poked, prodded, and thoroughly examined, first-timers were taken into the doctor's office and informed in a serious voice that they were pregnant. The doctor's assistant would usually let the girl know that he was kidding, but... Well I'm only assuming that all of the wrist-slicings were the result of a post-coital breakup. Several could have been post-doctoral humor.

Anyway, when Jackie came in with her gauze wristlets, she was invited to a table with several concerned girls. Later several guys paid attention to her and helped her get to class. But Jackie was just the beginning. Two days later, another sweet girl, call her Debbie, came in to breakfast with wristlets. She was another innocent freshman with short blonde hair curled at her chin-line and wondrous blue eyes. If her hair had been shoulder length, she'd had a slightly fuller figure and stronger self-confidence; she could have been one of the princesses. Debbie was followed by two girls the next day, one of whom only had flesh tone band aids on her wrists, two stuck side-by-side lengthwise on the inside of each wrist. Those band-aids actually became the norm after the first few weeks. Perhaps the girls used band-aids so they wouldn't have to visit the doctor. But the band-aid wearers no longer got the support that the first girls had received. In fact, they became the butt of the morning jokes. "Who's wearing band-aids this morning?" was a common breakfast icebreaker at any given table. Wilds even found out that you couldn't kill yourself by slitting your wrists. Well, you could, but you had to be very determined because your tendons protect the larger blood vessels. You have to cut through the tendons to get the job done. Needless to say Wilds' discovery was not an acceptable breakfast topic. Donna and another girl actually left our table that morning. Another reason for our lack of popularity? – quite possibly...

Several weeks into the post-season mutilations, Donna arrived with a different story about... let's call her Saundra. Like many at school, Saundra was lovely in her own way, although not my type. She had long dark wavy hair that she parted toward the middle. The result was that her dark, sad eyes just peaked out between the sides of her cascading hair, and her chin and blood red lips seemed very pronounced. She was built soft and luxurious, like some young, sexy version of mother earth; and she loved wearing flowing silk dresses with lots of lace. Saundra had jumped off the third floor balcony only to be saved by Kaeti. Donna didn't know the whole story, but Saundra was taken to the hospital with a broken arm. I went in search of Kaeti to get the whole story, but she wasn't anywhere to be found.

As usual, after dinner that evening I went to Le Nord for a beer and a game of *zim-zim*. Then I remembered the story about Saundra and figured that I'd find Kaeti at the snack bar. She had started the snack bar to give people someplace to hang out besides the local bars. Kaeti had been successful at finding ground beef that tasted similar to hamburger, a bun that wasn't too bad, and had perfected a method of deep fat frying potatoes twice to make them taste like the french fries you find only at the beach. The meal really reminded me of home, even if the Chasseur's *pomme frites* were better. Guys would come in early after dinner for a hamburger and fries and leave for the bars. Later in the evening, you typically found the place pretty empty with only a few girls drinking sodas or tea. Still, Baby John and Alice would occasionally come with his guitar and draw a crowd, Willie and I often had good philosophical debates, and I even learned that Colleen wasn't from Ireland sitting around those tables. Oh, and Tiny and Kaeti had started dating again, so Tiny would come here to meet Kaeti when she was closing. Maybe the place wasn't so empty after all. And the snack bar had a jukebox with a good selection of American songs and some popular European ones. Kaeti had the key so we could load new records when we found good ones.

I got to the snack bar after the hamburger rush and before any girls had arrived. Kaeti was alone, sitting behind the counter with her head resting on her arms and her long hair covering her face. "Love Me, Please Love Me," a sad, slow song by Michel Polnareff, a popular young French singer, was playing on the jukebox.

"Hi!" I said as she noticed me.

"Hi, Jim," she said softly as she raised her head and absently pulled some of her hair over her right shoulder. She had dark shadows under her eyes like she hadn't slept the night before. That wasn't the Kaeti that I knew, so I sat in front of the counter and waited quietly.

"You heard?" I nodded my head and waited.

"I don't understand," she said looking down at her hands.

"What?" I mumbled.

"She was so beautiful, so creative... I don't understand... why?"

"What happened?" I asked.

Her eyes glazed as she started her story. "Her door was open last night, and I thought I saw something move on her balcony. I almost walked by when I saw her getting up on the railing. I yelled to her and ran. She didn't say anything. She just bent down and slipped off. I caught her arm by the wrist, but I couldn't hold her. She fell... I... knew she was dead," she said with finality. Then she stared down, her eyes focused somewhere beneath the counter, her mouth open slightly. "I looked down, but it was so dark." She trembled slightly and swallowed. "I couldn't see her body."

I saw a glistening like a tear in the corner of her right eye and covered her hands with mine. "But you do know she's okay, don't you?"

She slowly focused on my hands then looked up at me. Her eyes with areas of green and brown flecked with gold looked confused... lost. I could see wet trails on her cheek now. "Someone said she landed on the balcony below and broke her arm, but I can't... I let her fall," she said softly as she looked back down at our hands.

"You do realize that you probably saved her life? You caught her arm and held her long enough for her to swing in to the lower balcony."

"Maybe," she said so quietly that I wasn't sure I'd heard it. I lifted her hands and held them tight. We sat in silence for a long time. Kaeti stared into space most of the time, but occasionally she would look at our hands and then hold my eyes for a few seconds before drifting away again.

Finally, she looked into my eyes, and with a little spark and a hint of a smile, squeezed my hands and said, "Hey, kiddo I'm closen' up early, gonna get some sleep. Want some left-over fries?"

"Never turn down free food!" I said as we broke our hold.

"Who said it was free?" she said flicking her hair over her shoulder, and we both laughed. Tiny wasn't there yet, so I helped her close up and walked with her the two flights up toward the girls' dorm. It was early so no one else was there. We hugged briefly at the steps up to the dorm.

"Hey, hero – get a good night's sleep, you deserve it," I said as I gently squeezed her hand. She turned and walked slowly up the stairs toward the dorm, her head forward, her arms folded protectively across her chest. As she turned the corner, she stopped, reached out for the hand rail, looked back through her hair, shot me a little smile, and then walked with a bit more spring up and out of my sight.

That was the last suicide attempt I heard about in the girls' dorm. No one chose to follow Saundra's example, even with all the attention she got in her new cast, which she decorated with black silk and white lace. When I relayed the story of Kaeti's heroics to Willie, he told of a similar episode the year before. This girl was at the Messange nightclub. She went out onto the balcony in the back. It wasn't far to the ground, but the slope was very steep, and she could easily have broken her neck tumbling down the mountainside. Stallone was the hero that night. He had stepped onto the balcony as the girl fell off the railing. He caught her by the ankles and was wrestling her back onto the balcony when Willie and some others walked out. It would have been interesting to learn Willie's perspective of the mating season... but I wasn't sure that I was ready for his answer.

You know a bizarre fact – I or Wilds or a half dozen other guys would have treated those girls like princesses if they had given us the slightest bit of attention. They typically were aloof around us, nose in the air sort of thing. It's hard to ask someone out with zero eye contact! It didn't make any sense to me. Anyway, the mating season marked the end of walking through the villages unaccompanied after dark for all but the most secure coeds. Therefore, the mating season was followed by the pairings. They were often more unreal and cruel. Like Dennie, the Association treasurer, and his girlfriend, Lee. Lee was cute with short dark brown hair and light brown eyes that sparkled with mischief when I first met her. Dennie treated her like a piece of crap – but she followed him around like a whipped puppy and kept coming back for more. She was young, a bit immature, and lacked self-confidence, but I will never understand why a woman would put up with that shit. There were far too many sick relationships like that, girls waiting hand and foot on guys just to keep their attention. Guys, like little lords, allowing them to stay around provided they were useful and put out. Wilds and I use to joke, "Hey, they could have us!" Well, maybe that wasn't such a joke...

Chapter Sixteen

La Neige

Early in October we woke to a heavy mist in the village. It was what I used to call an Oregon rain, a heavy, cold mist that happened every morning as I walked to school in Portland when I was eleven. While we hiked up the cowpath to the main, Tiny said the mist meant snow up top. Kaeti seemed to agree because she was in a "tizzy"– one of her favorite words, usually reserved for the other girls. After school the sky cleared, and we could see that the top of the Chamossaire across from us was outlined in white snow, which meant that there was snow on our mountaintop because it was a little taller. The arrival of *la neige*, as the French Swiss call it, was the talk of the school and the village.

That same afternoon the American high school in the upper village was having a used ski-clothing sale, and I had asked Stallone to guide me. He helped teach the high school athletics and was heading that way. I knew the general route but hadn't been there before. A strong, cold wind was blowing as we started the walk up. We walked with our hands tucked in our pockets and shoulders hunched. I attempted to start a conversation.

"Cold tonight!"

"Yep."

"Hey, did you see the snow? Pretty cool, huh?"

"Uh huh."

"Ski season's coming. Are your excited?"

"Yep."

"You teaching basketball?"

"Yep."

With his monosyllabic responses, I couldn't keep it up for long, so we walked for a while in silence. As we walked past an area with no buildings on the downhill side, a freezing gust came blowing up the mountain at us.

"God! That was cold!" I said as I looked between the buildings. But what I saw was beautiful! Apparently the sun was setting behind our mountain, and the snow on the top of the Chamossaire had turned crimson; the mountain was black and the sky nearly so, but the red outline of its multiple jagged peaks floated in the darkness. "WOW!"

Stallone turned. "Wot?"

"The mountain!"

"Wadabout it?"

"It's beautiful!"

"Geez kid, I thought you saw somethin'. That's always there."

We went back to walking in silence. As we passed the switchback where the road went on up to the upper village, we stayed straight. Streetlights were on in this section, and they illuminated some low clouds racing by just above the buildings. Suddenly, a locomotive-sized chunk of cloud broke free from the mass and sailed down the road straight toward us. As it flashed through us, or us through it, I ducked and covered my head thinking that I was about to be hit by something solid. The cloud felt like a chill breath from the grave.

"WHOA!" Stallone exclaimed!

I looked up to see him standing chest out and arms spread, ready to take on the world.

"Now that was somethin'! Those clouds are crazy sometimes! I remember when I first came here some stupid cloud came bargin' in my room like it owned the place. I thought I'd have to chase it out with a broom or somethin'."

That was the longest speech that I had heard Stallone make. His accent was definitely from Philly, but the way he talked out of the side of his mouth, almost like he had had a stroke, made him sound really strange. I wondered if he felt as out of place at this school as I did. Some of these guys could really be snoots. What was I thinking, this was Stallone! Nobody messes with Stallone!

We talked a little more after that about the ski clothes sale.

"You know this stuff is from the high school kids, right? They're kids, you know, you won't find very big stuff."

"I'm just going to see what's there. Probably won't find anything."

Stallone kind-of sized me up and said, "You never know, kid."

At the high school I found the ski clothes sale. It was in a rather small classroom, and there wasn't much there. As Stallone had guessed, most of the stuff was girls' clothes, and almost everything was too small. There were a lot of young girls hanging around staring as I checked out the stuff. Some of them were cute, but high school! Anyway, most of the ski pants I tried on were too tight in the butt. Some, I hate to admit, were too long in the legs. Finally I found one pair of medium blue pants with light blue stripes down the outsides of the legs that fit and were pretty cool looking! You could see where they had been altered to shorten the legs, but they were perfect for me. Ten dollars later and I was on my own, back down the mountain without Stallone.

Dinner was starting as I walked into the Main. I tossed the pants onto a ski locker as I walked toward the stairs.

"Hey, did you get something?" Kaeti said as she stood next to Tiny at the top of the stairs.

"I found some cool pants!" I said as I reached over, picked them up, and showed them off.

"You can't wear those!" Kaeti said as Tiny started laughing.

"Why not?"

"Those are the high school ski team's pants, and you can't even ski!" Tiny said.

"So?"

Kaeti explained, "Only ski teams wear stripes down the sides of their legs or on the arms of their sweaters. It's a rule. You can't wear those."

"I didn't know. Crap! You know what? I'm going to wear these by the end of the season because I am going to be on the ski team," I boasted.

Kaeti gave me the once over, smiled and said, "You just might. I'll help!"

Not to be outdone, Tiny chimed in, "Me, too!"

"Great! That will make three of us! You two willing to start tomorrow?"

"Start what?" Tiny and I both said together.

"Meet me at the steps tomorrow at 7 a.m. Oh and get to bed early and not too much beer."

I had only one beer and got to bed by 10:30, but the morning came too early! I don't know how Tiny felt, but it was hard to raise him. We dressed warmly but loosely and walked to the steps behind the main building. The steps ran several hundred feet up into the upper village. Kaeti was waiting with a broad, evil smile. "Okay, let's go!" and she started running up the steps. Tiny and I groaned and followed. About fifty steps up, Tiny's breath became labored. I threw it into long distance running mode and started long deep breaths: three steps inhale, and three steps exhale. Another hundred steps and Tiny had slowed and dropped several steps behind. I was still tailing Kaeti, but I was starting to feel it. A hundred more steps and I was in autopilot; my mind had blanked out, and I was running on long-trained soccer instinct. I didn't dare loose focus and look around to spot Tiny, but I didn't hear him anymore. Come to think of it, my total focus was on Kaeti's backside and the way her long ponytail whipped back and forth across it.

I doubt that I could have passed Kaeti at this point, but she wasn't moving as fast so I could easily pace her. Before we reached the top, my legs were past rubber; gone! I was pumping my shoulders and arms to lift them up each step. At the top we stood gasping, barely able to talk.

"You're (puff) alright (puff), Henderson (puff)."

"No sweat (gasp) I play soccer! (gasp, gasp) – just not at five thousand (gasp) feeeet! (gasp) What now?"

"Now (puff) we bounce down."

"Let me stretch out first." I used the stretching to catch my breath.

Kaeti showed me how to hop between the steps. First you hop to the right and land with all your weight on your right foot with your right knee angled inward behind the left knee, then you reverse that in the other direction. Back and forth, down and down the dozens of steps until we found Tiny resting at one of the switchbacks. We stopped for a while as Kaeti showed Tiny the hop. It was good for me to hear it again. Part of the way down, I had stopped hopping on the outside foot and had started my crazed mountain goat hop on both feet. We started off again bounding down the steps. I was in the lead followed closely by Kaeti, then Tiny.

At the bottom I turned and caught Kaeti as she tried to avoid me, and we looked up. Tiny was several steps behind us, hopping back and forth like some out of control monster robot. Kaeti shouted up, "Keep your knees together! Land with your outside knee bent inwards!" We both stepped as far to the side as we could get to allow Tiny's large frame to land beside us. "Great!" Kaeti said as she hugged him. "Ready for breakfast?" She didn't have to twist our arms. On the way in I stretched against the wall and Kaeti chimed in, "Meet you guys again tomorrow?"

"Sure," I said grimacing. Tiny grunted his response.

Kaeti laughed and threw one arm across my shoulders and the other around Tiny's waist, "Just kidding! You'll be stiff tomorrow. Give it a day or two! When you're ready, I'll be here."

I was stiff for the rest of that day, but it was a good feeling. I hadn't done much running since last spring's soccer conditioning. Sunday morning, I was up bright and early. I tried to rouse Tiny, but he just turned his back to me and told me to get lost. When I went outside, there was a chill in the air, and a light dusting of snow covered everything. I sprinted up the cow path to the main and around the side to the steps. It was exactly 7 a.m. and no Kaeti. I waited about ten minutes and was starting to get really cold when I decided that she had been joking about the run so I headed up on my own. The snow on the steps was cold enough that it wasn't slippery. It wasn't as easy to maintain my speed without Kaeti pacing ahead of me, but I pushed myself, and the crisp air helped spur me upward. Plumes of smoke flew behind me with every breath. I was serious about the ski team. Getting to the top wasn't as hard this time, but I probably didn't hit it as hard. I began bounding back down, trying to perfect the landings as Kaeti had instructed. I was so focused on landing correctly that, when I reached the bottom, I almost jumped right on top of Kaeti. "Sorry!"

"Looking good!" she said as she caught me.

"Thanks. You're late!"

"Hey, it's Sunday; they don't serve breakfast until 8:30." I hadn't thought of that.

"Ready to go again?" she asked.

"Ah... okay, let me stretch out."

"I was kidding!"

"I wasn't! I'm going to make that team. Hey, what kind of a coach are you? You should be kicking my butt not letting me off easy!"

"Then let's go, tiger!"

As we started off, I told Kaeti to be careful. The light dusting of snow didn't seem slippery, but it was starting to warm up.

She responded, "Give it a couple of more weeks, and you won't be able to walk up these steps. We better make the best of it!"

I was stiff, but I'd caught my breath on the way down. However, it wasn't long before I started loosing it and slowing. I could tell that Kaeti was also slowing because she didn't want to get too far ahead of me.

"It's alright," I shouted between breaths. "Run ahead! I'll catch... you... way down!" I was two-thirds of the way up when I saw Kaeti come bounding around a corner above me; her long ponytail bobbing behind her.

She shouted down to me, "You lead, I'll follow!"

"I'd rather follow you!"

"Who's the coach here? Turn and jump, kiddo!"

I did. At the bottom again we steadied each other and tried to stretch out. Then as I took my first step toward the main, the ligament between my quads and my hip cramped up. "Ah!" I grunted. I bent over and started rubbing the area with the heel of my hand.

"You okay?" Kaeti asked, concerned.

"Just a cramp, I need to stretch it. Mind if I balance on your shoulder?"

"Sure." I stretched my quads as best as I could and hobbled through the revolving door into the main.

Still concerned, she said, "Maybe you overdid it."

"Hell, you should have seen us at early season last year. Eight hours of running the first day. Everyone had rubber legs and walked like zombies into dinner that night. The second day of running and practice and the cramps started. This is normal, I guess. Same time tomorrow?"

"Actually I run after school's out on the weekdays. But tomorrow I'm helping Stallone with women's basketball. What about Tuesday?"

"It's a date!"

"A date huh? You're going to have to run faster than that!"

That took me by surprise, and I stood on the stairs chuckling. *A date with Kaeti? Nah, too tall, besides she's dating Tiny. Just friends… But now, my coach,* I thought.

Kaeti was right; two weeks later, and the steps were buried. Snow had covered the village. Early that Saturday morning, Gil came in and woke Tiny and me.

"Let's see what you guys can do. Grab your skis."

Gil was wearing a black sweater with gold stripes down the arms and a school patch. I hadn't realized that he was on the ski team. I was a little groggy from Friday at Le Nord but dragged myself out of bed and got dressed. My parents had bought me a couple of plain blue ski pants, no stripes. I put one pair on and a maroon Earlham College sweatshirt.

We went to a small bowl area in the lower part of the village. Tiny had skied before and was sliding down the slopes before Gil was able to show me how to put on my skis. He had me attach a leather strap to a boot buckle, claiming that it would keep the ski from running off when I fall.

"It also protects the other skiers. These things can become spears if they get free on the steeper slopes."

Gil had me put my skis in a big "V" that he called a snowplow and start sliding down the almost level slope I was standing on. Not two seconds into it and I did a face plant! The snow was solid rock here. "Oof! What happened?"

"You caught an edge. When you snowplow, you need to lean forward and push the heels of your skis out."

Two more face plants, and I was ready to give up the dream of ever skiing, let alone being on the ski team.

I was picking myself up after the fourth plant when Kaeti walked up behind me. "I thought I saw you guys! Having trouble?"

"No, I'm good!" I lied.

"Yeah, I saw," she said with a grin. "Put your knees together first, and keep them close as you push your skis into the wedge."

I did as she instructed and made my first successful slide down the tiny slope. I fell on my butt at the bottom, but I hadn't done another face plant.

"Better to fall back and to your side. You don't want to land on your skis and start sledding," she shouted down to me.

When I got back up the hill I asked, "Okay, but what just happened? What was I doing wrong?"

"Your skis were flat on the snow. Keeping your knees together in the snow plow raises the outside of your skis so you don't catch an edge."

"Gil keeps saying that. What does 'catching an edge' mean?"

"Simple, the sides of your skis are the edges. The inside edges are between your boots, and the outside are... the outside. You want to ski on the inside edges of the skis; if you get your weight on the outside edge, it plows into the snow, stops your ski's forward motion, and – you're down!"

"I know the result. Thanks for the help, Gil!" I shouted over to the side where he was watching.

"Sorry, it's been a while since I snowplowed," Gil shouted back.

Kaeti spent a couple of hours with us, and by the end I felt much more confidant. I could turn, and I could stop, sort of, by turning up the slope. I was still on my butt a lot but felt better about the whole skiing thing. She showed me a faster way up the slope than the sidestep Gil had shown me. It was like some exaggerated duck walk with the huge skis on your feet and your poles planted behind them. She called it the herringbone because of the pattern the skis made on the snow. Kaeti's departing word of advice was, start in ski school as soon as it begins.

Apparently some Frenchman named Bennie was a great instructor and a nice guy.

I followed Kaeti's walk with my eyes as she strode confidently up the hill.

"Hey, watch it Henderson!" Tiny's voice boomed from above my head. "She's my girl," he added as he lost his balance, plowed into me, knocked me over, and landed on top.

"Great, man! No need to crush me! I get your point!" And we both laughed. I looked up the slope and saw Kaeti looking down and laughing at our pileup.

When the ski lifts finally opened, I spent Saturday morning on the bunny hill. Then my killer friends, Gil, Tiny, and Wilds, dragged me onto the chair lift and took me to the top of the Riondaz, the lesser of the two ski-able peaks on our mountain. Gil encouraged me, saying that this was the intermediate slope and that I could handle it. The first run down, I was on my butt and trying to put my skis back on more than on my skis. The others would soar by and laugh at whatever new position I had gotten myself into. However, by Sunday, I could make it down with only one or two falls. I was improving! One certain fall was on one especially steep switchback in the trail. I never made it around that turn! In fact, I started falling in anticipation of falling. That way I knew where and how I would land.

The following week the guys disappeared up the Riondaz right after school and left me to walk up to the bunny hill on my own. Getting down the bunny hill wasn't a challenge for me. I just snowplowed "S" curves down the slope. The challenge was the getting up. You had the choice of a *pulma* lift or a "T" bar. The *pulma* was easier. The seat was a round dish on the bottom of a two-foot long pole attached to a retractable cable that was towed by an overhead cable. Kaeti had warned me about this lift one dinner. She mentioned that the lift "helpers" liked to play tricks on the newbies. They would hold the seat until the retractable cable played out then put it between the skier's legs – especially the females. That way the skier would find herself snatched into the air by the seat and riding the pole like a witch on a broomstick! Kaeti really did not appreciate their sense of humor! The description actually sounded dangerous for a guy. I learned how to deal with the *pulma* by watching my friends. They grabbed the seat away from the operator right away and put it between their own legs. That way the cable played out slowly, and the seat pulled them gently up the slope.

The "T" bar, on the other hand, operated similarly on a tow cable with a retractable cable, but the seat, or in this case, seats, consisted of a large upside down "T" made of wood. Two skiers stood side by side while the helper slipped the "T" between them. The top, or was that the bottom bar of the "T" was then positioned so each skier sat on half of the bottom bar and held onto the central shaft. This was tricky because you had to get the bar safely between the two beginners and then position it so it was beneath two butts that were frequently not the same height. Then, even if this was successfully performed, if one skier fell, the other would quickly join him as the "T" bar readily slid away from the remaining skier when the other half was empty. As with the *pulma*, the "helpers" liked to have fun with the beginners, just to keep themselves amused. Waiting until the retractable cable played out and then misplacing the bar, usually behind the knees, was a favorite. This threw the beginners into synchronized, but not pretty, back flips. Anyway the "T" bar line was always shorter because it was more challenging for a beginner, and it took twice as many people up, so I preferred it. I even perfected a way of riding it by myself. I held it diagonally across my lower back, holding the opposite side with my arm. It wasn't fancy, but it got me up, and I wasn't destroyed by the fall of another passenger. I saw more experienced skiers put the whole "T" between their legs, like the *pulma*, but it took some expertise to not lose a valuable part of your anatomy during the dismount.

About two meters of fresh powder fell that week, mostly at night, making everything a winter wonderland! That next Saturday, my "friends" took me for my next session on the Riondaz. The snow was softer and deeper, which made it easier to turn. First time down, I lost track of where I was and passed the bad turn without knowing it. I got to the bottom and had not fallen the whole way down the slope, outstanding! My second trip was much different. Overconfident, I raced around the evil switchback and lost control. I sailed off the side of the path, just squeaking between two trees. It would be more accurate to say that I made it between but my skis didn't. They were sideways when I went through and caught between the bases of the trees. My bindings did not release, and I was left hanging upside-down in several meters of fresh powder. I couldn't see anything but the snow. It was light enough that I could move fairly freely, but I couldn't find anything solid to push against to get myself righted. I managed to find my poles, which were still attached to my wrists; but I couldn't find any base to push them against either. Finally, I gave up trying to push off anything and started to curl up and grab behind my knees. I then walked my hands up my legs to my boots and bindings. Releasing one binding let my leg fall away, only to be caught by the safety strap. Damn! I searched blindly in the snow, trying to undo the safety straps before releasing the other binding. Luckily I had grabbed the free ski when I released my second binding, or I might have fallen deeper into the snow. As it was, I hung for a moment from my skis, pulled myself up onto them, and squirmed back onto the slope. Passing skiers stared, and several fell as the abominable snowman came up from the depths and stood dusting snow off his body. I was amazed to find that my poles were still around my wrists.

With *le neige*, the nightlife of the village changed. Leysin was small and inexpensive, and the skiers came on the weekends. We didn't get a lot of foreign tourists because little was known about our village outside of Switzerland. Well, the upper village did draw some foreigners: the French came to some hotel called the Club Med, and hostellers came from all over the world to a small youth hostel called the Vagabond – oh, and occasional busloads of people speaking German would invade our ski slopes and barge through the lift lines walking across our skis. But the lower village near the college didn't get many foreigners. Our hotels began filling with local weekenders from Geneva, Lausanne, and Montreux. For me, the amazing thing about those weekenders was that most of them were women! It seems that the Swiss men were attracted to big name areas, like San Moritz, where there were lots of foreign tourists.

My interaction with these women was limited by language –both of us tired quickly of communicating in a second, and in my case, very basic, language. But dancing was different. I have always loved to dance – jitterbug, twist, rock-n-roll, folk dance, even an occasional square dance! – and dancing involved no linguistic skills! Also, given that bars often had a four to one average, girls to guys, they were asking and often buying the drinks. Not a bad situation for a young guy, even if I didn't look much over fifteen. Women were often desperate enough to ask me for a dance. However, it did spoil me later for the American bars, when I was old enough to go to one! Now the Swiss version of fast dancing involved a very rigid, stylized version of the twist, where partners shifted their heads back and forth pretending to ignore each other. Slow dancing was the same as back in the States – and very pleasant I might add! BUT their fast dancing was slowly driving me crazy! I wanted to move, jump, spin, and rock it out!

Tiny helped me with my problem… or, rather, Kaeti did. You see Tiny didn't dance, and he trusted me – probably because I was his roommate and because he knew he could squash me with one hand! Anyway together Kaeti and I got to jump and spin! It was fantastic! The only hassle was our first slow dance. Tiny immediately gave us the hairy-eyeball, and I retreated quickly to my beer. He trusted me only sooo far!

One evening, after watching me dance with Kaeti, a brunette Norwegian girl with deep blue eyes that seemed to curve down at both ends and a bright smile asked me to dance. Odd, I guess that I had always imagined Scandinavian women as blonde, but she explained that many are not, especially in Norway. She was almost as tall as Kaeti and thin, but not athletic. I suspect she stayed thin by not eating much rather than by exercising. Her face was thin and long with a nose that appeared to stretch down out of her forehead, a little longer than I thought was attractive. But she shared my love of dancing and was fairly fluent in

English. After a few drinks, which she bought, we shared a few kisses as we rocked gently together during the slow songs. Then later I offered to walk her back to her hotel.

At the hotel door when I went for a kiss, she opened the door and invited me in. *Whoa!* That got me excited and frightened at the same time! *What's she expecting? For that matter, what's her name? Perhaps she just means to share a kiss in the warmth of the hotel.* However, once inside she took my hand and started up the stairs. My arousal and nerves intensified with each step. As she opened the door to her room I half hoped to find a roommate. That would definitely define the expectations – but we were alone. Inside I stood momentarily as she took off her coat and helped me with mine. I then paced the room nervously for a minute, looked at the painted picture of the Swiss mountains in the spring over her large double bed, and barged out onto the balcony. The freezing air blew some of my nervousness away. She, whatever her name was, followed.

"Is it O K?"

"Ah, What? – sure," I replied, shivering and looking up into the night sky. *It's freezing out here without my coat!* "I love the stars up here," trembled out of my mouth. "Do you understand? – stars?"

"Yes, of course. They are beautiful!" She moved close to me, and I put my arm around her. I could feel her shiver, too.

"You're shivering."

"What? I know not this word."

"Cold."

"Ah yes, is cold here. Inside is warm," she said as she smiled.

Yes, but I'm not sure how to explain a confirmed virgin to a person who doesn't know the word 'shiver.' "I think I need to go," I blurted. *Oh, this is nuts!*

"Why?"

Why? I don't know. Why am I here? What do you expect? All I wanted was a long kiss goodnight. "I had a really good time," I said as I leaned in for a kiss, but she pulled her head back, spun out of my arm, and walked inside.

"It was very nice. Thank you for dancing," she said very formally as she walked to her door and opened it. I grabbed my coat and tried once more for a kiss at the door, but was offered a cheek as I left. *Shit! Shit! SHIT!* I thought as I walked down the stairs. *What is wrong with me?*

Back at my room, I berated myself for being such a coward. Why did I have to panic like that? Was it the alcohol? Had it been that long since a girl had paid attention to me? Could I have controlled the situation? – set the limits? What if she didn't understand them? Would it have been better to stop half way – or would she still have been upset? As I slept, I dreamed about what might have happened and had to change my underwear halfway through the night. I looked for her the next day on the slopes, but couldn't spot her – or wasn't sure what she looked like except for her longish nose and I still didn't remember her name.

That evening I stayed away from the Messange and dancing. Just chicken, I guess. Late in the evening Wilds caught me watching a game of *zim-zim* at Le Nord.

"Not dancing tonight?"

"Nah, not in the mood," I lied.

"I was just up at the Messange, and Kaeti was asking about you. She looked pretty bored standing around with Tiny."

"Yeah?"

"Hey, and Garbo was looking for you, too."

"Garbo?"

"Yeah, I don't know her name. That girl you were dancing with last night. Something about her face and hair makes me think of Greta Garbo."

Yeah, I don't know her name either. "Greta Garbo? That old time actress?" *Her nose was a little long for her face, too.* "She was asking about me?" *I wonder why? I thought sure I blew that one.* "She still there?"

"She was when I left." I went up but neither Kaeti nor Greta, or whatever her name was, was there. Will I ever understand women?

Chapter Seventeen

Bennie

The Monday that ski school started I took the chair lift to the top of Riondaz and skied down the mountain to the bunny hill. I spotted several schoolmates standing in a semicircle around a short man in a puffy red-orange jacket with a red, white, and light blue stocking cap that had a large white ball on top. I skied over and stopped behind the others. The short man stood confidently on his skis, leaning nonchalantly back onto one of his poles with one hand while his other was pressed backwards against his hip. He looked up at me and asked, "Can I 'elp you?"

"Yes, I'm joining your class."

"You come from there?" He indicated the path down the mountain with his chin.

"Yes."

"Then you come back in hour *pour l'intermédiare* class."

"If you don't mind, I'd like to start here. I want to learn to do this right."

The man barked out a hearty laugh and said, "*Bon*, join zee line. Monsieur?"

"Henderson, call me Jim."

"*Bon*, Monsieur Jeem."

I'm glad that I joined the beginners' class because it turned out I was doing everything wrong. I leaned back in my snowplow. I shifted my butt to turn. I flailed my poles ahead of me. As I said... nothing right! Bennie, the instructor, was meticulous, exacting. Every angle had to be right, every balance point... One move that I followed but could not understand was the way to turn in a snowplow. He had me turn my body and lean over the ski I wanted to turn on. This meant that I ended up facing uphill through the first half of my turn. It just didn't make sense because I couldn't see where I was going, so I asked him about it after class.

He replied, "Ees too early, you weel no understand. You must TRUST!"

"Try me!"

"*Qu'est-ce que c'est?*"

"Ahhh… Try to explain it, please."

"No, you weel understand later. Now you are backwards. Later, you weel be forward on zee fall line. TRUST!"

He was right. I was backwards, so I let it go until I spotted Gil. I told Gil about it and got a blank stare. "No clue."

"Well then what's a 'fall line'?"

"That." And he pointed down the slope. I looked but didn't see anything. "It just means straight down, like a ball would roll if you dropped it. You're supposed to face down the fall line when you ski." *That doesn't help! In fact, it's backwards from Bennie's lesson!*

Later, I caught Kaeti with the same question and got the same blank stare. "Don't worry about it kiddo. Bennie knows what he's doing."

I gave up. "Okay, I TRUST!"

I advanced quickly to the intermediate class and learned the "Stem Christian" turn and parallel traverse. It was in the stem christy that I learned what Bennie's body positioning was all about. The turn happened so quickly that I never looked back up the hill as I had in the snowplow. Moving the body out over the turning ski kept my shoulders angled down the slope with all my weight ending up on the downhill ski. In fact, Bennie was trying to retrain most of the other skiers in the class, and he began using me as an example. Not that my being used as an example for skiers like Tiny and others with two or three years of experience won me any friends. I learned the parallel traverse, or running across the slope with skis together and all of my weight on my downhill ski. The downhill knee was tucked behind my uphill knee, like Kaeti had shown us hopping down the stairs. This position also was supposed to keep my skis from crossing because my boot and the tip of the downhill ski were supposed to block the uphill one. However, I still managed to get them crossed. My solution – sit down! Bennie's solution – all your weight should be on your downhill ski, so just lift the uphill ski and put it back where it belongs. Easier said than done!

Anyway, the stem christy was a modified snowplow turn where you moved your uphill ski out of the traverse and placed it up the slope into the "V" as you squatted down. Then you planted your pole near your ski tips where you wanted to turn, stood up taking the weight off the tails of your skis, and quickly transferred weight to the uphill ski as the ski tails slid around. This move caused a rapid turn around the pole and back the other direction across the slope. You then squatted down again and tucked your new downhill knee behind the other while leaning out over that ski. This move set the inside edge of the new downhill ski into the snow and carved your turn. You also ended up in the parallel traverse position for your trip back across the slope. Over and over again Bennie shouted "down – up – down, look down zee fall line!" I was great turning to my left but sucked at turning to my right and would often fall. I could not get the strong carving action in that turn. Bennie just said, "Practice! Get all zee weight on zee downhill ski – and don' worry about falling. You are no learning eef you are no falling!" That was not the last time I would hear that expression. I was learning and had the bruises to prove it.

After class one day, I was carving turns down the Riondaz when I noticed a fallen skier in my favorite switchback. I pulled to the high side and stopped. Did I mention stopping? – no problem now that I could carve a turn; in fact it just took a down – UP! – down without turning or a sharp turn where I stayed up a little too long, and hit an extreme carve at the end. Again, my left-hand stops were superior! I could toss copious amounts of snow with my stop! Anyway, I had stopped decisively and was about to ski across the trail to offer help to the downed skier when I saw one totally out-of-control skier sailing down the slope from above with his poles flailing in front of him. I held my position and waited, knowing full well the impending disaster on this turn. I did not want to be part of it! I'd done that enough already…

The flailing skier screamed into the turn and headed straight at the downed skier. I watched as he tried to turn by throwing his shoulders in the direction he wanted to go, knowing that move would put all his weight on the wrong ski and prevent his turn or cause him to turn the wrong way. In the last instant he hopped the backs of his skis into the turn and planted both his poles in front of him to push himself the rest of the way around. Unfortunately, he was on top of the downed skier, and his right pole stabbed into the poor man's right thigh and got caught. The impaler's skis smacked into the wounded skier and that helped finish the turn for him, but the trapped pole remained upright in the victim's thigh as the attacker screamed down and around the next turn.

I scooted across the path as the victim pulled the pole out of his thigh. There was no blood visible in his black ski pants, just a wet area; and the stretchy material seemed to seal up around the wound. Not knowing what language he spoke, I took his hands and had him push down hard on the wound, as I had learned in Boy Scouts, then raced on downhill after the attacker and for help. I did not see the out-of-control skier again. Perhaps he found a convenient exit over one of the steeper cow pastures. Then again, I probably looked very much like that guy not three weeks before; would that everyone took ski lessons. When I got to the bottom of the ski lift, I used my pigeon French to explain what had happened, but learned that they were aware of the problem and had already sent a *luge*, or rescue sled, to pick up the victim.

I ran into Kaeti before supper that evening and told her about the incident. She bet that it was one of the Club Med skiers. She said they were nuts on the slopes. She would race their classes to the lifts because most didn't even know how to get on and off the chairs and would fall, one after another, virtually shutting down the lifts. Then at the top their instructors would line up a class of over twenty people and shout, "Follow me!" and ski away. The fall of one student frequently took out a half dozen others, effectively blocking the slope down. Kaeti said they were awful skiers with worse manners. "Keep away from them, kiddo!"

I had only seen the one, but I kept my eyes open after that and began spotting the Club Med classes. Nothing like Bennie's!

Returning to my room that evening, I walked in on Tiny with the tip of one of his skis wedged into our hot water radiator. He was pushing on its tail like he was trying to bend it in two. Forgetting the story about the impaler, I asked, "What the hell?"

"These are too stiff. I can't turn on them. I have a warrantee on them; if they break, I get them replaced for free. I'm hoping to talk them into giving me the money so I can buy Rossis, like Bernd's. You ought to do the same. Yours are way too long!"

I convinced him that the PX didn't have warrantees on its skis and I was stuck with what I had. Tiny didn't return to class. In fact it took almost a month to get replacement skis in his length. Not too many six and a half-foot tall Swiss.

Another thing happened about two weeks after I discovered Tiny bending his skis; he found and moved to a vacant room on the second floor. Its original occupant or occupants had departed without my even getting to know them. With Tiny gone I had a large room to myself, quite a luxury! On nice nights I would pull Tiny's mattress out onto the balcony and sleep under the stars. His poof, as the Swiss called their feather-stuffed blankets, and mine combined to make a giant and toasty feather fortress for the frigid nights on the mountain. The experience took me back to scout snow camp on Mount Hood, and further back to sleeping with my grandfather in the middle of the winter on the unheated sleeping porch off his bedroom.

Chapter Eighteen

Paris Nights

For Thanksgiving the school had to deal with an American holiday that wasn't celebrated in Europe, so their solution was to offer a weeklong trip to Paris. Perhaps half the students hit up their parents for the money to go. Gil, Wilds, and I were packed and ready the day before and comparing notes on things to do and places to see. I had been to Paris before but only for one night while I was searching for a college last summer. I really hadn't seen anything. Wilds didn't have much more experience, but Gil had been there several times and talked at length about the beautiful women, fantastic clubs, and beautiful women... I related my encounter with several French girls on the Mediterranean beach the previous summer in Marseilles and how they generally disliked Americans, but Gil seemed to feel Paris was more cosmopolitan and accepting.

On the train across France we left the snow and entered a grayer world. The white world of the mountain was in my blood now, and the grayness was a little depressing. Gil was otherwise occupied with Sam, not that we blamed him, so Wilds and I were left to our own imaginings. We kept our spirits up by talking about our fantasies of Paris. We both agreed that Brigitte Bardot was one of the sexiest actresses alive, and she was from Paris, wasn't she? We had to climb the Eiffel Tower, see the Arch of Triumph, Notre Dame, the Louvre, and the castles. Gary, a freshman in the car with us who claimed vast experience in Paris, began to tell stories about French hookers. Gary was a stocky, round-faced guy with glasses and some acne problems. His bowl-cut hair across his forehead above his glasses made his face seem twice as wide as it was long. It seemed that Gary believed it was cheaper to spend the night with hookers when traveling across Europe. "That way you got a room and entertainment for the night."

Wilds asked, "Aren't you afraid of catching some disease from the hookers?"

"Nah, in Paris the police inspect the hookers to make sure they're clean. Actually there are some young, call them trainees, in the eastern part of the city who aren't, but the police try to control them. Anyway, the doc at school will give you a shot of penicillin when we get back, if you ask. I can show you around, if you like!"

Wilds and I didn't exactly turn him down because what he was talking about was so alien as to be intriguing, but my curiosity had its limits.

When we arrived at the Gare St. Lazare, one of the Paris train stations, the chaperones told us to catch cabs to the hotels. It seems that the girls were staying at a different hotel somewhere by the Royal Palace, and the guys were to stay at a hotel near Pigalle. Gary was all smiles at that. It seemed Pigalle was the area were the best hookers worked. I guess each of us needed a reason to see Paris… As we left, the chaperones gave us typed directions to the hotels and warned us not to pay more than forty French francs, or about eight dollars, for the cab ride.

"It isn't far to the hotel," they said, and then added, "the cabbies will rip you off, if they can."

The cabs were small and would hold only a couple of guys. In seconds, Wilds and I were in one and traveling ninety miles per hour through the narrow streets. Two turns later and we were no longer following the directions that we had been given. The driver claimed that he didn't understand a word we were saying. A lot of good French class was doing! We raced into an enormous circle around the Arch of Triumph and were in what looked like a gigantic bumper car ride – no lanes, no signals, and cars switching directions at random. Man, it was amazing that we didn't hit anyone. Half way 'round the circle and we sped off to the south. Wilds was sure that we should be heading east, but the driver wasn't listening. He seemed to be carrying on a conversation with himself in French. Perhaps he thought that he was giving us a guided tour. Zoom and we were across a bridge.

"Rive Gauche," the driver announced.

"Left bank?" Wilds questioned. "NO, no rive gauche, Pigalle!" he exclaimed.

The Eiffel Tower flashed into full view. We had been seeing bits and pieces of it above the buildings, but now we were sailing around its base.

Another bridge. "Notre Dame!" the cabbie announced, "Le Louvre!"

This is getting out of hand! I grabbed the instructions out of Wilds' hand and held them over the seat to the driver. "We - want - to - go - here!" I yelled while pointing at the sheet.

"*Oui, oui...*" He said annoyed and went back into his guided tour voice. We were told to give the cabby forty francs, but when we arrived at the hotel he wanted one hundred. We split the difference and gave him seventy. The driver cursed us loudly in French and passable English as he departed.

From the outside, the hotel was a dump, a narrow, dirty, old building with a sign that had last been painted during the French revolution. Inside wasn't much better. It was dusty with worn wood floors and a decrepit wooden counter. A middle-aged woman with too much make up was standing behind the counter in a choking a cloud of cigarette smoke and perfume. We walked toward her, but my eyes started to water and my sinuses burn and run. Damn my allergies! I stopped, but Wilds walked up to her as I reached for the Kleenexes I kept in my back pocket for just such an emergency. She greeted him formally, but when he said that we were with the college group, she said that was impossible, that they had all arrived and the rooms were all full. He assured her that we were from the group and asked about the chaperones. She explained that there were none at this hotel, only students.

Frustrated and tired, he started pleading for a room with no success until Roark walked into the lobby on his way out. "Troubles?" he asked, and we explained the situation. Roark looked at the woman behind the desk and smiled; her face brightened, and she smiled back. He began talking to her in French as he leaned onto the counter across from her. Before long, they were laughing and conversing with foreheads almost touching. I was beginning to think that we had been forgotten when she reached back and picked up a key attached to a light bulb-shaped wooden fob from the hooks behind her.

"You're on the second floor. That's special. Most of us are on the first," Roark said and walked out. That was the last we saw of Roark until the train home.

Wilds and I signed in and went up to find our room. Without an elevator we toted our bags up the stairs.

"So much for special rooms!" Wilds said as he dragged his bag up the two flights.

Opening the door revealed a room with a rose-colored throw rug and matching color coverlet on its one double bed. The two windows had frilly off-white-toward-pink curtains.

"Cute!" Wilds exclaimed sarcastically.

"Gross!" I added. "There's only one bed!"

"Hey, at least we have a room," Wilds, the voice of reason, countered.

The room had a sink and what at first appeared to be a toilet. Upon further examination, we found that the toilet had no water in it and when I turned the handle water squirted like a drinking fountain across the floor onto the rug.

"What the hell?" I asked.

"You know, I think it is one of those women's things that they use to clean themselves after sex; a douche," Wilds decided.

"Okay, would it hurt anything if we peed in it? It's been a while."

"Don't see why not; just don't squirt it across the room. The douche, I mean." We laughed.

After finishing, I held my shoe in front of the spout to be sure it didn't spray too far and turned the handle slowly.

"You know, this might be good for washing your feet!" I joked, and we laughed again. *A douche instead of a toilet in the room; what kind of hotel is this?*

It was evening, and we went in search of schoolmates and dinner. Gil, who hadn't figured out how to find Sam at the girls' hotel yet, was on the floor below us.

"Gil, has your room got a footbath?" I asked as we met.

"A what?"

"Just kiddin', you know, a douche, a woman's thing like a toilet that squirts water."

"A bidet you mean? No. Why? Does yours?"

Gary strode out at that time and added, "all the classy whores' rooms have bidets. It keeps them clean between customers. Where's your room?"

"Third floor, I mean European second!"

"Wow, that's prime real-estate. How'd you score that?" Gary asked.

We explained the cab ride, the mix up on rooms, and Roark's assistance as we went in search of something to eat. We wandered the streets in Pigalle past innumerable prostitutes standing on the corners or hooting down from the windows until Gary led us to a sleazy looking bar with more pros than customers.

While we waited for our food, several heavily made up women, reeking with perfume, came over to offer their services to our "lovely group of young men."

I stayed quiet but was curious, especially after one middle-aged woman with a garish shade of red hair spoke to us with an American accent. After she left, I asked Gary if she was an American. He said, "No, they have to be multilingual in their profession."

To my embarrassment, when I followed up with a question about why they did what they did, Gary called the redhead over and asked her to explain it to me. She sat next to me, put her arm on my chair with her hand just touching my shoulder, leaned in so I couldn't help but look down her front, and said, "We are a public service, like the water company. There are many lonely men who need companionship. There are also busy men who have no time for… do you say, 'beating around the bush'?" That is funny, no! There are also men who would be dangerous if they found no way to relieve their tensions. We have that relief; to others we are companions. We help keep things happy, no? Is this so bad?"

"I guess not," I said conflicted but interested in the concept.

"You are so young. You will understand. I would be delighted to instruct someone so young as you!"

"Thanks, but I don't need instructions. I'm quite, you know, knowledgeable," I lied.

Gary got up and left the table with the redhead, and Wilds said, "Looks like Gary is cutting in on you!"

"Geez, she's almost my mother's age. Besides I don't..." I was saved by the waiter as he brought the food. It wasn't much to talk about, breaded meat cutlets in a white sauce that tasted like dishwater. The meat was not to be identified – too dark and stringy to be veal or pork and didn't taste like beef. I asked Gil what we ordered, and he said, "Veal." Not likely! And the wine, well, I kind of expected great wines in France, but this wasn't; it was dry to the point tasting like red rubbing alcohol, yuck!

Wilds, with a fake nasal French accent, said, "Mayhaps, we no have ah sophistique palate to apprecia zeez meal?"

Gil and I laughed, and he actually had a couple of the prostitutes laughing, too. I am not sure whether his accent was that funny or the pros knew how bad the meal really was.

The next stop, the Moulin Rouge. Gary had promised to take us there, but he was otherwise involved with the redhead. One of the laughing hookers gave us directions and told us that the midnight show was the best. It wasn't far, and we scored tickets at a student discount; so they said. The seats weren't great, but we could see most of the action. Women with lots of makeup doing the can-can and showing their panties. It was pretty much what you see on TV, but the waitresses or hostesses or whatever they were – well, they were young and good-looking. They were continually coming up and checking our drinks. One even sat on Wilds' lap, wiggled, and giggled. Talk about a red face!

After the show, we compared notes on the way back to the hotel. We had each expected something sexier with more nudity. In all, it was kind of disappointing. During the walk back we ran into Dick, the sergeant's son. He had apparently spent twenty francs for a handful of "nude" pictures from some guy on the street. The other guys with him were ragging on him because his twenty francs had gotten him half a dozen pictures of nude statues and nudes in classic paintings. One night and Paris was already making an impression!

Getting into the hotel after two o'clock was very difficult. We banged on the locked exterior door and yelled for almost an hour before some half-naked Frenchman came out to unlock the door just to shut us up. In the room, Wilds and I used the facilities, such as they were; I cracked a window for fresh air, and we lay down head to foot on the only bed. Sleep came easily, and the noises of the morning were coming in the window before we knew it.

The sound of multiple voices talking outside got me up, and I peered out the window to see several small trucks unloading groceries at stands and stores just below us and up the street. We dressed hurriedly and ran outside to see what was going on. The entire street for several blocks was a kind of farmers' market. All kinds of fruits and vegetables, breads and pastries, and almost any food imaginable were at the various stands. Wilds and I feasted while other early rising students started joining us.

I was particularly intrigued by a butcher who had hung several skinned rabbits up on hooks in front of his store. I wasn't used to seeing rabbits in stores. I knew they were rabbits because I had hunted them for most of my teenage life and I recognized the paws, which hadn't been cut off. That seemed strange to me so I tried my basic French and hand signs and asked the butcher why he left the paws on? I couldn't understand his response other than something about cats.

Gil had walked up behind me, laughed, and said, "The butcher wants his customers to know they are not buying cats."

"Cats! They're afraid someone might sell them a cat to eat! Seriously?" I exclaimed.

I kept a close eye on the other butcher's stands but didn't see one with paws with claws, thank God, but it made me wonder about the

breaded mystery meat that we had eaten the night before and
confirmed that I wasn't eating there again.

Gil had directions to the girls' hotel, and we went hunting for a
Metro station. Several blocks later, near the Moulin Rouge, we found
one and were on our way. The Metro, the Parisian subway, was pretty
cool, but it was nearly impossible to tell where we were going. For
some reason they identified the trains by the last station on the line, but
the maps weren't color-coded, and it was hard to tell where each line
started and ended. With Gil's help we found the right train and were
soon hopping into a half-full coach. We got out at some station that had
signs outside directing us to Notre Dame. We walked the other way up
a large avenue to the hotel. The place wasn't big, but it was nice, and
the entryway was clean and spacious. No expenses spared for our coeds
and our chaperones. Yes, none of the chaperones stayed at the guys'
hotel; not that I can blame them. This hotel was on a beautiful tree-lined
boulevard near everything, except the hookers and the open market.

Gil picked up Sam, and we were joined by two other girls who I had
seen a few times at school: Janet, who looked a little like Jana, innocent
with long dark hair and square-cut bangs but with eyes that were not
as large and never seemed very happy, and Kathy, who had collar-length
red hair and bangs and whose young, cutesy face reminded me too
much of my sister. The two were not seen outside of the main building
very often, at least not after dark. I can't fault them either, given the
results of the mating season. They seemed to be nice girls, just ones who
were overshadowed by the princesses. Actually Wilds and I probably
had a lot in common with them, except that we got out of our frat house
after dark. Apparently what princesses had come to Paris had already
left for a shopping trip; they were nowhere to be seen.

The girls had the action mapped for the day. We hit a Metro that took
us to a large viewing area west across the river from the Eiffel Tower.
Great place for photos! Then we walked to and went up the tower. We
had lunch at a sidewalk café by the tower and then saw all the tourist
traps that we had wanted to see: the Notre Dame, the Louvre, and we
walked the Champs Elysées to the Arch of Triumph. Luckily, there were

tunnels under the bumper car circle around the arch, or we would not have made it alive. We saw some lunatic setting up a camera tripod in the middle of the Champs Elysées, where it joined the circle. Cars were missing him by bare millimeters, but he ignored them.

An odd thing about crossing French streets that I had first noticed in Marseille was strongly reinforced in Paris. When you cross, you dare not make eye contact with the car drivers. The rule seems to be if you stare ahead or at your feet, the drivers must miss you. They will pass you as closely as possible, but they will miss you. However, if you make eye contact with the driver, then you take the responsibility for getting out of the way. You dodge or they will hit you! In Paris, I noticed that our female companions had a slightly different experience. As the automobiles raced by, a hand would frequently come from the nearest window and pat their butt. That caused some serious problems between the girls and us because Wilds, Gil, and I couldn't help but laugh whenever it happened, and it happened several times. However, everyone was rolling on the sidewalk laughing at my expense after one car narrowly avoided me and a hand grabbed my butt! I swore that they were trying to pick my pocket, but no one cared!

Dinner that night was on the Champs Elysées in a rather large street-side restaurant. We saw a number of other ACS students at various tables inside and out. There were also several people with their dogs at the table; most were under, but one was actually eating off a plate with its owners. I wondered how the health inspectors dealt with that one. Oh, did I mention the poop on the sidewalks? Dog shit was everywhere, especially after dark. The morning wasn't bad; someone must go around cleaning it up at dawn. But at night you had to be careful where you walked. Wilds actually stepped in some one night on the way back to the hotel. Geez, did that stink up the room! We also found that bidet thing was handy for washing shoes!

Back to the restaurant. It became our usual meeting place after that first day. It was half way between the guys' and the girls' hotels, and the food and service were great! In fact, this one tall, thin waitress with straight blonde hair cut and curled on the front of the sides so as to point to her pink lips was unusually attentive to me. In an odd way, she kinda reminded me of Kaeti; maybe it was her strong legs and small butt or her athletic walk. Wilds burst my bubble by insisting that she was a he. I couldn't tell whether he was right or not, but after the butt grab, I wasn't taking any chances. *Paris is so bizarre!*

The next day we met several of the girls for a Metro and train trip to the Château de Versailles. The castle was amazing! I especially liked the concept of the hall of mirrors and all the gardens, but it seemed an extraordinary waste of space. Maybe it was the Quaker in me, but the place was one hundred times the size of my boarding school, and my school housed and educated over one hundred students each year. The German and Swiss castles were much more, what, practical?

The town adjoining the castle was far more interesting to me. The place was more French than Paris, if that makes any sense. It had real people's houses, yards, and fences. Actually, the fences were pretty cool. I had seen them before on my trip to Marseilles, high concrete walls with broken glass embedded in the top. A great way to protect the house from robbers and reuse left-over wine bottles. There was also something kind of pretty on a sunny day about the colored glass and the light it deposited on adjoining walls. Then I spotted a weird decoration that I had seen on many walls in the south of France. It was a line of pockmarks that, if you used your imagination, looked just like it had been made by a spray of machine gun bullets. Last summer, my buddy Gary and I had played combat running through the streets in one town after seeing several of these decorations. Wilds had wandered off when I spotted the spray, and I called him back. "Hey, check this out! It looks just like the wall was hit by a machine gun!"

"It was."

"What?"

"Those are bullet holes."

"Bull shit!"

"For real."

"No shit? Gangs have automatic weapons here?" I looked around warily.

"No, those are left from WWII."

"You're pulling my leg. That has to be twenty years ago. You can't tell me that glass has been there for twenty years. If you can concrete in new glass, you can patch bullet holes. Get serious!"

"No, my dad said it's something like a memorial or reminder for the French to not forget the war."

"The shit you say! That's a long time ago."

"Dad didn't seem to think it was that long."

Staring at the bullet holes got me thinking. *Quakers are supposed to be against all war, but what happens if your neighbor or your family gets gunned down in your front yard by some invading army. Could I hold my pacifist beliefs then? War doesn't make sense. Nobody wins unless you over-run some weak neighboring country. Even then you spend a lot of time and money controlling the country. Vietnam, what the hell are we doing there? It was a French colony, right? They gave up, and Americans are dying there now. What is that all about? But these holes are evidence of a real at-home war. I doubt that I could be a pacifist in a real war.*

"Hey, Henderson, we haven't got all day," Wilds called from the next block.

When I caught up, Wilds asked, "What's with you and cussing? I don't remember your talking like that at the beginning of school."

After thinking for a while I said, "Not sure. The Quakers didn't allow it and my dad actually washed my mouth out with soap."

"Really? Cool!"

"Not really, it tastes like crap. I guess that it's just this school and it is kinda fun, but I'll try to control myself around you."

"Go fuck youself, Henderson," he said with a smile.

We spent an hour in a flea market that had all kinds of great stuff like German helmets and Iron Crosses before catching the train back. I actually bought a royal blue and navy ski sweater for less than five bucks – twenty-three francs. The thing was heavy with an extremely thick weave. I swear it made me look like a knight with chain mail and a breastplate. Pretty cool! Besides I needed something warmer than a sweatshirt for skiing.

That night at our hotel, it started. We had gotten in early and hit the sack. Just before midnight, there was a knock on the door, and a man's voice first hooting, "OOoowoo" then *"Mademoiselle, combien?"*

What the hell was that? I went to the door in my underwear, opened it to a chubby French guy smelling of alcohol and BO, and asked "What do you want?" He looked a little surprised, smiled, excused himself, and staggered down the hall.

"What was that all about?" Wilds asked as I returned to bed.

"Probably looking for his whore."

We laughed and were just about to fall asleep when the same knock and hooting occurred. Wilds went this time. The same guy was there, and he started when he saw another guy at the door.

"Go away," Wilds yelled! "Nobody here! Just us guys."

We didn't answer the door after that and just yelled from the bed in as gruff masculine voices as we could muster. It was a long night, and the remaining nights were not much better. Apparently the natives believed that the regular occupant was about to return from wherever she was.

Wilds and I were on our own for a couple of days while Gil joined the girls on their shopping trips. By Friday, he had had enough and suggested going to the USO by the American Embassy. It sounded like a good idea. We could get cheap souvenirs there and some American stuff, possibly even a real burger. We hadn't counted on the fact that Wilds wasn't a military dependent. He didn't have an ID so they wouldn't let him past the front desk. Gil and I wandered for a while. I found some free postcards and took a few to Wilds along with a couple of free cokes. They didn't have burgers, but recommended a place called Blimpies not far away.

Wilds and I walked into a nearby men's clothing store while Gil talked to some of the other American dependents in the USO. The two female clerks at the store were really cute and very attentive; "flirting" might be the best word for it. They stayed close to us, closer than I was used to, and they touched a lot when you tried on a shirt. Sometimes I'm so ticklish that any touch drives me up a wall, but I tried to resist the response. The shirts were expensive, but if I had found a shirt that fit, I might have bought it whether I needed it or not. But the shoulders were too small and the arms too tight. Besides, they were all bright colors, and I was more into blues and browns. Wilds did find a shirt that he liked, and it fit him all right. The clerks also had cute French nicknames for us that they said in Brigitte Bardot sexy voices. Man, did we have a great time waiting for Gil!

We relayed the story to Gil as we ate at Blimpies. The hamburgers were wretched. I guessed that a lot of cats were missing in this neighborhood. Gil seemed a bit surprised at how good a time we'd had because his experience with the girls was that the store clerks were all unfriendly and ridiculed their group in French in front of their faces. He would pretend he didn't understand so he could listen in. When we told Gil about our nicknames, he broke out laughing and told us that the clerks were lovingly calling us "bean pole" and "sheep's ass." *Sheep's ass! Damn! I'm glad I didn't buy a shirt.*

This last night in Paris was to be a big one. We were all to meet at a bar on the left bank for a party. Wilds wasn't feeling well, something he ate. Hopefully not the cat burgers! Anyway, I joined a gang of the sophomores, including Stallone, Cliff, and several others. The place was down a half flight of steps from the street level. Loud music was playing, and a batch of the students and local French youth were there before we arrived. We started drinking early and didn't stop. We were dancing, and the French girls would join in occasionally. It was pretty cool. About 9 p.m., I was just starting to think about getting food when there was some shouting and angry voices coming from the dance floor. One voice sounded like Cliff, so I moved where I could see. He and an older French guy were in each other faces, shouting and shoving. Stallone was standing to one side of Cliff looking on protectively. Who knew what this was about? Probably a girl but Cliff always did have a hot temper. Suddenly a knife appeared in the Frenchman's hand. Almost instantaneously, Stallone pushed Cliff to the side and grabbed the hand with the knife. He snapped the hand around and pushed it back into the French guy's stomach. I didn't see the knife at this point and have no clue to what happened afterwards. I flew out the door, up the stairs, and was several blocks away before I slowed down.

As I staggered down dark streets looking for a Metro stop, I replayed the events in my mind, trying to remember if I had seen the knife fly out of the attacker's hand. Maybe I had! I found a Metro entrance and started asking how to get back to Pigalle. At first, nobody had the time to stop and try to understand me. One twenty-something guy finally took me to a train and said he would help. As we rode along in the car, we talked in my pigeon French and his pigeon English about school and our trip here. We stopped at last at a station that was near where he lived, and he invited me up to see his place. It was ten at night, and I just wanted to get back to the hotel; besides he was starting to freak me out. Then he grabbed me by the arm and started to bodily pull me off the Metro car, saying, "You are a student. We will study, no?" I may be small, but I am strong and was I pissed! I let him pull me toward the open door, resisting slightly; then, as the doors started to close, I pulled back, hoping to trap his arms in the door. He dropped his grip and got out of the door in the last instant. I know pure hatred was flaring from my eyes at him through the door window.

The train pulled out, and I had no clue where I was. At this point no one in the car would talk to me. They just kept their distance. I got out at a stop that sounded familiar and began wandering the streets. I was in luck! Coming down the street in a suit with a bowler hat and umbrella was a Brit, if I ever saw one. I ran up and asked if he spoke English, a stupid question, I know; but his paced, pompous response was, "I speak English, not American!" and he walked off down the road leaving me standing and staring in shock. Once I had recovered my wits, I started to spot the familiar sight of hookers on the corners and decided that they also spoke English, if Gary was correct. I asked a not bad-looking, if over-done, woman for directions, and she politely told me the way, even offered to escort me for a price. I politely declined.

Wilds was standing in front of the hotel with our bags when I arrived. "What's going on?" I asked.

"Been kicked out! The hooker whose room we were in came back."

"And they didn't have any place to move us?"

"Didn't seem to care."

We went in to talk to the manager, but Wilds was right, she didn't care. She let us put our bags behind the counter for the night but showed us the door. We waited outside for some of the other students to come back without luck, and then started wandering the streets. It was dark and getting misty when we finally walked halfway down a flight of Metro stairs and sat with our backs against the wall with the bums. One of us tried to stay awake while the other slept, but it was hard. I was surprised to awake with my wallet and passport still on my body. Wilds had lost his shoes, but an old beat-up pair had been left in their place so he had something to walk in. I was glad to be leaving Paris and planned on never returning.

Wilds and I managed to score a case of German beer *especiál* for the train ride back to Switzerland. Think malt liquor! The bottles were small, but powerful! Late afternoon, Wilds dragged our suitcases while I carried the case into the train station. While we were waiting for the train, Roark arrived with two young, sexy French girls, one on each arm. The kisses goodbye seemed to go on forever with one trying to outdo the other. What can I say? Among my stockpile of fantasies, I added that scene, but I put myself in Roark's place, of course!

We dragged our way onto the train and found that the school had sprung for sleeper berths for the way back. Wilds and I grabbed the bunks on one side, Stallone and Cliff on the other. We broke out the beer. We didn't have a bottle opener, but the edges of the bed worked well. Stallone and Cliff had brought their own beer but tried a couple of ours. I briefly thought about asking about the knife fight but decided that they would tell me if they wanted. They didn't. About an hour before the border, Cliff said that customs wouldn't let us into Switzerland with the beer, so we proceeded to try to chug the rest. When the border came, we were unconscious. It was getting light when we caught the cog up the mountain. I had sobered up, but a pounding hangover was clouding my vision, and the brightness of the snow was like a spike in my forehead. Mercifully, I passed out again on the cog train. Don't remember getting there, but back at Hell House we slept all Sunday, and I was still slightly hung over Monday morning as I crunched my way through the snow up to the main building. Just before lunch, Kaeti caught me in the hallway and said, "Sheep's butt, huh! Kinda cute!" while jokingly checking out my derrière. "The nickname, I mean."

"Gee thanks! Don't pass it around, please!" *I'm going to kill Gil! The whole school knows! Please God, don't let that nickname stick!*

Chapter Nineteen

The Berneuse

A couple of weeks of stem christies after I returned from Paris and Bennie said that I was ready for parallel turns and should move on to advanced. The advanced classes were taught by Bernd on the Berneuse, the upper peak that I had climbed my first week at school.

My trip up the Berneuse in the telecabine was thrilling and frightening. I saw skiers going across the trails that were once grass covered. Except for the skiers, the gray escarpment was almost the only color in a sea of white. Snow clung precipitously over the top edge of the cliff, and the steel avalanche barriers had all but disappeared – just the very tips of several crosses were visible. The small trees that grew near the top were just cone-shaped piles of snow with the tops bending over like the curly tops on soft serve ice cream. The cleft in the rock spire was wider now, but I suspected that was because snow had filled the narrower area near its bottom. The expert trail along the edge of the cliff and through the cleft had the trails of only two skiers across it. The snow there looked windblown and icy and the drop deadly!

At the top of the lift, I may not have been on the Tour D'Ai, but today it was the top of the world for me. The sun was bright, and a freezing wind was blowing hard from the valley below. I put my skis on and started looking for someone I recognized. There was no sign of a class forming on top, so I skied to the edge of the bowl and looked down. The area below was filled with skiers up and down both sides. I went behind a rock for shelter from the wind and stood watching. The scene was amazing! Little kids, maybe six years old, streamed off the nearby chair lift and sailed through a wide field of moguls or bumps in the snow. Their legs were spread wide, and they were in a deep tuck as they flew into the bottom of the bowl. Older skiers were flowing over the moguls like their skis were part of their bodies. I heard someone singing as he came from the telecabine behind me. As he passed beside me, I realized that he was yodeling. Even better, the guy had only one ski on! – his other leg was held out to the side and ended without a foot. I had been astounded to see a lot of amputees at the swimming pools, or *swimbads*, in Germany. The war had taken quite a toll there. The Germans weren't embarrassed about their losses, but it took me a while to get used to them. However, this was the first I had seen in Switzerland. But to consider this person handicapped was impossible as he yodeled, slammed down his poles, and swooped cleanly over the tops of the moguls, down the slope and out of sight.

Two minutes later I spotted Kaeti in a pale blue outfit with white panels and her matching ski cap. She was floating down a smoother area to the left of the moguls. Her long body arched left then right as her skis, held together like a single ski, moved smoothly back and forth under her. Two seconds later, I saw Bernd sail around the turn in front of me in a tuck with his legs spread about a foot apart. His racing strips were emblazoned on his arms and legs. He hit one of the upper moguls and flew over several others then landed smoothly and soared into the bowl without turning. I started to turn my skis to face downhill when I saw Gil and several others race past, some jumping moguls, others just flowing and caressing the slopes with their skis. *If this is the advanced class I'm in trouble!* I thought. I traversed and stem christied my way after them and pulled up next to Gil in the lift line.

"Hey, Jim, finally made it to the mountain!"

"Yeah, it's unreal up here! Hey, where are the cow sheds?" I asked as I looked down were the pond and sheds had been.

"You got me! Probably buried."

Kaeti spotted me, waved, and shouted from further up in the line, "Hi! Meet you up top!" I raised my hand with the pole swinging from my wrist and waved back at her. I realized that this was the first time that I had seen Kaeti on skis. She hadn't visited me on the Riondaz.

"Hey, Gil, is this the advanced class?" I asked, concerned.

He looked up at the group confused and said, "You know, I'm not sure there is an advanced class anymore. We're just skiing together."

I was concerned but decided to ask Bernd up top. He was supposed to be the instructor. However, when I reached the top Bernd was gone and only Kaeti was waiting for me.

"Great to see you up here! I can't wait to see how you ski."

"It's not much compared to you guys. Hey, what's the deal with the advanced class? I'm supposed to join it."

"Oh, I don't know." She looked concerned. "Bernd only spent a couple of weeks before he turned us loose. Most of us have been skiing all our lives. I'll talk to him, but I doubt that he wants to be tied down teaching anymore. What about Bennie?"

"He sent me up here. What about you?"

"Me? I'm not a teacher, I... its kinda instinct. I wouldn't know how to teach it." We skied, and she watched and gave me pointers for keeping my skis closer, but she was right. She didn't know the mechanics that would take me to the next level.

I met Bennie the next day on the Riondaz and explained the situation. "*Bon*, my beginners zey 'ave moved up or given up, and my intermediates... some can advance to l' Berneuse. We weel start zee advanced class, no?"

"Great! Thanks! When?"

"Next Monday at zee top, five hour. Let's see those turns, Monsieur Jeem."

"Great!" and I sped off down the all too familiar trail, at ease among my equals.

Monday couldn't come soon enough. The rest of the week I went to the Berneuse to ski with Gil and Kaeti, but I could tell they often had to wait for me to catch up. Kaeti did make it official. Bernd wasn't teaching anymore. He was coaching the ski team, but all he seemed to do was set up occasional courses for them to practice on. Otherwise he just led whoever would follow him.

Monday was a fairly warm, sunny day. I grabbed my skis and was on top the Berneuse as soon as school was out. I skied the smooth part of south face down and across under the chair lift, but checked back periodically to see if Bennie had showed up. A little after 5 p.m. he showed up with three of the better female skiers from the intermediate class. Colleen was there. Her green eyes sparkled and reflected the peaks in front of us. She greeted me with a smile. A rumor was going around that she was dating some Swiss guy in the village. *"Dans* zee advance class," Bennie began. "You weel learn zee parallel turns, zee moguls, and zee *autre* things you need for to survive *dans l'* mountain." The traverse we were using was the same; even the down – up – down motion. The difference was the turn; your upward motion was supposed to allow the skis to slide across without separating. That was easier said than done. I was back to sitting on the slope more than skiing. "You are no learning eef you are no falling!" echoed in my ears.

Bennie would demonstrate and exaggerate the moves. "Down – UP Hoopa!" He would throw the backs of his skis together through the air and land in the opposite traverse position. "– down and carve – face down zee fall line!"

I felt like an idiot imitating him. "Hoopa!" The tails of my skis would fly through the air, and I'd catch an edge and fall.

"No, no, no! You must land on zee inside edge of zee downhill ski! *Mon Dieu!*"

An hour of that, and I was battered, bruised, embarrassed, and ready to go back to the Riondaz and stem christies.

As class ended, Bennie said, "Don' worry Monsieur Jeem. You weel learn. Eet takes practice. We weel no look so foolish when we learn zee edges."

Tuesday wasn't much better until I saw Kaeti skiing past me. "You know 'er?" Bennie asked. "She skis *tres beau*! Watch as she moves and learn."

I didn't need orders to watch Kaeti, but this time I watched her knees and skis as she carved through the snow. Instead of hopping like Bennie was showing us, her down – up – down was rhythmic and smooth. I could almost feel the way she moved on her skis. I found myself moving my legs and hips, imitating her as I would when I watched a new folk dance being demonstrated at boarding school. I started down the slope, eager to try what I thought I had just learned, and managed three parallel turns before I caught an edge and fell. Bennie raced up beside. "*Bon*, you learn by watching, *Tres bien! Encore!*" I tried again, but I had lost the rhythm. I waited until another skier came by with a rhythm similar to Kaeti. Bennie saw my focus. "*Oui*, thees one!" Again, I felt the skier's motion in my legs as I watched him and started off after him. One, two, three, four, five successful turns and I started feeling my edges. I spun into a snow-throwing stop and turned to see Bennie pulling into a stop beside me with an enormous smile. "Fantastic! I 'ave no seen thees before! *Encore!* Oh, there ees your friend!" He pointed across the slope.

I turned and spotted Kaeti sailing by and waving. I waved back. Then realizing that we were alone, "Bennie, where's your class?"

"Oh, *mon Dieu*, I 'ave left zem up zee mountain! Aaaloow!" He shouted back up the slope and waved them down to join us. As they were hopping their skis back and forth down the slope Bennie said, "I 'ave an idea. You ski and wheen you pass I weel point skiers for you to imita'e. Zat way I can work weeth my class."

"*Bon!*" I agreed.

That week was spent doing just that. I even convinced Kaeti to lead and let me follow and imitate her. Things were going smoothly!

The next week was moguls.

According to Bennie, "Moguls, zay are very easy once you geet zee rhythm. Down - as you approach *le* mog'l, pole out and plant like - I pick zees one!, Up - as you rise on *le* mog'l and zen Down as you slide down zee backside. Zen you are ready for *le* next mog'l. Zees ees easier zan turning on zee flat snow because *le* mog'l lifts zee tail of skis, but ees harder because you MUST turn left - right - left - right. You can pass over *le* mog'l and turn on zee next, but you must absorb zee bump weeth your knees keeping body level or eet weel spill you. You do not wish to fall *dans* a field of moguls because zay weel punish you!"

And punish me they did!

Actually it wasn't too bad or too hard to learn provided I kept it slow. Each mogul really did help turn my skis. The trouble began when I started trying to imitate passing skiers. They were faster and cleaner. They didn't let their skis slide all the way into the depression before setting up for the next mogul. I could get started across one or two moguls and then my ski binding would pop open leaving me on – well, I was going to say one ski… but the truth was my butt, my face, or worse – Splits! – OUCH! Bennie kept trying to help, but he couldn't find anything wrong with my style. He tightened my bindings, but I still popped out. He finally decided that the problem was my skis. My skis! I couldn't afford new skis! My parents wouldn't understand… I took my problem to Gil, and he went to Bennie. They decided that new bindings would do the trick and would cost a lot less. Bennie suggested that I go to the ski shop in the upper village and ask for Yves. "Tell 'im to geev you my deescount on zee bindings."

I was in luck that evening. Bernd was heading up to the ski shop to order some replacement equipment for the ski team, and he said he would take me. The walk wasn't much different from the one I had taken with Stallone. Except that I was carrying my skis and boots, and we were in a hurry because the store was closing soon. I mentioned my ambition to be on the ski team before the end of the season, and it was met with polite indifference. It was dark when we arrived at the shop. The lights reflected gold and cheery out of its windows. The golden windows were the only light on the dark block because nothing else was open in that area.

As we walked in I noticed a couple inside break apart, and the dark haired girl moved to look at some stocking caps on a display.

Bernd greeted them, "*Bon Soir*, Yves, I brought you a customer. Colleen."

The girl turned and I realized it was Colleen. Her dark hair usually hidden by her ski cap and the subdued light caused her green eyes to flare. She smiled as she recognized me. *She's definitely one of the friendlier goddesses at school.*

"Colleen, I didn't expect to find you here," I said as I set my skis and boots down.

"Hi, Jim," Then to Yves she said, "He's okay! Tiny's roommate." Yves moved closer, and she put her arm around his waist. "Please don't tell anyone. Some of the girls don't approve."

"I won't," I promised. *Although, my conversations with the opposite sex rarely... NEVER have anything to do with someone else's love life.*

Yves asked, "What can I do for you two?"

I watched Yves as Bernd gave him his order. He was built stocky and wasn't much taller than me. He had a strong square face with a gentle look in his eyes, and his thick, light brown hair fell in several commas across his broad forehead. Colleen had found a handsome partner in this guy, and with what little I knew of her, Yves was probably a pretty nice guy, too.

After a bit, Bernd said, "This guy needs new bindings. Give him the school discount." He moved to sit on the ledge of the store window by the door.

"What do you need?" ask Yves.

"Marker turntables and Geze toes."

Bernd snorted from the window ledge. Yves looked at him and back at me. "Are you sure? Those are pretty aggressive. You will have no heel release."

I'd talked this over with Gil and Bennie. They agreed that I could handle them, especially since I probably couldn't afford to replace my bindings a second time. "Yes, Bennie said that I could handle them. Besides I'll need them when I move up to the racing team," I said.

Bernd snorted again, this one more of an exasperated chuckle. Yves looked at him again, and then quickly back to me with a questioning look. "Did you say Bennie?"

"Yes, I've been working with him."

"Wait a moment, Bennie's Jeem..." imitating Bennie, "from the school? Are you Bennie's protégé?"

At that Bernd got up and walked out followed by all of our eyes.

Protégé? He's never called me his protégé, but I am the only one from the school who's getting almost private lessons from him. "I guess. I almost forgot, he told me to ask for his discount, but I guess that's the same as the school's."

"No problem! He talks about you all the time at the Vag. Were you really hanging upside-down in a tree on the Riondaz?"

I told him the whole story, and the three of us got a good laugh at my expense.

"Bernie says that you are making unbelievable progress. You'll get his discount. The school's is... how do I say it?" He looked over at Colleen and shrugged, then back to me with a smile. "Not so good!"

I discovered that they actually added a surcharge to the American students on bindings, in fact, on anything that didn't have a price tag. I felt pretty sure that Bernd knew that.

I got the bindings for almost wholesale price with a little added for installation. I might have to reduce my alcohol intake for a while, but I wouldn't have to stop drinking altogether.

"I'll have them ready for you next week," Yves concluded.

Next week! That felt like a body blow! Colleen saw my reaction and whispered something in Yves ear that brought a great big smile followed by a laugh. "Okay, tomorrow after school, if I have the parts. Hey, with Bennie's discount you should buy something else."

I had been eying the Uvex ski glasses with the interchangeable lenses. Gil had a set and loved them. "What about these?"

"Sorry, no discount on Uvex. Although, I guess I could give you the school discount," he said.

"Gee thanks! What's that, five francs more?"

"Ten, at the very least!" We all laughed. "I will do this. Buy the glasses at Swiss price, and I'll toss in several replacement lenses. These blue and clear lenses are overstocked."

"Sold!"

I was at the shop right after school. I had changed to my ski clothes and ran almost all the way up. The skis were ready. Yves showed me how to wrap the red leather long-thong safety straps. Apparently, just like the judo belt, if you didn't wrap them correctly you looked like a fool, plus they helped keep your boots tight in the heel binding. The correct wrap for long-thong put a red "X" across the back of the boots. I practiced it until I had it down, then put my hiking boots back on, grabbed my skis and boots, and jogged back down the street to the telecabine.

I had missed class, but practiced with my new bindings on the moguls. The skis were solid against my boots. I hadn't realized how much play there was in my Solomen toes and cable bindings. Was I perfect? No, but when I fell I didn't loose my skis and popped back up. The next day Bennie had me following some serious mogul skiers. The guys would almost jump onto the moguls and roll their tips up over the top round, cleaving the mogul about two-thirds up one side or the other while keeping their upper body level and facing the fall line. I could do this for one or two moguls but not the whole field and quickly grew frustrated, again. I looked to Bennie.

"Each person 'as zeir own rhythm. You must find your song."

Then, as if on command, the one-legged, yodeler came singing and crashing over the moguls in front of us.

"*Tres bien*! You see! Thees man's song… I no understand but eet ees 'ees song. You find yours." Then waving his hand dismissively, "Oh, don' follow 'ees style. 'e uses 'ees poles too much. You do not need crutches. Zee poles only le Beat –" he said as he snapped his pole into the snow beside him, "– of your song."

I took Bennie at his word and went through a dozen songs before settling on "Mellow Yellow" by Donovan. "I'm just mad about saffron… They call me Mellow Yellow. Da-Da-Dum!" That was my song. I could feel it through my whole body as I bounded over the moguls.

The dead of winter brought a couple of other things to the dark of night. First, someone cooked up the idea of putting on a play, and I was asked to play a role. I didn't mind; in fact, I kinda liked acting in high school and had taken an intro course in my stateside college; but, Stu, the guy who wrote and directed it, just came up to me and asked me to play a part. It wasn't like I auditioned or even knew Stu very well. I got the feeling that someone was playing a practical joke by volunteering me, but, "What the hell!" It was dark out, and my other options during the week were drinking and *zim-zim*. My character was this young guy who finds out that some older guy who has been on the run from the mob for years has given up and decided to wait for his death. My character is so innocent that he can't comprehend the older guy's decision and fights to get him to save himself. After a week of practice I began to wonder if Stu had typecast me for the part...

Dick, the sergeant's son, was also type cast – or at least he loved playing the part of the mindless assassin sent to dispatch the old guy – besides he didn't have to memorize too many lines, and he got to carry a big gun. I got to know him a little better when we grabbed a beer at Le Nord each evening after practice. He really didn't like the freshman dorm, and he had completely lost that devilish spark I had originally seen in him.

The other amusement was the Searcher's Club. My favorite rat-faced dean, Zagier, caught me in the main one day and invited me to attend a debate club he was starting. That kinda floored me because I didn't think that he liked me after I had told him, in so many words, that I thought his English class was a remedial high school course. The group met once a week. Willie was there; maybe he had recommended me... Dean Zagier supplied the wine or hot tea to drink and snacks. The discussions ranged widely, but the topics were generally philosophical in nature – life, birth, death, infinity... Also the class distinctions, which were evident before and after the meetings, seemed to melt away during these sessions.

We frequently talked about religion, and I shared my view of Quakerism. My favorite story explaining the reason that we had no preachers was that of the blind Indian wise men who happened on an elephant. The first grabbed a leg and thought it a tree, the second the tail and thought it a rope, etc. They had no clue of the nature of the beast until they all compared notes. Quakers believe that each person has communication with God through what they call the "still, small voice" and that each person can discover and attempt to understand some small portion of God. But without sharing your discoveries with others, there can be no understanding of the totality of God. That is what their meeting for worship is about, a gathering of people to sit in silence listening for the still, small voice, and then a sharing of your discoveries. It is also the basis for Quaker pacifism. Destroying another human, in effect, stills his internal voice and denies that small portion of God within him.

Our group was diverse, an equal mix of guys and girls with a couple of Moslems, a Catholic, a variety of Protestants, and also an atheist – but there was no talking with him. He was so sure that there was no such thing as a God that he really wouldn't debate. In my stateside college these bull sessions were fairly common, but they usually involved only one or two other guys in the dorm parlor who had different Protestant beliefs. Here this diverse group sitting in this darkened parlor with glasses of wine or tea was quite civilized and intriguing. It was a pleasant break from the drinking and carousing.

Chapter Twenty

Christmas

About a week before Christmas break we had a "third strike, you're out" meal! Before I go into this I should say that most of the meals at ACS were better than my boarding school or stateside college. Also, the kitchen staff was a group of good-natured Italians with a top-notch German chef, and they seemed to really enjoy their work, especially BJ. She was called BJ because she made the dining room echo with her *"Bon Journo!"* She was a small, round waitress who looked like a tiny but jovial Italian baker right out of an operetta. She would prance in and out the kitchen bringing our fare, always cheery and usually always polite. At times she would seem to steam up when everyone wanted seconds of something especially appetizing. "BJ! BJ! *Encorra! Encorra!"* she would shout as she stomped back into the kitchen. She seemed ticked, but she would prance quickly out with the seconds and present them with flair! I suspect that she was proud when we loved her food enough to ask for more.

As I said, most of the food was good with a few exceptions. One exception, American chicken, arrived with all of us expecting southern fried, and we got great tureens of stewed chicken parts, bones and all, in broth mixed with onions, tomatoes, potatoes, peppers, and Italian seasonings. No one had a clue where the name came from, and it wasn't a bad meal once your mouth got over the craving for deep fat fried chicken. But the third-strike meal was tripe, cow diaphragm wrapped around an inedible purée of garbage that had been baked inside. The two other times I had carefully cut the meat from the diaphragm and attempted to chew the tough, rubbery chunks. Admittedly, after those meals my next stop was Kaeti's snack bar for a burger and fries. The meal was so bad that nearly the entire student body had signed a petition to have it removed from future menus and had taken it before the student government.

The third time it was served, Willie, the student council president, who had proven that he would eat anything else, led the revolt. He grabbed his table's platter of tripe and flipped it upside-down on the school president's table. Not two minutes later there were at least two-dozen platters upside-down on that table; ours was included as Wilds and I tossed it on. As the platters stacked up, the entire dining room emptied, leaving the president and his staff among the mounds of puke-filled cow diaphragm.

Tiny, Wilds, Gil, and I left to find food elsewhere. Tiny mentioned that the Messange was close, and we started hiking up the crunchy, snow-covered road toward it. As we entered we noticed Prince Paul alone at one of the tables. His bodyguards were at a table on the opposite side of him facing the door where we entered. He greeted us and moved to a bigger table so we could join him. As we ordered we talked about our plans for Christmas break. With the exception of Tiny and Prince Paul, all of us were heading home. Tiny's folks were stateside, and he was thinking about staying at school, so I invited him to come home with me. Prince Paul then announced that he would be taking the embassy airplane to Stockholm for an Ethiopian Christmas party there and a meeting with the Swedish Royal Family, then on to New York City for New Year's Eve on Times Square. Man! Envy surrounded him at the table. Several of us were actually salivating – not only from missing diner! Then, Prince Paul looked at each of us with a gleaming smile and asked, "Would each of you care to join me?"

"YES!" we shouted as one… then reality set in. Except for Tiny, we'd have to check with our parents. When the food was served, I bolted my veal, offered to pay for mine, but Prince Paul would not allow it, so I thanked him and dashed for the phone in the main.

The only telephone with an outside line was in an alcove in the front lobby of the main, and it often had a queue. When I arrived, I found that I was in luck, both because the phone was free and because my parents were home. It took some talking, but I convinced them that I would be in safe hands, especially with Prince Paul's bodyguards, and they agreed to let me go. I raced back up the hill only to meet the group walking down and announced that I could go. Wilds and Gil later found that they weren't so lucky.

That next week held one more surprise from the kitchen. It may have been the direct result of our revolt, and it might have been believed to be a punishment for our misbehavior, but it didn't turn out as the staff expected. As we came in the dining room we spotted one large table covered with white butcher paper set up across the back wall in front of the stage. With several dozen other earlier tray dumpers, Willie, Wilds, and I were asked to eat at that table. The table was bare, with no plates, silver, or drinking glasses. The servers arrived with whole roast chickens, mashed potatoes and gravy, peas, and pitchers of bug juice, or the Swiss version of red Kool-Aid. The pitchers were set down, but the platters of the other food were dumped in piles between every set of four diners. As the food was deposited on the table, the gravy started flowing toward the low side, away from me, thank God, and the peas rolled everywhere!

Not to be undone, Willie ripped a leg off the nearest chicken, grabbed a handful of mashed potatoes and dug in laughing like some Victorian lord in his castle! Soon the table was a riot of greasy students ripping chicken meat off the carcass and tossing the bones down the table to Willie, who was making some kind of macabre sculpture from them. After the legs and wings had been torn from one bird, Tiny had grabbed the entire torso and begun gnawing on it like a great cave bear. Wilds was the first to manage the peas by dabbing them up with a handful of mashed potatoes. Soon all of us were following suit. The pitchers of bug juice were passed from person to person around the table. Several couples, including Dennie, the Association treasurer, and his cute, if abused, girlfriend Lee, began imitations of the erotic food devouring scenes from a recent movie called "Tom Jones." This was some sex flick about Victorian England and had nothing to do with the grotesque crooner of the same name.

After a while, Lee got upset with the fact that there were no napkins and began trying to flick the cold excess mash potatoes off her hands, only to have some land on Dennie's shoulder. Dennie got back at her by smearing potatoes and gravy across her face. When Lee left the table we assumed that she was going to find somewhere to clean herself up, but not two minutes later she came sneaking back into the dining room with a large bowl of mashed potatoes and gravy which was immediately deposited onto Dennie's head. There the bowl sat like some goofy hat until Dennie threw it against the wall, shattering the plastic bowl, and stormed out. We thought that was the end of it, and Lee was getting a round of applause when Dennie returned with a bowl of dessert, chocolate pudding! Now I don't usually like chocolate pudding, and Lee may never eat another bowl, but there was something delicious about the way it dripped off her chin and into her cleavage. A fantasy to be stored for another day because Lee was now in tears and running for the exit. Whatever the rationale behind the supper, it became known as a Tom Jones meal, and we had at least two others before the school year was out.

Soon the day of departure had arrived. Tiny and I, with suitcases packed, met in front of Prince Paul's room. We should have noticed that the bodyguard was missing, but we were too excited as we knocked. After a second attempt, Willie came to his door at the other end of the hall and said, "He already left."

"What? We're supposed to go with him. Where is he?" Tiny demanded.

"Settle down! I believe that I heard he left this morning with Sandra. Don't look now, but I suspect he's engaged again."

"Engaged, Shit!" Tiny shouted. "What about us?"

"Hey guys, who would you want to travel with, two guys or a cute bird?"

Tiny and I stood there in shock for a while until an errant thought hit me. "He went with Saundra, the jumper?" *Admittedly she doesn't appeal to me, but she might to someone else. However, the episode on the balcony doesn't speak well for her sanity!*

"No, Sandra, the thin-faced blonde with the pointy nose."

"Oh!" I laughed, "Sandra!" *I wondered why Willie used the English term 'bird.' Baby John frequently used it, but Willie never does. She did kinda look like a bird. But what does that do for us?*

"What the hell are you laughing at, Henderson?" Tiny boomed from above me.

"Cool it, Tiny! We'll just grab our skis and catch a train for my home. It won't be Stockholm and New York City, but it beats staying here."

We descended the cog and easily made our connections to Lausanne, where we sat for hours waiting for connections to Basel and on to Germany. A late dinner at a local restaurant provided *rachelet*, a couple of thick slices of Swiss bread smothered in molten fondue cheese. Remembering Willie's earlier warning, we finished a bottle of Fendant wine while gorging on the meal. It was surprising how filling that stuff was. I felt like I had eaten Thanksgiving dinner, and Tiny was satisfied, a difficult task, at best. We snuck another bottle of wine on the train and took over one of the compartments. The train sped through the night as we sipped wine and catnapped. We changed trains in Basil and again in Heidelberg. Early the next morning, as the sun was rising, we were nearing Landstuhl. Germany was shades of gray and brown – overcast skies, dirt, and wilted farmlands. There was no snow, and I was already feeling like I needed a fix. Just one snow pile – something, anything white! There was a cold heavy mist falling when I called from the train station and told mom I was home and had brought a friend. She sounded surprised but very pleased and promised to be right down to pick us up.

When she picked us up, she let us know without a doubt that she preferred our coming home to our taking embassy flights around the world, but she reminded me of dad's golden rule: I wasn't allowed back in the house without a haircut. This rule had been in place since I had started boarding school six years ago, and having a friend visit didn't make a difference. In fact, she told Tiny that he should get his cut as well, handed us both the cost of a haircut, and dropped us off at the post barber. We left the bags and skis in the station wagon and said we'd walk home after. I was embarrassed. I should have remembered it on the train home and prepared Tiny, and I should have insisted that Tiny be excluded, but he hadn't seemed to mind. He had laughed, saluted, and went along like he was following the family marching orders. Mom later told me that Tiny had actually thanked her. He didn't like his hair long, but his girlfriend didn't want him to cut it. Somehow that didn't sound like Kaeti, but what did I know...

Christmas was like every other Christmas. Mom always decorated to the hilt, and Germany had provided a treasure trove of new and exciting decorations. Nutcrackers, incense burners that had smoke curling out of St. Nick's pipe-filled mouth, red and white mushrooms, bubbling candle lights, and a variety of wooden ornaments the likes of which I had never seen before on a Christmas tree. Mom was in heaven! And Tiny... well, he was part of the family! With his size no one would believe that he was a blood relative, but he was treated and put to work just like the rest of us.

Seeing mom's fascination with everything Christmas, Tiny bought the family a candle-powered wooden windmill of the three wise men coming to the manger with the Christ child. With the heat from the candles moving the fan blades, the wise men sailed around and around in circles, never quite reaching the manger. I, on the other hand, bought practical things like ski gloves and stocking caps from the PX for all of them. Mom got Tiny a German beer mug with a cast iron top that would have fit in to the collection I was starting. It was unique because it had a handle made to look like a red fox walking up its side. I wondered briefly if one of my presents had been renamed until I got the same mug. He also got a pair of XL ski gloves from my sister, Millie, and was kind enough not to mention they were too small until we returned to school. Millie actually paid an inordinate amount of attention to Tiny, and I began to suspect that she had a crush on him. When I warned Tiny that my sister was an innocent from the same Quaker background as me, he said, "No offense, but she's not my type, too short." That was the curse of our entire family! I already had an inch on dad.

After Christmas came the problem of what to do in the drab, dreary German countryside. I had the Opel station wagon, and we hit my favorite pub over by Ramstein Air Force Base. After a couple or three wonderful German beers, the trip home became a near disaster as I jumped the car over a railroad crossing. We must have flown a full car length before touching down.

"Shit, Jim! What are you trying to do, kill us both?" Tiny shouted.

"Shit!" I shouted as I wrestled with the steering wheel to get control of the car. "Sorry, I guess not having a car at college is a life saver." We hit the teen club dance in Kaiserslautern or K-town, but most of the girls were teeny boppers, fifteen and less. Now, I could easily pass for a high schooler, but Tiny was totally out of place. Afterwards I mentioned having dated one of a pair of twins from K-town last summer. Tiny perked up at that and pressed me to see if they were around. I was reluctant since we had officially broken up before summer was over, but Tiny's encouragement finally caused me to drive by Kathy and her sister's quarters. I was a bit disappointed but a bit relieved when we saw no lights on at her place. Likely their family had gone somewhere for the holidays. Then when we had seen all three American movies at the nearby military posts, celebrated New Years in front of the one and only U.S. military TV station, and were about to fall into total boredom and nightly drinking, dad came home with reservations for the two of us for three nights at the military recreation center in Garmish. The tickets included meals and lift tickets for the Zugspitza, one of the highest Alps in Germany. Outstanding!

We loaded our suitcases and tied our skis to the roof rack because they were too long to go inside. Then as we left, dad tossed in snow chains he had sized for the Opel saying, "You never know." They seemed pointless because there still wasn't a flake of the white stuff in this gray wilderness, but I didn't argue. The trip on the autobahn was much as I had expected. The Opel just didn't have the power to get up and run with the big dogs. We were lucky to pass the semitrailers, and our passing speed was so slow that at least three Mercedes stacked up behind us and rode our tail, flashing their lights, until we were able to pull back over to the right.

We were on secondary roads from Munich toward Garmish when the snow started. The further south we got, the heavier the snow fell. The snow was wet enough that it clung to the windshield wipers. Tiny and I took turns reaching out the side windows and snapping the wiper blades to clear them of snow so we could see. Tiny's arms were long enough to grab the right blade as it slushed across the window. The road signs were worse. We had to stop close to them, and Tiny would reach out and swat the post, before we could read the sign.

Somewhere on that route we missed our turn, and the signs no longer mentioned Garmish, but we kept plodding southwards. After almost an hour of driving blindly we approached a lighted building near the road with a snow-covered sign that spanned the roadway. It looked vaguely like a turnpike tollbooth. We stopped and went inside to ask where we were. I recognized the interior as a border-crossing guardhouse and knew we were in trouble. The guard, who spoke some English, told us what we already knew: that we had missed our turn thirty K's back and that we were entering Austria. We hadn't brought our passports, but he let us go on my military dependent ID. He also told of a short cut a couple of K's south that would take us back into Germany and straight up to Garmish. But he warned us not to miss that turn, or we would be heading into the Austrian Alps, and the nearest town of any size, Innsbruck, was many K's away.

We made a left-hand turn a few K's down the road but weren't sure we were on the right road because it was only a single plowed lane through window-high snow banks on either side and we were the only vehicle in sight. Drifts spilled off the snow on the side of the road and filled large portions of the opening between the banks, forcing us to skirt them when we could and plow through them when we couldn't. I was beginning to think about turning around if we could find a wide enough area when we spotted a red and white barber pole blocking the roadway. We approached it slowly, hoping that this meant something good as an old gentleman walked into our headlights in forest-green clothes with a military cap. He pushed down on the counterweight at the end of the barber pole, causing it to swing up out of our path. We stopped beside him and asked if this was the road to Garmish. He said "*Garmish, ja, geradeaus!*" I began laughing – *geradeaus!*

"What's that all about?" Tiny asked. "Are we heading in the right direction?"

"Yes, he said straight ahead."

"So what's so funny?"

I told Tiny of my trip with dad to K-town city hall to get my international driver's license last summer. We had stopped to ask directions from a local, and his answer was "*geradeaus.*" Now dad's college German covered left and right, but he had no clue what the guy had just told him even after repeatedly asking. Frustrated, we drove on hoping to find someone else to guide us when we passed the city hall. "*Geradeaus–*" dad had laughed, "–must mean straight ahead!"– something apparently not covered in German class.

The snow got worse after that. Now it was no longer sticking to the windshield wipers, but it was blowing sideways across our headlights, giving me the feeling that we were in a continual curve to the left. After about a half hour, the plowed lane widened, and we started seeing other cars coming at us. We even found ourselves following someone's taillights through the snow tunnel. But almost as soon as we caught up and began feeling secure, the taillights disappeared around an unseen corner ahead, and we plowed straight into the snow bank at the end of the curve. Tiny and I got out and began trying to pull the car out by the doorframes, but we were stuck. We grabbed our skis from the top and dug in front of the car to give us a place to stand. Then, with our backs pressed into the snow bank, we pushed the car back onto the level surface. I am not sure that I could have done this without Tiny's power. Another friend and I might have had to wait for rescue.

I remembered the snow chains that dad had so thoughtfully provided. It seemed a good time to put on them on, but neither of us had a clue how to do it. After draping the chains over the tires and rolling the car forward, only to wrap the chains around the axle, we decided to try driving onto them and lifting them up either side. This seemed to work, but trying to clip the split rings together was nearly impossible with our frozen fingers. Once the tightening bungee cords were clipped on, we continued our journey jingling down the road.

In town we found lots of helpful Americans on the street, and they directed us to the military rec center hotel. It was too late for dinner, but junk food and cokes from the snack machines were readily available, and we crashed on twin beds, dreaming of the trip and tomorrow's skiing. We rose leisurely and found the dining room. Our reservations included anything we wanted from the menu; sooo - steak and eggs, pancakes, bacon, hash browns, toast, orange juice, two cups of coffee for each of us, and we were ready to hit the mountain. It was still snowing at ten the next morning when we hopped into the bus to the slopes. It was empty, but we figured the others were either too frightened or didn't realize that the top could be clear while it snowed below. However, the actual reason became clear as we approached the ski lift. It wasn't moving. When we asked we were told that over three meters of new snow had fallen up top and it was closed.

"Three meters! Ten friggin feet of snow! That's impossible!" Tiny bellowed. "How soon before the slopes will be open?"

"*Ich weiß nicht.* (I don't know.)" said the ticket collector. "Maybe tomorrow, maybe next week. Ve can do nothing until it stops snowing."

"Crap!" I said. "What's open?"

"They've groomed the bunny hill, *aber* it has several centimeters of new snow so not many people are using it."

Tiny and I spent the day on the bunny slopes. The snow covered our boots but was light enough that it did not affect our turns. The snow stopped falling about noon, and we skied every inch of the hill. There was one fairly steep section with a couple of trees on it that provided some challenge. We were pretty sure that this section was not on the bunny-hill skiers' typical route. We soon had carved some adequate moguls on it and treated the trees as gates in a ski course. It was fun but too short. As other skiers ventured out after the storm, we drew quite a following through our course. One young teen actually complimented us, "Hey, you guys are great! Are you on a racing team, or something?"

"Yeah, we're on the American College of Switzerland racing team," Tiny lied. "Can't wait until the top opens." The kid became our shadow for the rest of the afternoon.

Dinner that evening was steak, of course, baked potatoes, and sour cream. Tiny ordered a glass of Burgundy wine, but when I tried they carded me. We were back in the U.S. as far as the hotel was concerned. Not that he was older than me, just taller; but Tiny got his glass, and I had to settle for a coke. Over dinner we talked about school. Tiny was getting bored with skiing and of doing the same thing night after night. I probably bubbled on too much about my lessons with Bennie.

When Tiny started complaining again, I said, "Well, at least you have Kaeti. She's great, and can she ski!"

"Kaeti, hell, she plays too many games! She's always on the slopes and, when she's not, she's working at the snack bar. She doesn't like to go to the bars, play *zim-zim*, or anything!"

I sat quietly listening intently to this tirade. Then after chugging his third class of wine, Tiny quietly admitted that Kaeti wouldn't have sex with him. "Shit, she won't even come to my room after that first time at the purple passion party! You know, you broke up what was a very promising evening!" At that, the angry look on Tiny's face made me more than a little nervous.

"I said I was sorry," I said with my hands up in surrender. *Whoa! No sex! I thought that Wilds and I were the only ones not having sex at the college. Tiny and Kaeti have been dating for months now! Since he has his own room, I assumed that she was popping in and out like Sam from Gil's room.* This was a surprise but not an unpleasant one, although I made sure I wasn't caught smiling. Tiny could crush me like an ant!

Day two and the lifts to the top were still not open. Half of that day on the bunny slopes was enough, and we decided to explore. Munich was only thirty or forty K's up the road, so we hopped in the car. Unlike Garmish, the snow in Munich was black and slushy from all the cars. We cruised the town and ended up at the Hoffbrau Haus across from the

University of Maryland extension. I told Tiny about visiting here when I first arrived in Europe and being driven away by its German *stallag*, or prison camp, look. Tiny didn't think it looked bad.

"What would you do aside from drink?" I asked. "We have the mountain and the skiing."

"Hell, what's wrong with drinking? This German beer makes Swiss beer taste like Schlitz! You could take weekend trips to the Zugspitza for skiing," Tiny added laughing at his own joke.

"That would get old a whole lot faster, and this place looks like crap – dark, gray, slushy crap! Not for me!"

We were about to continue when the bartender pulled out an accordion and started singing, *"In München, stat der Hoffbräu Haus, ein, swei, sofa!"* I had learned that song over the summer at the beer festivals. Soon the whole bar was singing, rocking back and forth, and toasting. We were lucky to safely find our way back to the hotel that night.

Day three and the top was still closed, so we gave up and headed home. The trip was uneventful. Just south of Heidelberg, we ran out of the snow and drove back into the gray world. Dick from ACS was at our house when we came in. He was talking with my sister, Millie. He seemed to be in much better spirits away from school. We had another week to kill before heading back. The bars called, but I had to control how much I drank because I had to get us home safely. As Tiny, Dick, and I pulled up outside my favorite Ramstein bar one evening, we saw a high schooler who had tried to chug a pint of Cognac. *Stupid little punk! Alcohol poisoning is not a pleasant way to go...* The ambulance was already there when we arrived. As it pulled away, taking his thin, pale body to the nearest hospital, its eerie sound was like the SS sirens in some old Anne Frank movie. The bartender said that the medics believed the kid would live, but he sure hadn't looked like it on that stretcher.

Inside the bar Dick spilled his guts. He hated the school, and he was pissed that his dad wouldn't let him join us on the trip to Garmish. This was the first that I had heard about that, but we convinced him that it wasn't worth the trip, especially with the top of the mountain closed. But he really put a downer on that night.

Tiny and I ditched Dick after that. He was just too depressing to be good company, and it was hard enough to find two girls who would be interested in a six and a half-foot tall Adonis and a shorter, curly-haired ah... skier? Near the end of the week we went to an early movie in K-town and decided to make a second try at Kathy's. This time the lights were on. I was really nervous and felt that flowers might add the right touch. I had seen an open shop a few blocks back. The owner greeted us, and I asked about some roses. He asked what color and to help me decide he explained that different color roses meant different things: red was for passion and white for true love. Tiny encouraged red, but I chose six pinkish-orange roses that were new and apparently had no meaning, yet.

The lights were still on when we returned. I held the flowers behind my back and knocked at the door. Kathy's twin opened the door. Was I sure? No, but she was always the first to the door last summer, and she just stood there trying to remember my name while thoroughly checking out Tiny. I hoped that Kathy would have remembered my name and been focused on me; therefore, I was pretty confident in my guess. Telling them apart seemed to be really important for Kathy last summer. "Is your sister home?"

"Yes. Kathy, it's that guy from last summer!" While I waited Tiny secretly pulled three flowers from my batch.

Kathy peaked out tentatively from behind her sister. "Jim? Hi. What are you doing here? Is your school out?"

"Yes, these are for you!" I brought forward the three remaining roses. "There used to be six," I said as I gave Tiny a dirty look.

Then he bent forward and said gallantly, "And these are for you... ah?"

"Sally! Thanks!" Kathy's sister supplied her name as she took the flowers Tiny offered and looked at Kathy. "He knew I wasn't you!"

"Really?" Kathy then took my flowers and gave me a quick hug. "Thanks!" *Something's wrong, but I can't put my finger on it.*

"Do you girls want to go for a ride?" Tiny asked, and Sally responded, "Great!"

Tiny hadn't been in the back seat of the Opel wagon before, and he didn't fit facing forward. He managed at the diagonal with the passenger seat as far forward as it would go. On the other hand, Sally didn't seem the least bit shy as she climbed into the back seat throwing her legs across Tiny's lap. I am not sure how we ended up there, Sally seemed to be directing, but we drove the winding road up the hill to Landstuhl castle. We stopped where the road overlooked the town. This was a favorite make-out spot for teens during the summer. In fact, it was the place where Kathy and I almost lost our heads. Given the memories, this would have been the last place to take Kathy before we had a long talk, but here we were, and Tiny and Sally were already kissing, fondling and laughing in the back seat. Tiny's legs jumped and rocked Kathy's seat as they laughed. I looked over at Kathy, who was sitting there uncomfortably, and I shrugged my shoulders. "Want to take a walk?"

"Sure."

We got out into the misty, cold night air. Kathy shivered and wrapped her arms around herself. I stuffed my hands into my pockets. I started talking about college and bragging about my success skiing, and then asked how her year was going. Instead of answering she stopped, looked into my eyes and asked, "How did you know it wasn't me at the door?"

"I know you by your smile," I said.

"You didn't!" She said angrily.

"Didn't what?"

She looked down at her feet and said softly, "I'm sorry but... we tricked you last summer. My sister took my place on our date. She said you didn't know it was her, and you almost..." again facing me challengingly. "I was so angry! but... but I had played the trick so I couldn't tell you."

Floored, I just looked at her. "That wasn't you that night?" staring at her not knowing what to say or do.

We stood in silence for a while. Then she said, "I'm sorry!"

"Me too. I... I should have known."

"Why?" she asked, looking up at me, her eyes pleading for something to hold onto. Thinking about that night, it became obvious...

"You were so forward. So... like that," I said, looking back at the car. "I should have known it wasn't you."

"Do you want to hear something funny?" she said. "My sister thought that she had been discovered when you stopped." She looked at me confused, "Why did you stop?"

I thought about telling her about wanting to stay a virgin but said, "I didn't think that we were ready."

She curled shivering into my arms. "It's cold out here!"

"Yeah, they've been in there long enough!" We walked back to the car. The windows were already thoroughly fogged. I knocked just in case.

"Just a minute!" Sally said.

We waited, huddled in each other arms. We kissed. It was nice, like I remembered it, and not like that night last summer. "I should have known."

"I wish... It was a stupid trick. I'm sorry." I suspected that it wasn't Kathy's idea but didn't say anything.

When we got in, Tiny and Sally were still adjusting their clothes. I looked at the two and said, "You know Tiny, her dad is a Master Sergeant in the Green Berets. He could kill you with one hand."

"Now you tell me!" Tiny laughed.

"Don't worry," Sally said, "He just left for Vietnam. We're heading back to the States as soon as school is out."

That next day we borrowed the family station wagon and picked up the twins for a movie. Tiny and I had already seen them all, but we weren't planning on watching. Necking in the theater was fun and a little warmer than the hilltop! It had been a while for me. It did wonders for my confidence after those ego-bruising months on the mountain. On the drive up to the Landstuhl castle that evening, I told a story I had heard last summer. It seems that a feudal lord was taxing his people to death and was spending all the money building this castle. One evening at midnight he was surveying the construction from the top when he fell and impaled himself on the scaffolding below. A wooden upright had speared through his heart! "The legend goes that his ghost

is condemned to walk the top of the castle at midnight! BoooOOOooo!"
We all laughed!

It was nearly midnight when we arrived. We parked on the backside
away from the restaurant where I'd had my first German beer with my
folks. Sally dared us to climb to the top of the castle. A dare is a dare! We
offered to lift the girls up first, but they decided to stay and watch. Tiny
lifted me easily over a lower section of the ruins. Getting Tiny up was
tougher. Both girls pushed from below while I pulled from above. Once
up we walked blindly through hallways that I had passed through only
a half dozen times last summer. The castle was in sufficient ruins that
large areas were open, allowing some ambient light into the interior.
There was no moon, but the lights from the restaurant were shining
through openings in the ruined walls. I showed Tiny a dark room with
the steel barred gate and explained that it was the torture chamber.
Then across from that was a narrow roped-off staircase that led to a
small hole in the earth, which I had snuck away from a tour to explore.
I explained that I thought that it was another small dungeon, but the
tour guide said that the stairs once led to a tunnel that crossed the valley
and opened on the far hill not far from my home. That would have
been one hell of a tunnel! It would have had to travel down the hill
underground, then under the village of Landstuhl, and up the far side.
I couldn't imagine anyone in the Dark Ages digging and shoring it by
hand.

We were just about to move on when a loud thunk followed by two
smaller thumps came from inside the torture chamber. Why a stone
would choose to fall at that very instant, I don't know and it didn't
matter. I panicked, and since Tiny was standing between me and the
way back I ran up the stairs toward the upper level, and Tiny was hot on
my heels. Running through old castles is not something a person even
my size does, especially in the dark. I could feel the tops of doorways
brushing the hair on top of my head. But Tiny! – after hitting the first
doorway headfirst – held one hand in front of his face, leaned well
forward, and yelled as he smacked into each stone door frame.

We finally came out on the top of the castle and looked over the low-walled open area. Haze hung over the top like something out of a Frankenstein movie. Tiny started to walk over to a raised area on the far side above where the girls waited when he stopped and stared. I walked up to see what he was looking at. It was just the fog, but a part of it was glowing; a vertical area about the size of a large person was illuminated near the far wall. I suspected that the lights below were shining up through some crack in the castle wall and walked bravely forward to prove my theory. I was about three steps past Tiny when we heard the scream! Actually it was more of a low wail. I froze! *It's the girls playing a trick on us, right? But that sound was too deep… more like a man's tortured howl.* I heard Tiny sprint for the stairs. That was all I needed, and I was running close behind him. Just inside the first entrance Tiny stopped, and I plowed into him. "What?" I asked.

"You lead, I don't know the way!"

"Shit!" I exclaimed as I bolted past him. I barely touched the stairs on the way down. I was running blindly back through the narrow passageways and under the short doorways. I don't know how Tiny was following and fitting through at this speed, but I kept running. Terror building with each step! I reached the wall we had climbed up and leapt off letting my legs absorb the shock of the ground and rolled on my side in a parachute-landing fall. I then raced to the car where I could see the girls huddled together in the back seat. Tiny wasn't far behind. When he reached the edge he didn't jump. Instead he turned and lowered himself off the wall. Tiny ran to the car and piled in the back as Kathy climbed over the seat to the front. "Did you hear that scream?" the girls asked as we hopped in.

"Yes," I said, out of breath.

"That was you guys trying to scare us, right?"

"No, we thought it was you!"

"It couldn't be! That was a man's voice! Please say you did it."

"No, it wasn't us."

Kathy huddled close as I heard Sally ask, "Tiny, what happened to your forehead?"

"It's nothing," Tiny said. I looked back quickly and caught a glimpse of a bloody scrape, likely caused by his hitting a doorframe in the castle.

"Geez!" I grabbed a Kleenex from my back pocket. "Hold this on it. We'll get some Bactine on that when we get home," I said. *Whoa, being short has advantages. Although, how often will I be running through a castle being chased by a ghost?*

That was the last time I saw Kathy. They got grounded for staying out too late, and Tiny, Dick, and I needed to catch the train back to Switzerland. The cog up to our beautiful, sunny, snow-covered village was exhilarating.

Upon our return, we learned that Prince Paul had not taken Sandra on his travels; instead Colleen had gone with him. I caught up with Colleen later in the snack bar. She said that the trip with Prince Paul was completely platonic. In fact he was a perfect gentleman, but I did see a hint of mischief when she mentioned escaping from the bodyguards one night to go to a club. She then sat silent for a moment, and I watched her green eyes flash with fear, and then anger, as if she were reliving something in her mind. Then she told me that his bodyguards found them later that evening, and pulled their guns on her. Paul managed to settle them down, but that was too much. Prince Paul left for New York by himself, and she returned early to the school. Prince Paul returned to school almost two weeks after the end of the break.

Colleen's story got me wondering what had happened between her and Yves, but I didn't have the nerve to ask. However, not a week later, I spotted the two of them dancing together at the Messange. With eyes like hers I guess that I'd forgive her anything... *Geez! Prince Paul's bodyguards carry GUNS! I hadn't even considered that!*

I also learned that the French professors had indeed taken separate vacations. Wilds said that he heard that Monsieur Bailet had spent the weeks with an unnamed coed. Madame Bailet had taken their kids to Paris. Likely she just visited her family, but who could say for sure.

Chapter Twenty One

La Grande Neige

Wilds and I compared notes when we returned to school. Scotland was just as dreary as Germany, but he didn't have any adventures to talk about. I built up the wonders of our ski trip and neglected to mention that we didn't get to the top of the mountain; the Hoffbrau Haus story became an oompah band and dancing in the isles, and the walk on the haunted castle had everything but werewolves. I left out the parts about the twins, even though I wanted to brag about Kathy, for fear that Tiny's role would get back to Kaeti and hurt her. I briefly considered sabotaging Tiny because he put down Kaeti in Garmish, but I decided that would just hurt her and do nothing for me – except get me pounded.

I also caught up with Willie and Baby John comparing notes in Le Nord. Willie had the beginnings of a significant Afro and had added a spindly goatee to his chin, and Baby John in his red and white striped shirt and clashing flowered pants had new rose-colored lenses in his glasses; his hair was almost touching his shoulders... and my dad thought that I needed a haircut! Willie's Christmas story made my adventures seem small, although, after my exaggerations to Wilds, I took his story with more than a grain of salt.

He alleged that he had spent Christmas with friends in Geneva, but on a drunken dare he had headed off to hitchhike to Paris in a major snowstorm. His trip spanned several hundred K's and a couple of nights, but he claimed to have walked large portions of it in the snow. He had been turned out by hotel owners, like Mary and Joseph from the inn, but continued his dogged walk into the night. He claimed a few rides – with Italians who said he would never get Frenchman to pick him up and invited him back to Italy, and with a French couple, the wife of which had made a serious impression on him and he described her down to the chips in her red nail polish. He and she shared cigarettes – his Marlboros for her Gauloise. *Yeah right,* I thought, *I'm calling his bluff if he starts talking about a menage-a-trois in some roadway hotel!* But he didn't go there. He also claimed to have ridden the Paris metro for proof because they had dated ticket stubs before taking the trains from Paris to rejoin his friends for New Year's Eve in Zermatt, at the foot of the Matterhorn. Baby John and I smiled and looked at each other skeptically until Willie slowly pulled out his dated metro stub, the ticket stub for the train to Zermatt, and finally the empty Gauloise cigarette packet with a lipstick stained butt in it from the truck driver's beautiful wife. *Sometimes it's what Willie doesn't say that speaks the loudest – menage-a-trois? maybe…* Baby John and I just sat there with our mouths open – dazed.

Out of curiosity I went to the snack bar late that evening and found Kaeti closing up. I repeated my stories but included the fact that the top of the Zugspitza was closed by ten feet of snow and asked about her adventures in Paris.

"Paris is not my kinda place," she said matter-of-factly. "I'm just not a shopper, I guess. There are too many people, and most of them aren't friendly."

"My impression exactly!" I agreed.

"Oh, I've been there before, but I figured that I'd have more fun with Kayanna. The place was so gray. After two days, I needed a snow fix!"

I reached over and shook Kaeti's hand. "Actually it only took me two hours in Germany!"

"And all the guys we met were way too short!" Kaeti said, shaking her head and laughing. *Too short!* I thought as I sat up straighter on my stool. "Jim, what's this I hear about twins on your trip?"

What? I tried to control my reactions. I looked down and closed my mouth. *How had she heard about that?* "Did Tiny tell you about that?" I asked as I looked up.

"Ahh... Yes," Kaeti said while shaking her head no. She didn't look at me when she said that. *She's heard something but wants details*, I decided. *Well, I'm not going to provide them!*

"He's ahh..." *We had a good time? No!* "Tiny helped me out."

"Oh, yeah?" Kaeti said skeptically.

"Seriously, I had dated one of the twins, Kaeti... I mean Kathy!" I sputtered, embarrassed, "– last ah... summer and really liked her, but we broke up. Tiny encouraged me to visit her. He even helped me pick out flowers."

"Flowers?" Kaeti said, showing a little annoyance.

"The flowers might have been my idea. Anyway, he got us back together. It was really great!"

"What about Tiny and her sister?"

"I... They... Tiny took out the other just to help me out." *Change the topic!* "I found out why we broke up! Kathy's sister played a trick on me. She pretended to be Kathy, and went out with me. Kathy got pissed because I couldn't tell the difference."

"And Tiny..." Kaeti started.

"She really hated it because I ended up parking with her sister, and things got a little out of hand."

"How out of hand?" she said with a smile and an excited sparkle in her eyes!

Yes! Got it changed, but now I have to finish the story! "Ah... pretty far... We didn't go all the way, but it was pretty extreme. Kathy was really pissed!" Kaeti smiled and actually gave me a serious once over. *I dodged the bullet!* We went on to talk about the new snow up top the Berneuse and getting back on the slopes tomorrow.

The following day Bennie got the class together and announced, "Now I weel show you 'ow to survive any slope zat 'olds snow. Theez you call shortswing."

He went down a steeper area poling and hopping his skis back and forth violently, his edges cutting fiercely into the snow at each landing. "Attack, attack, attack!" he shouted as he bounced back and forth down the slope.

It looked like great fun! "Attack, attack, attack!" I shouted as I bounded after him. After the third bounce it hit me. *I've done this before, but where? The steps! With Kaeti! Of course, our fall training routine! This is what Kaeti was training us for!* "Attack, attack, attack!" I burst out laughing for the shear joy of it!

As we gathered at the bottom Bennie explained, "You can use thees anywhere, almost. You must no try eet at too high speed, but you can use eet before you are skiing too fast *dans* a very steep slope." We rode the lift up and went to the steepest section of the slope on the right of the field of moguls. Bennie first, "Hoopa, Attack, attack, attack!"

I was next, "attack, attack, attaaaahhh!" My uphill ski hit my boot and kicked out my bottom ski. *This slope is too steep!* I was rolling down the slope and ended up sliding headfirst. My skis were still on so I rolled over again on purpose and slammed them into the snow below me to slow my slide. I slowed it but did not stop it and ended up lying at the feet of Bennie at the bottom. "Still learning!" I said as I looked up at him. The others chose to walk back to a lesser slope to practice their short swing. I followed suit after I regained my pride. I caught Kaeti that evening and told her that I now understood the steps drill. She seemed confused, but when I mentioned short swing she thought about it for a while and agreed it was the same motion. Apparently she just did it because the ski team practiced there, and she hadn't thought about the similarity. The earlier practice on the steps made learning short swing a breeze, and by the end of the week I had even mastered the steep area. You just couldn't let your skis come too far across the slope. The angle was so severe that your skis could not stand next to each other without the upper ski being shoved into the lower boot.

The next week brought more snow and lots of it. Monday morning it was whiteout conditions as I walked up to school for breakfast. It didn't stop all day. At 4 p.m. I grabbed my skis and was walking through swirling snow in powder over my knees up to the lift. No one followed. Bennie was inside the lift housing, talking to the operators, when I walked in. When he saw me he said, "I knew you would be 'ere! Zey are talking about closing zee lifts because zee wind ees so bad up top, but we can make one run een deep powder, eef you like!"

"I like!"

You couldn't see anything from the telecabine as we rose toward the top of the Berneuse, and they were right about the wind. With the two of us inside, the cabin was swinging dramatically back and forth. We even banged into the guide bars for one of the pylons before we reached the top. It wasn't snowing on the top of the mountain, but it was blanketed with waist deep snow. They closed the lift when we got up so there was only one way down. The sun was out, but the wind was blowing the snow sideways into our faces. The chair lifts were also closed.

Bennie said, "forgeet everything you know about skiing today. Powder ees different! You mus' lean back and float. Zee snow weel leeft you and slow you. You mus' keep your skis apart so zey do no cross but zey must not go too far out. Zat weell 'urt! You turn by moving your *derrière* back and forth slowly, like zee dance. Everything ees like dance. When enough weight ees on zee right ski you weel drift left. Slowly balance back and forth. Watch as you tips rise and you weel be sure zey are align. Follow me, but not zee same path. Zee snow slows you. Eef you follow my path you weel ca'ch me, *comprend?*"

"Okay... I think."

We started right down the steepest part of the slope. Floating was right. I am not sure about dancing; I was too nervous. You couldn't see your skis, except occasionally when the tips popped out. I imagined them floating somewhere between the packed powder below and the top. If you put too much weight on one foot, the ski started to sink; and it felt like you were going to fall over. I didn't make one complete turn before my skis separated and I went down into a white cloud bank of snow. Suspended in the powdery snow, I found the bottom; therefore, up was the other direction, but turning my skis across the slope was impossible, and I started going again straight down. I slowly shifted my weight and came around across the slope. Then I made an enormous curve back around to where Bennie was waiting.

"Fun, no?"

"Yeah, great... I don't suppose they can bring a *luge* through this if I break my neck."

He laughed, "probably no. But don' worry, zees ees like falling in feathers."

"Why did you pick the steepest slope?"

"Ees too slow. You would be walking on zee *autre* slopes."

At the bottom of the bowl we did just that. I saw why the chair lifts were closed. The chairs at the bottom were buried. The walk wasn't far, but it was tiring as we plowed through powder almost up to our chests. The next slope we took was another that I had never dared before. If it wasn't part of the escarpment, it was damn close to the edge. I watched Bennie as he floated through it in large snake-like turns. I tried to match his pattern but couldn't, or was too damned scared to turn as frequently or as prettily. The snow tended to pile up in front of my face as I skied. It blocked my vision so I had to push the pile out of my face as I floated. I asked Bennie about it.

"Turn more and you weel leave eet behind."

I began to feel the motion of balancing and floating through the deep snow. It was kind-of like trying to balance on a large beach ball. You didn't want to put too much weight on one foot, and you continually shifted your weight back and forth as you plowed through.

As we neared the village, the snow started coming down heavy again. It was only thigh deep on the slopes here, but the more level areas, like the streets, had drifts and were almost impassable.

We skied to Bennie's chalet, and we brushed the snow off as his wife came to the door. He introduced me to her. She was a very young and pretty blonde, maybe just out of college and at least ten years Bennie's junior. *Bennie, you dog!* I thought! At the door Bennie asked me to stay for dinner, but he got into a little argument with his wife in French after making the invitation, so I said that I had to get back to school before dark. We agreed on another night in the near future.

I skied through the streets of the upper village and down the slope behind the main. The snow was so deep and forgiving – like plowing through feathers – that I skied down the extremely steep face where I was sure there were large buried rocks and the railing for the stairs.

As I walked into the main, everyone turned to see who had just come in from the storm. Then they stood there staring at me like I was some monster from outer space. As I put my skis up, I caught my reflection in the mirrored wall. A stranger stood there with white hair and a red face. Startled at my own appearance, I laughed, pulled off my ear band, and shook the snow off my head to reveal my dark hair. Then, as I removed my glasses, people started to recognize me. Gil had come to the top of the stairs and said, "God, Henderson, you were out in that shit!"

"I met Bennie at the lift and we skied it from the top. It was fantastic!"

I wore my damp ski clothes to dinner and regaled the table with my adventures. Five of us were ready to skip school the next day and hit the slopes before the sun made the snow too heavy to ski without some grooming.

That next week Bennie invited me and a date to dinner. I mentioned it to Kaeti that night, and she offered to come as my "date." I didn't ask but figured it was her business to tell Tiny. He wasn't my roommate anymore, and I hadn't talked to him since Christmas break. The hike up to Bennie's was enjoyable. Kaeti was easy to talk to – both of us loved talking skiing and the snow. We also enjoyed the meal, but I learned the reason for my invitation when Bennie said, "I 'ave taught you all zat I know about skiing. You must follow your 'eart now. Treat zee mountain as a beautiful woman." He hugged his wife. "She must be caressed genteely at times, strong at *aut*-ther. Do no fear 'er, love 'er an' she weel love you! I weel always be 'ere eef you need 'elp, but you must now esperimont and learn on your own." Kaeti and I got quite a laugh at that speech on the way back to school, but I soon realized that he was right, especially after Kaeti's lessons.

Kaeti took me under her wing after that. "Jim, you have the skills, you just need to let it all hang out! You're too careful on the slopes. Skiing is supposed to be fun. Raise a little hell! – Ski the edge!"

Her lessons took me to the Chaux de Mont, the steep slope on the sunny side and known for breaking legs, and into narrow trails between the trees that I didn't know existed. We *schussed*, or skied straight down holding a tuck along the intermediate trails. We did jumps that threw us into the air as the slope vanished beneath us; our arc would carry us five or ten meters along the slope before we touched down again. Oh, and I started falling again. More bruises but a lot of laughs with Kaeti! She took a few tumbles herself, and each time I echoed Bennie, "You are no learning eef you are no falling!"

One jump and one dare almost cost a couple of lives. **The jump** was our favorite. You came off the top of the chair lift on the Berneuse and *schussed* into a narrow slot that led to the shoulder of one of the drops near the bottom of the lift. Once you were locked into the slot there was no getting your skis out or turning. Kaeti and I would wait at the top until the landing area was clear of skiers and make our jumps. On one run I got into the narrow slot and leaned forward, preparing for the jump, when I spotted the head of a kid skiing on the side of the drop and across in front of the takeoff. His timing was perfect, and if I didn't do something he would end up shish kebabbed on the ends of my skis. I threw myself onto my back into the slot, flipped my skis up, and held them with the flats toward the junior skier. I was still moving at high speed when I hit the kid and carried him down the drop across my skis. Seconds after we stopped sliding he popped up crying but alive and apparently uninjured. No parents came to curse me out. He was one of the town kids up for a few runs after school. After that experience, Kaeti and I took turns watching the landing area from below as the other jumped.

The dare... Bennie had taught me to imitate others to learn new skills, so one day when Jean Paul, the Swiss junior national champion skier, and his friend Benard Russi came to town, Kaeti dared me to follow him. I had seen Jean Paul *schuss* by a couple of times that day and was fascinated by his style. He was fast and fearless! I took her up on the dare and stood at the top waiting for him to arrive again. His red hat with the white Swiss cross was easy to spot. Soon he went soaring past me from the telecabine, and I took off in hot pursuit! He flew to the right across the steep area beside the moguls, and I followed. He didn't drop down the steep slope but continued to traverse the cliff-like surface. The angle was so steep that my uphill ski was above the top of my downhill boot. He then *schussed* across an unskied area that I may have visited with Bennie during the deep snow, but I wasn't sure where it led. The downhill angle was taking us faster and faster. My two skis were locked into the two paths his made through the virgin snow. I had no idea where we were going. *There's a secondary bowl to our left, but no one skis here!*

I had the impression that I was catching up to him by skiing in his trail when he disappeared before my eyes. *What the hell just happened to him!* my mind screamed as I came to the edge of the earth. The bowl I had just been thinking about spread out beneath me as the snow under my skis ended. As I fell off the cliff I held my position as Kaeti had taught me, like I was making an intentional jump, but I was frozen in that position with fear. I vaguely remember seeing Jean Paul's trails beneath me and thinking that I needed to land one ski in each. *Preferably my right ski in the right side!* I also saw Jean Paul blow out of the far side of the bowl, fly head-high into the air with his momentum, land, turn to the left, and sneak between two large rocks that sat high above a field of moguls that you usually approached by zig-zagging back across the side of mountain. I noticed brightly-colored skiers making the standard crossing on the far side of the bowl. All this and I was still falling. By now my hands were well over my head, and my ski's stretched downward, hoping to find land again. My ski tails hit first, and the fronts flopped into Jean Paul's trails; the impact sat me on the tail of my skis, but I popped up and locked my boots parallel. The landing slope was steep! I had *schussed* many like it before, but I didn't like being locked in those two ski trails, and I was still moving at the speed of gravity! I flew like I was on rails straight through the bowl and was thrown up out of the other side. My landing wasn't fancy or even remotely controlled, but I managed to stop without falling and looked back.

The stone wall behind me didn't look like much from this distance. It was only about three meters in height, but the snow hung well over the top edge, hiding its upper wall, and snow had built up against the wall beneath it, hiding its base. The bright blue sky exposed two notches in the snow near the crest, and our trails started again a good ten meters below! A thirtysome-foot fall on my head would have been the end of me, and a poor landing would have been the end of my skiing for the year, if not forever. I skied over to where Jean Paul had disappeared. There was a drop of a couple of meters into the field of moguls that I didn't bother to follow.

I found Kaeti later that day, teased her for almost getting me killed, and showed her the cliff and the trails.

"Man, you're insane!" she said, laughing nervously as she looked at the jump.

"I'm insane? He's insane! I was just stupid for following him! Besides, who got me into that, huh?" I asked.

"I'm really sorry!" she said, as she leaned over on her skis and gave me a hug. "Unbelievable! I wonder…"

I saw Kaeti measuring the jump with her eyes. "Don't even think about it! I've got few enough friends around here!"

The next afternoon after school, as I rode the lift up to the precipice, I saw a ski trail of what, at first, appeared to be a tragedy. It started down the expert slope along the cliff's edge toward the cleft in the stone spire, then it disappeared over the edge. Over the winter the snow had been building up from the base of the two hundred-foot-high cliff below a notch in its face. The result was a narrow stalagmite of snow starting at the bottom of the cliff that reached up to just below the top overhang. The ski trail dropped off the overhang and landed near the top point of the stalagmite. Then there were the marks of three sharp turns and traverses down the stalagmite until the skier had reached the base and skied away. His drop over the edge to land on the stalagmite must have been sheer trust in fate because it was unlikely that he could have seen its top as he went over the edge. He had to have been an expert like Jean Paul or a madman.

Chapter Twenty Two

Saas Fee

About two weeks after my jump, which had made the rounds of the school rumor mill, we took a weekend trip to Sass Fee, a town next to the Matterhorn, and Zermatt. As usual, someone had brought a couple of cases of beer and the drinking started as soon as the doors closed. The trip was pretty carefree until we started up the mountain to Saas Fee. That's when the beer hit the bladders, and, typical of Swiss mountain roads, there was no place to pull off. Mile after mile we ascended as the pressure grew. In desperation the bigger drinkers started to refill the bottles they had just drank. Wilds and I soon followed suit. It was not easy, especially as the bus rounded the corners, which it was doing continuously, one way or the other. However, the girls had a bigger problem. There was no way they could hit that small a target, and they were getting desperate. Finally Cliff got the idea of opening the side emergency door. After he successfully peed out onto the side of the road, the girls started to line up. One by one, with Cliff holding the door open and Stallone holding their arms, they stuck their derrières out the door and peed onto the roadway, the side of the bus, and any unfortunate car that happened to be following too close. I had noticed earlier that several of the second-year girls, including Kaeti, had abstained from drinking the beer, and this sight made it impressively clear that they knew what they were doing.

Like Diablerets lifts last fall with my parents, there were two separate lifts that took us from the town up the Mittelallalin, and once at the top lodge, you were still not on the top of the mountain. Giant cats with tow ropes would pull you up from there. The view was unreal with the craggy vertical face of the Matterhorn off to the side. We didn't get up there until late afternoon and were told that the lifts to the top closed at 5 p.m. Since we were staying in the lodge on the top, a trip down the six thousand-foot trail to the village was not on the menu for those who feared being stuck in the village without a way back up. Most of us just skied the upper bowl. It was small but filled with perfect powder; so cold and fine that as you descended the slope, your skis whispered *hush*, like a Quaker mother at meeting trying to get her baby to settle without disturbing the silence. A dozen or so short runs and we were in for the night. Inside, our teachers/chaperones took small groups up a flight of stairs from the main area into an attic of sorts. Mattresses were strewn across the floors and into the eves. There was a separate smaller room on one side, also filled with mattresses. The chaperone for my group waved his arm toward the smaller room and said, "That's the girls' dorm, and this is the boys', officially!" Then we marched back downstairs so the next group and chaperone could go up.

Tables were set around the interior of the main area, which was circular with windows on all sides. It was only 5 p.m., but the sun had set behind the Mittelallalin for us and the village below. However, the sides of other peaks that faced the sun were still illuminated and starting to glow orange. As we sat the wine was served, and it was dark before the meal was brought out. It was basic fare, brats and buns, but it tasted great!

Dinner was over by 6:30, and someone started the music. We danced and drank for another hour or so. I had only had maybe three glasses of wine, but I was already feeling the effects. The altitude was really affecting my tolerance of alcohol. The smokers were also getting frustrated because they would set their cigarettes down for a minute or two and they would go out. Wilds and I started talking and fanaticizing about the official dormitories upstairs. He mentioned that he had heard that Paula, with her short brown hair and almond-shaped eyes, was an "anybodie's." In fact, he heard that her boy friend had told her to come to Europe and get as much experience as possible. With the alcohol and reduced oxygen, the idea fascinated me as I watched her dancing with another guy. Soon, with a little encouragement from Wilds and Gil, I got up and staggered over to her. She and I danced for what seemed like a long time; then, as the music slowed, we writhed together on the dance floor. A short while later we were helping each other up the stairs to the "dormitories." I was far enough gone that Paula had to half carry me up. At the top of the stairs and just around to the left were two unoccupied mattresses. That was all the further we got. As we knelt down onto the mattresses I noticed Jana with her long dark hair and large brown eyes watching us momentarily. Then she curled up behind a tall guy with curly blond hair who had to be her boyfriend, Little John. Little John was curled up in a fetal position, fast asleep and snoring softly.

Paula and I started slowly and quietly kissing and touching. Soon her blouse came open, and her bra was loose and I was kissing her breasts, down her stomach, and up under her neck. We were dancing together on the floor with no music, and our rhythm was increasing. She touched me, and I her. I had never been here before, and I was clumsy. Finally her pants came down and off; mine were around my knees. I moved over her, trying to push her legs apart but she held them together. The harder I tried, the tighter she held. Frustrated, we wrestled for several minutes before I came to my senses. She wasn't having any of it. Was I too clumsy, or not tall enough? I sighed and rolled onto my back. After a little while she put her head on the crook of my right arm as I fell asleep.

My dreams were dark. I was skiing in the dark between unseen trees that I could hear rushing by me. The snow was crusty, making it hard to turn. I felt like I was being chased by something in the darkness behind me, and I couldn't stop for fear of being caught, but I was afraid that my next turn would be my last as I struck a tree or went over a cliff.

Then someone was trying to wake me. They were pushing my hips. No, they were sitting on me. I looked up, but it was dark, and all I could make out was a vague silhouette. Then I realized that I was erect and buried in something very warm and wet. It hit me, Paula had decided I wasn't so bad after all and was sitting on me, riding me like a horse. No, this could be some strange wet-dream. Although I had never had one with the girl on top, but there is always a first time. I reached forward to where her hips should be. I felt hips, warm full hips, sliding back and forth, pressing me into her. Unbelievable, she had started without me! How could she not know that I was asleep? But what did it matter, this felt great, no better than great, bloody fantastic!

My hands slid up to her waist, and I started to pull her down to kiss me. As she leaned forward, her long hair fell onto my stomach and tickled its way toward my chest. We kissed; her breathing was coming so fast that she couldn't hold the kiss long. Wait, Paula has short hair… Kaeti! I realized that I was dreaming, a wet dream like I had never had before! Kaeti was over me, making love with me. I slid my hands to her exposed breasts. They were fuller than I had imagined in earlier dreams about her. That was confusing, but hell, it was my dream, and I was going to enjoy it! I rolled her over to a more traditional position and thrust deeper into her, my breath now coming in gasps. There was a controlled quietness in our mixed breathing as if, even in our dream, we were afraid of waking others. Soon there was that familiar stabbing pain and shooting fulfillment. "I love you, Kaeti! I love you!" I said as I collapsed onto her.

She rolled me off to the left onto my side and moved away as my dream changed once again. This time I was skiing in the bright sunshine. The slope was shaped like a reclining woman covered in soft, white powder snow. The black tips of my skis were just peaking through the powder. I *schussed* down the mound of her left breast and across the furrows of her ribs. As I slid onto the flat area of her stomach, I looked to my right and saw Kaeti paralleling me not twenty feet away. She wasn't wearing her ski cap, and her long hair streamed behind her. We matched the rhythm of our turns as we sped for the valley below.

I awoke once again in the dark. This time a little light was just starting to come through a window near the top of the stairs. I heard the noises of people starting to wake around me. What a dream! Ouch! While reliving it, I realized that my pants were still around my knees. I didn't want to sit up until I was decent, but I didn't want anyone to walk by with me half naked, so I reached down to the sides to pull them up. Once they were fastened and zipped, I looked over at Paula. Her short hair covered her face, and she was breathing deeply.

Realizing that my dream had probably left a wet spot the size of Lake Michigan somewhere on my mattress, I sat up cautiously. I could still hear Little John snoring softly. As I stood I looked around the dark attic. I could hear an occasional rustle, but I couldn't see anyone else moving. Jana then rolled from her position next to Little John onto her back and stretched one arm high over her head. She had a large smile on her face, making me wish that I woke up feeling that great. Actually, I didn't feel that bad. My usual morning-after doldrums hadn't hit yet. The light from the window was falling across Jana's body at an angle that highlighted her right breast as it pressed tightly against her blouse, and I could see her long dark hair as it flowed off her mattress onto mine. Looking at her tickled a memory in last night's dream, and I stood there looking back and forth between Paula with her short hair and Jana with her long hair on either side of my mattress. That dream was so real, so like nothing I had ever experienced in dream or reality before. Could I have awakened with Jana riding me? In the darkness could she have confused me for Little John? It didn't seem possible that she could mistake me for him. He was much taller with longer hair, and... I saw a flash of light, a reflection from Jana's face in the shadows where her large brown eyes hid under her long lashes. Was she peeking at me as I stood there confused? I turned and walked quickly down the stairs.

My thoughts were warring as I went into the bathroom, washed my face, and brushed my teeth. *Was it a dream? Was it sex? With who? Why would Jana have sex with me? She had Little John. They had been together for months. Women don't have random sex with people in the dark! – a guy would, but women don't!* Once it hit overload, I just told myself, no matter what happened *IT WAS A DREAM! – a really, REALLY nice dream!* There was no way to find out the truth, and I wasn't sure that I wanted to know. I sure wasn't going to ask Jana. 'By the way, did we have sex last night?' And would Little John love that! OUCH!

The sun reflecting off the snow outside coming through all the windows in the main area was so bright that it almost hurt my eyes. As I walked out, I spotted Kaeti sitting by herself at a table chowing down. There were only a couple of others up this early. When Kaeti spotted me, she smiled and flipped her head back, inviting me over. Her long hair flashed gold in the sun. From her casual smile and attitude, I knew in that instant that nothing had changed – for her…

"Where's Tiny?" I asked as I sat down next to her.

"Don' know, upstairs I guess."

"Seen Wilds or Gil, yet?"

"Nah, we're the two early birds. Did you have a good sleep?"

That question flipped me back into my earlier mental tug-of-war, and it hit me. *If that wasn't a dream, then – had I yelled out that I loved Kaeti? Had she heard me? Oh, my god! If it wasn't a dream, then… I'd yelled it out to Jana! No wonder she pushed me off and rolled away. I could have woken Little John and who knows who else!* I looked over and Kaeti was looking at me with a curious, sideways stare. "You feelin' alright?" she asked.

"Sure!" I said, and I was feeling pretty good, physically. *In fact, I feel great!* "This altitude must be good for me! I don't feel like I have my usual hangover."

"The altitude does that for some people," she said and added, "Besides you get high on a lot less alcohol."

*Yes, the altitude and the crisp air had left me without a hangover and provided me with one… **unbelievable**… dream,* I thought as Kaeti caught me staring at her.

"What?" she asked as she flipped her hair over her shoulder.

I turned away, ordered some hot tea, and grabbed a couple of croissants and jam packets.

We began talking about the day's skiing. She had made a quick run last night and was concerned that the trail was a little dangerous. "It's really long and fairly straight," she said, "but the sides are dangerous. There's a lot of glacier ice with crevices."

Crevices! I remembered back to my experience at age eleven by the parking lot on Mount Hood in Oregon. I had wandered over to play on a gigantic mound of snow that came from the parking lot. As I got to the top, the snow broke under me, and I fell into a crevice barely catching myself on its sides with my elbows. My feet couldn't get any purchase on the icy sides and swung uselessly below. I yelled for help but couldn't see my parents. Soon a man passing in the parking lot spotted me and came to my aid. He lifted me up and out. Afterwards I looked down into the crevice. Its blue-white ice descended and narrowed until the blue was so dark and the sides were so close that I couldn't see the bottom. I imagined myself sliding down into the blue depths and being wedged between the icy walls. Kaeti's use of the word "crevices" brought back a half-forgotten but primal fear. *Would I have the nerve to go down?*

Sensing something was wrong, Kaeti said, "Hey, don't worry! I'll make sure I'm back up here when you're ready to head down to the bus."

"Hey, yourself, I'm not worried!" I said with false bravado. "The snow's so beautiful up here that I'm not sure I want to go down until the last minute. What time do you want to meet?" I asked. As we made our plans Bernd came out of the dorm, grabbed a croissant, a coffee, and headed to his skis. As I headed up to find my gear, I saw Kaeti strapping on her skis to join the student coach.

The top bowl was even better in the morning – snow like talcum powder dusting the slopes and flying up like clouds as you turned. I was in heaven! *Glandesprung* or leaping off the moguls – tip rolls – I could do no wrong! Too soon came the time for the descent. Kaeti showed up at the lift. Tiny, Wilds, and I joined her, and we went to the ropes behind the giant cats. They pulled us further up the peak, and we started our descent. Kaeti was off to my right as we paralleled together. Unlike in my dream, her stocking cap hid her long hair, but her long lean body and her flowing movements took me back to that part of my dream. As the trail disappeared around a turn we stopped. At this point I was definitely into stopping and reading the trail ahead before crashing blindly down some new passage. Kaeti pointed out all the glacier ice on our sides and warned us to stay away from the side of the trail, where the crevices hid beneath a snow cover. I could see the sides of the chunks of blue-white ice forming mounds beside the trail. I shivered, but I wasn't cold.

Tiny struck out on his own after that. I guess he thought we were being too careful. The trail was long but not hard. We stopped a lot as

Kaeti pointed out steep areas and narrow passages and told us how to navigate them safely. The snow got a little warmer and heavier as we descended, but was still a nice packed powder. The bus awaited us as we arrived, and we were the last to get there. We loaded our skis and got into the bus. Kaeti led the way, and I followed. Tiny was in the back of the bus with Stallone, Cliff, and a bunch of other guys. I didn't spot either Paula or Jana, but I didn't look too hard. I saw curly blonde hair that might have been Little John.

Kaeti grabbed the last vacant double and invited me to join her. Wilds grabbed a seat up front. As we headed down, I wondered why Kaeti and Tiny weren't together but wrote it off as my luck.

"Looks like Tiny's in the back," I said, trying to sound casual but hoping to get some insight.

"You do know that we aren't dating anymore, don't you?"

"I guess not. I'm sorry."

"I'm not. Didn't you see him dancing with Pat last night?"

I guess not, I must have been lost in my own fantasies, I thought. "Wait a minute, Tiny dancing? Tiny doesn't dance!"

"Not with me, anyway."

"What happened, if you don't mind my asking?"

"I do... personal things... We just disagreed on stuff. We actually broke it off several weeks ago. We're still friends."

"Oh, I guess I lost track when Tiny moved out." I let it go at that but cheered inside.

"Besides," Kaeti leaned next to my ear and added in a whisper, "he's a horrible kisser! He slobbers too much, yuck! I kinda got a kick out of thinking about him and Pat last night. That's an awful thing to say, isn't it?"

"Nah, kinda funny, actually!" We shared a secret laugh. *I'll have to remember that, if I ever get a chance...*

I listened to the conversations around us. Dee Dee and Lenore were just ahead of us, and Dee Dee was saying something about never trusting a naked bus driver. I heard agreement and laughter from a couple of other girls ahead of us. I have no clue what it was about.

I don't remember what the driver looked like and couldn't see him from where I was seated, but I doubted that he would have stayed with us in the lodge. It did seem to be a great joke, and it actually became a common saying repeated on many occasions after that trip. As the sun went down behind the mountains, exhausted from our weekend, we grew quiet, and people started to fall asleep. The wonder of Kaeti's recent announcement, the fun on the mountain, and my previous night's dreams kept me wide awake, but Kaeti had fallen asleep. I watched her surreptitiously as she slept until one curve brought her head over onto my shoulder. Then I couldn't take my eyes off her tawny hair and dared not move for fear she would awaken and move away. I hadn't noticed before, but she smelled of a sweet men's cologne, Canoe, I think. That was odd, but it seemed to fit her. Somewhere along the route that night I decided that I would try to ask her out.

When we got back to school, I dropped my stuff in the entryway and helped Kaeti with hers up to the entrance of the girls' dorm. At the base of the stairs, I took her hand and stopped her. Then, trembling in my boots, I said, "Ka-eti" *Shit, my voice is cracking!* "I know we're friends and all, but would you think it crazy if I asked you on a date?"

She caught my other hand and tipped her head forward so that she was peaking up under the long sweep of hair that crossed her forehead, that sexy look that I'd seen her melt Tiny with so many times, and whispered, "I was wondering if you would ever ask. I was afraid that I would have to." Then she kissed my lips. It wasn't a long kiss, but it wasn't a peck; it held a little promise. She then picked up her bags and walked lithely up the stairs toward the dorm. As she turned the corner, she flicked her long hair over her shoulder, looked down on me, and smiled. Starting with a tingle from the kiss, my whole body was now vibrating. I can't imagine what a fool I must have looked like when I smiled back. I would like to say that I floated to our frat house, but I was moving so fast that I slipped and almost broke my neck carrying my suitcase down the snow-covered cow path. I did hurt the ring finger of my right hand. I didn't sleep that night. Not because of my finger – my mind was flashing a hundred miles per hour. I had to get control of this, or I was going to make a real fool of myself. The next day I discovered that I had broken my finger. Stallone provided a finger splint from his boxing days that I wore for a short while, not too long because it interfered with my skiing.

Chapter Twenty Three

Kaeti

The next day at school I was beat! I didn't remember sleeping a bit. I felt so bad that I worried about running into Kaeti and looking like an idiot, so I started avoiding her. In fact, I was in such sad shape that I avoided the slopes and took a nap that afternoon. A little sleep and a quick shower – well that isn't exactly the truth... they didn't have showers in our house, just a tub with a handheld sprayer but no shower curtains so showering was a challenge – anyway that spray-off made all the difference! I had mixed feelings when I spotted Kaeti at dinner. Her table was full so I couldn't join her even if I wanted to, but I wasn't sure that I did want to because I was afraid that I'd make a fool of myself in front of the others. I definitely had it bad!

The snack bar was my next chance. When I walked in Kaeti spotted my finger splint. "Whoa, what happened? Take a fall on your skis?"

"No, just fell..." *how can I say walking to the frat house!* "walking to the frat house." *That's how... Really smooth – Damn!*

Kaeti looking concerned, "What did the doctor say?"

"Doctor? – Oh, no, Stallone gave me the splint. He's pretty sure that I broke it, but I can get this thing in my ski glove so it won't slow me down."

Kaeti gave me a big smile as she ran back to catch the fries. She was busy feeding several guys who hadn't liked the evening's dinner. I got a coke and retired to a table to keep out of her way. When the guys left she came and joined me. We sat in the quiet for a while then she asked with a cautious smile, "Second thoughts?"

"What? No! Definitely not! Just trying to come up with something special for a first date."

"And have you?"

"Not yet... but I will!"

We crossed over each other's words with her saying, "It doesn't have to be special," and my asking, "Want to start with dinner at the Messange?"

"Sounds great! That can be expensive. Do you want to dutch it?"

She's right; dating could really break my bank, but this has to be impressive!

"I think that I can handle it. I'll let you know before we have to wash the dishes, okay?"

"Great! I get enough of that here!"

"Don't worry, I'll help. Hey, my first paying job was washing dishes."

"Maybe we better dutch it!" she said, teasing. I kept her company most of the evening, and we played songs on the jukebox. I stayed out of her hair when the coed shift arrived – still not knowing how the rest of the school would take our dating. *Dating? We haven't even had our first date! – I'm already getting ahead of myself. After one date she could decide that we'll only be friends... Man! – Not if I can help it!*

As we cleaned up the grill that night Kaeti asked about my dishwashing job. I explained that the students at my Quaker boarding school were responsible for doing all the basic janitorial work and the dining room service and cleanup. The work was done to teach the kids responsibility and to keep tuition down. The only paying jobs were organizing and running the dining room set up and cleanup teams. These were offered to four responsible seniors each semester. My best friend, Dave, and I had been a part of one semester's team. We worked about three hours a day for four months and were paid fifty dollars for the semester.

Kaeti studied me as I told that story and asked, "What's it like being a Quaker?"

"Well, I'm not your typical Quaker. My dad is a Lieutenant Colonel in the Army, and that's a big 'no-no' for the Quakers. I like not having a preacher telling you right from wrong in church; what we call meetings. I also like the fact that most Quakers believe people are born good and learn evil. Dad took me to a Calvary Methodist church when I was in junior high... You're not Methodist are you?"

"No, Lutheran."

"Lutheran? One of my uncles is Lutheran. He and I don't always see eye to eye, either. But, anyway, the Methodist minister spouted about man's evil nature, hell, and damnation until I got up and walked out, embarrassing my family. There wasn't a meeting house in that area, so dad started reading the Bible at home on Sunday mornings when I refused to go back to that church."

"So religion's pretty important to you then."

"Yes, I guess so."

"Me too!"

"Hey, if you want proof that there is a God, all you have to do is walk outside and look at these beautiful mountains!" That drew an enormous smile from Kaeti. *She knows what I mean, even if I don't say it very well.* "So, will you be able to get off for dinner Friday night?" I asked.

"Definitely, even if the regulars have to starve!"

Friday came quickly. I had gone to the Messange and met with Herr Dietrick, the German owner and my English student. Actually, I hadn't given many lessons since ski season started, but we were still friends, especially when I splurged and ordered a German beer. I told him that I had a special date that I really wanted to impress, and he chose the menu and told me not to worry. I also consulted Madame Linden, my French living teacher, and she recommended a 1965 Moulin à Vent Beaujolais wine. Herr Dietrick said he had several bottles and agreed that it was excellent without being expensive.

It was dark when I walked up to the main building in a light blue button-down oxford cloth shirt and black dress slacks under my navy ski jacket. I had already returned the finger splint because it interfered with my using ski poles. My knuckle was swollen and stiff, but I could manage without the splint. We planned to meet after the school's supper crowd had disappeared. At the bottom of the stairs waiting for Kaeti, I heard the sounds of the kitchen staff cleaning the dining room through the entryway. Then, I saw Kaeti as she walked down the stairs. *Beautiful!* We almost matched with her white turtleneck and black skirt. She carried a dark blue wool coat over her arm. Her hair was brushed and hanging straight with her bangs sweeping across her forehead and tucked behind her ear, not the ponytail she usually wore during the day. *I can't believe that we actually have a date. Now if only I can be cool about it and not screw anything up!*

"You look great!" I said lamely then added, looking up into her eyes, "definitely no second thoughts!"

Kaeti smiled warmly down as she paused on the last step and looked behind me toward the door to the library. "Come here for a second," Kaeti said as she stepped down, took my hand, and led me into the library. We slipped just inside the door. It was Friday, and the library was dark, but the light from the hall and the street lights reflecting off the snow and coming in the windows provided enough illumination for us to see.

Kaeti took my other hand and said, "Let's get this over with!"

She leaned forward, pulled my arms behind her, grabbed my shoulders, then kissed me full on the lips and held it for several seconds, moving her lips gently over mine, then looked out from under her hair with a sexy, mischievous smile.

Caught me off guard, again! Okay, my turn, I thought, and gave her my best predator look, then said, "I'd like to get that over with again – several times!" I smiled and slid my hand up under her hair and pressed my thumb and fingers on her neck, just below the base of the skull. I pulled her gently forward into a kiss that was at first gentle then a little more demanding. My tongue slipped out just for an instant to taste her lips, and I slid my lips around to a place on her neck just below her left ear. I kissed her gently there as I inhaled her scent.

When I pulled back, Kaeti looked a little startled, "Whoa!"

"I said I was a virgin, not a celibate. Now, not that I'm complaining, but what was that all about?"

"I, ah…" looking a little confused "– hate the tension of worrying about the first kiss. It, ah… mmmm…" She smiled and laughed quietly. "Let's do that again!" I complied. This time her tongue just brushed the tip of mine and it sent tingles up my back. *No, those are her fingers working skillfully up my spine and under my shoulders!*

"Whoa!" I said as the hair stood up on the back of my neck, and we exchanged mischievous smiles.

"When did you say you were a virgin?" she asked, looking confused again. *Oh, shit! I hadn't told her. Where'd that come from?* I just stood there with my mouth open, unable to speak.

"You know that does bring up something important. I get the feeling that we are going to have a lot of fun together, but... there are a few game rules." She looked serious but a little worried as she bit her lower lip. She reached down and squeezed my hands. "I have a boy friend back home that may be serious. So this has to be a fun thing! Better than friends, but no sex." Her right hand came up quickly and her pointer finger teasingly touched the tip of my nose as she made her point. Then she cupped my cheek with her hand. "I'm not going to your dorm room. Too dangerous!"

I interrupted, bubbling with excitement, "You may not believe this, but I understand. I... I really believe that you should be a virgin when you marry. The way this place is, I haven't been able to tell anyone that. They'd probably think I was crazy!"

She seemed to be extremely pleased at my response. In fact, when I said that, the pupils in her hazel eyes actually seemed to flare wider than they already were in this dimly lit room. This strange unconscious reflex occurred many times in our relationship, especially when I did or said something very right.

Then, with a challenging look, she said, "You mean I should be a virgin? – or you should?"

"Both! The man and the woman. It's only fair." We went into a clinch and held it for quite a while, experimenting on shocking the other with our tongues or hands.

As her hands flowed over my derrière, she whispered, "Nice sheep's butt."

I backed off laughing, and she laughed leaning back in. "Yeah, you can call me that, in private. I think I inherited it, but gymnastics helped solidify it."

"Oh yeah!" she said challengingly as she pulled me close again and squeezed my butt with both hands. "Solid!" she agreed.

I returned the favor, and she flexed her hips into me. Hers was small and round, – and hard as stone. "Not bad!" I said with the snooty air of many of the ACS upper crust. She punched me in the arm, and we laughed with foreheads pressed together. I looked into her eyes. *We really are going to have a lot of fun!* I thought. We held each other's eyes for a long time before I said, "I hate to be the one to bring this up, but we have dinner reservations."

"You guys and your stomachs. No time for fun!" Kaeti teased.

We walked the couple of blocks up to the Messange, holding hands and crunching through the snow. It probably was cold, but I was glowing warm. Herr Dietrick met us at the front door and escorted us to a corner table – about as private as you could get in the restaurant. Kaeti's eyes sparkled in the candlelight.

She smiled and said, "I think he forgot the menus."

"I hope you don't mind, but I had Herr Dietrick prepare a special meal for us."

"We're not going to have to wash dishes, are we?"

"I hope not!" As we sat, we did some small talk. "What is your perfume? It smells familiar." I was embarrassed to say it smelled like men's cologne.

"Ambush, it's by Dana. It's a lot like the men's cologne, Canoe. Like it?"

"Definitely, and it suits you – not too flowery or strong. I hate the strong ones like "My Sin," sometimes they start me sneezing so hard that I can't stop."

Kaeti laughed – *nice laugh*, then that mischievous look came over her again, "What attracts you to a woman?" *Dangerous question!*

"I like a woman who's outgoing, smart, a strong personality, but friendly, and helpful to others. You know I've liked you from the first because you were a good friend. I liked you with Tiny because you seemed to enjoy life..."

Kaeti held up her hand. "You tend to over think things. I like that about you, but what I mean is, are you a legs man, a butt man... you obviously aren't a breast man," she said, glancing down at her chest.

"Oh, a quick and dirty assessment," I said with a big smile. "Well, I still like the friendly thinker type, but first impressions... Hmmm – the eyes, definitely. I go crazy over beautiful eyes!"

"Mine aren't anything special," Kaeti said, seemingly serious. *Curious...*

"You're so wrong. First their color is unique, and they change constantly with your mood or clothes or colors around you. They positively sparkle at times when you're talking about skiing or something you love." That drew a huge smile from Kaeti. The wine steward arrived with the Moulin à Vent wine and served. I addressed the cork and tasted the wine like a professional, thanks to Madame Linden.

"Okay, turn about's fair play, what about you? What kind of guys do you like?" *Another dangerous question – hopefully she won't say tall!*

Mimicking me, "Smart, friendly, helpful, a good sense of humor, umm... athletic..."

I held my hand up. "Quick and dirty!" I couldn't come up with anything self-deprecating that wouldn't bring up Tiny, my polar opposite: tall, blonde hair...

"A nice butt!" she announced loudly, and we both laughed; then I "Baaaaaa"–ed like a sheep. The commotion was such that most of the diners in the room turned their heads to see what was going on. No telling if anyone understood enough English to have a clue what Kaeti had said; likely my sheep bray drew the attention. When things returned to normal, Kaeti reached out and took my hand. "And a real love for the mountain and skiing!"

"Your eyes are sparkling!" I said. Kaeti looked down, blushed, then looked up innocently from under her hair, and smiled.

With perfect timing, Herr Dietrick showed up with a portable burner and a skillet with a couple of filet mignon. "*Tournedos Flambé,*" he announced as he prepared them beside us. The waiter arrived with plates that had julienne beans and almonds and quartered new potatoes with butter and parsley. Then Herr Dietrick poured on the brandy and lit the mixture. He extinguished the flames with the skillet lid and served the filets. These were perhaps the two best pieces of beef that I had eaten since arriving in Europe. I hadn't thought about dessert, but Herr Dietrick had. He repeated his performance on the steaks with a couple of peaches in a cream sauce. In this case, he announced, *"Peche flambé."* The meal was fabulous! Kaeti couldn't help but be impressed; I was, and I thought that I knew what to expect!

At the end I pretended to have been called over by Herr Dietrick and then walked back with my head forward and shoulders slumped. I grabbed Kaeti's hand and held it with both of mine. She looked a little startled and concerned.

"I'm sorry," I said. "I have to go. I hope that you enjoyed your meal. They… need me in the kitchen." That drew a sharp poke in the stomach, and I broke out laughing as the dining room looked on perplexed.

"Ouch, geez! Why do I think that you have brothers?"

"One younger one and an older sister."

I haven't found out about her family; this is interesting! I sat back down. I ordered a cognac.

Kaeti declined and said, "I have a confession. When I first met you, I was reminded of my kid brother – so young and full of himself."

"And when did you change your mind about me?"

"Who said that I have?" Kaeti asked with her usual teasing smile.

"So, you're dating your kid brother…"

She looked in my eyes with a serious expression and said, "In all seriousness, that changed the night after I dropped Saundra. You were so… mature – you looked inside me. No one else even had a clue." I saw tears start to well up in the corners of her eyes.

"Kaeti, I've thought about that night and wondered if I could have done it any better. You seemed so sad."

"No, you were wonderful. I still can't believe that I dropped her," she said as she wiped the corners of her eyes with her napkin.

"Let me finish. I've thought about it. I've done gymnastics for years, and that catch was impossible, especially if she didn't want to be caught. I doubt that even Stallone could have held her by one hand once she was falling. You shouldn't beat yourself up over that. You really were a hero! Hey, break out of this mood! Our evening now continues with dancing downstairs. We really get to dance tonight!"

"Oh, and we haven't danced before?"

"You know what I mean."

Now we could dance slow dances without drawing Tiny's ire. After a while "Love Me, Please Love Me" by Michel Polnareff came up. Kaeti smiled and looked deep into my eyes, then said, "When you held my hands that evening after... Saundra, that song was playing and I knew." *Man, I wish I'd known...* That became our song – but I am getting ahead of myself...

Later we returned to the snack bar before curfew. We continued where we left off before dinner. More teasing and trying to shock each other. Man, was I aroused! I was a little embarrassed by being erect while we held each other tightly, but Kaeti didn't seem to mind, so I let it go and enjoyed it. I came close to climaxing just rubbing tummies together.

"Do you need a cold shower before we head upstairs?" Kaeti joked at my discomfort.

"Couldn't hurt!"

"Why don't you just head out the front. I'll find my own way upstairs."

"As long as I get kissed here."

"You need another?" she said with a smirk.

"Many more! I can't wait for my dreams tonight."

"Okay now! Watch what you're dreaming about!" she cautioned with a spark in her eyes!

The relationship grew from there. I loved lying with my head on her lap looking up, her hair cascading from her head and surrounding me like a warm, golden curtain, only our two faces within this universe.

She'd lean down occasionally to kiss my lips, or I'd rise within the curtained passage to kiss hers, her long cool hair tickling my neck.

The teasing was constant, but physically we became more trusting and open. I would frequently climax when we were together. Kaeti, always understanding and always practical, had a store of napkins to clean up the mess. One night I just could not seem to climax.

After a while Kaeti said, "Here, let me help." She started to undo my pants.

I grabbed her hands. "Wait! What...?"

"Don't worry," she said as she pushed my hands away. As she took me in her hand, I climaxed. I was embarrassed, but she took it in stride.

We lay there looking into each other eyes. After a few minutes a thoughtful look came into her eyes, and, choosing her words very carefully, she said, "You're really serious about staying a virgin, aren't you?"

I smiled, wondering where this was going. "Yes."

"Even if we were lying here naked?" she challenged.

I thought about that a moment. That dream I had on the mountain flashed through my mind. I smiled. "Well maybe not naked. Let's say we keep on our underpants, if only as a reminder." She smiled, her pupils flared. I rolled over and put my leg between hers. Her turtleneck had pulled out at the waist so I put my hand on her warm stomach.

"You just did something wonderful for me. Is there something that I can do for you?" Her legs pulsed around mine, her hips popped up like she had had a cramp, and she let out a startled gasp!

"What? Are you alright?" I said as I rolled off her. "Did I hurt you?" She started giggling with her hands covering her face. "What's so funny?" I said defensively.

She pulled me close to her. "Nothing, nothing" as she continued a stifled laugh. As I held her I noticed her body seemed to be shivering.

"Are you cold?"

"Shhhh... It's alright. It's great!" She snuggled into my neck.

After a while in silence I asked quietly, "What just happened?"

"I think I just climaxed," she answered equally quietly.

"What? How? I didn't... Do you need napkins?"

"A woman's not like that. No. I don't know why. I was just thinking about us, imagining us... and when you said... well, when you asked... I... I lost it. Mmmm... and yes."

"Yes, what?"

"Shhh..." She began unzipping her slacks on the side.

I stopped her hands. "Wait, What?"

"It's alright. Gosh, I can't believe that I am saying that to a guy! You are so cute!" *Cute? What the...* She took my hand guiding it inside her slacks past her curly hair to the moist area. *Oh my God!* "Ah!" She flexed away like she had been shocked!

"What?" I started to pull away, but she held me.

"No, no, it's okay. Just too sensitive there."

"Where?"

"It's my..." Her head down face hidden in her hair. *Kaeti embarrassed?* "you know."

I wasn't sure that I did know but pretended to. "Oh!"

She pushed my fingers gently around the lips. They were moist and hot. "Mmmm," she purred. I found the center and gently probed inside. She flexed a little and said, "Not to deep. I think you need to trim your nails."

"Sorry!"

"Just use the fingerprint and tease the edges. Come up front occasionally, but don't stay long, just tease." I moved my middle finger forward, and she jumped, electrocuted again. "Still too sensitive. This may not work tonight, but you've got the idea." She smiled.

"Let's not give up yet. I like teasing," I insisted.

She smiled seductively and began unbuttoning my shirt. She looked a little upset by my undershirt but started to untuck it. I took my hand out from her slacks, removed my shirts, and sat there half-naked. She sat up and looked at my chest a little curiously and began rubbing her hands across it. Anticipating her question I said, "Yes, no hair. I blame it on my Indian ancestors, but I'm not sure I really had any."

"Nice, soft, smooth... Mmm," she purred again as she kissed it.

"Hey, turnabout's fair play!" I said as I reached to finish untucking her turtleneck. She smiled and started to help. I pushed her hands away. "I think I can manage."

She reached up as I slid it over her head, and when it was off she shook her hair back into place again, although a few wayward strands crossed her face, giving her an extremely sexy look, which she emphasized by dipping her head slightly and looking through her lashes. She pulled the strands back as I reached to unfasten her bra. Then she leaned in and nuzzled into my neck. As the bra slid forward, her tiny beautiful breasts fascinated me. They were champagne-cup sized with small pink nipples.

Anticipating a question that I wasn't even thinking. "I know, small. I blame my mother…"

"Shhh…" I said as I leaned in to kiss one. As my lips brushed the tip, the nipple rose to meet them. I tickled the tip of the eager little one with my tongue as I held it between my lips. When I moved to the other, I noticed it starting to rise as I breathed on it. "Amazing!"

Kaeti pulled my head into her chest, and we lay back. "You're amazing!" she said. After kissing for a while with our warm, naked chests pressed together, I moved back to her breasts. Now, except for the nipples, which rose for attention as I gazed on them, her chest was almost flat. It didn't matter; the tiny erections were fascinating. My hand moved back inside her slacks, through the hair and to the lips. I brushed the front, and her hips gave a little involuntary twitch, but the area wasn't nearly as sensitive. We lay there kissing and teasing for quite a while until I noticed her hips rising into my hand instead of shying away when I touched her clitoris. The name had come to my mind from some sex ed class. It wasn't what I had expected, just a harder area no larger than a blood vessel beneath the skin. It yearned for my touch now, but I continued to tease and move away. Finally, I was rewarded with Kaeti's thighs almost crushing my hand as her whole body flexed and shuddered. She pulled me close to her, crushed me against her naked chest, and breathed heavily into my ear. That same controlled heavy breathing I remembered from my dream on the mountain, breathing as if she were afraid of awakening others around us. What a turn-on knowing that I'd given Kaeti such pleasure! I had an erection the size of Kansas! After she stopped shuddering, she reached into my pants again, but try as we might, it wouldn't come or get smaller. After a bit we started giggling and talking about how to hide it when we said good night on the dorm stairs. Just the thought of that caused it to flag fairly quickly. What a night! I believe that I did float down to our frat house that night.

It was hard to integrate our relationship, Kaeti and me, and our skiing. The love of the mountain and skiing probably brought us together, but as I learned from Bennie and from Kaeti, skiing was a very personal thing. It could be shared from time to time with others when you both were in parallel moods, but when you skied, your lover was the mountain. You caressed her slopes and explored her valleys with your skis. You were affected by her moods – bright blue skies and a soft hush of packed powder or heavy clouds and crystalline jewels of ice being blown in your face by a strong wind; you skied gently at times and roughly at others. Bennie was right. Kaeti and I met at times on the slopes to compare notes or to lead the other to a jump or something just discovered, but we usually skied by ourselves with our crystalline lover. We couldn't be jealous of our mountain because we both were in love with her, and she wasn't jealous of us when we shared a clumsy kiss from our skis after some exceptionally fun run down a trail or a stupid fall.

Tiny was right about some things. Kaeti was busy, but that made the time we spent together all the more special. And Kaeti wasn't a drinker or *zim-zim* player – but she was a dancer, and to me dancing was life – at least it was before I learned to dance on skis. But we also loved exploring little out-of-the-way places in the village. We found a tearoom with an unbelievable view of les Dents du Midi, and went to a bar in the lower village, not far from the freshman dorm, that had a bowling alley. That's probably an exaggeration. The lanes were a quarter the length of U.S lanes, but they made up for their shortness by being very narrow. The ball was wooden with a handle carved into one side, but the pins were the amazing things. They hung on strings, like puppets, and there were only nine of them in a diamond pattern. When you played, you got points for knocking them down, but you got extra points for leaving the middle one standing, called a picture frame, or something like that in French. Kaeti had the knack! She said the lane was so old that you could put your ball into the groove in the wood. That way you would either strike or picture frame every roll. Kaeti really knew how to twist those puppet strings in knots! I, on the other hand, rarely found that groove and was certain that the alley was raised in the middle. My ball rarely made it all the way to the other end without rolling into the shallow gutters on either side, but it was fun watching Kaeti! We also went to the French-German movies, but mainly to neck. We sat downstairs, well behind the fall line of the balcony, just in case they had had chicken noodle soup for dinner.

Kaeti and I also went to church together several Sundays. Since I was Quaker she had a better chance of finding a Lutheran church in Switzerland. But to my surprise, we ended up going to a Catholic church past the Parisienne and just up the street toward the telecabine. I guess that was because it was close and it wouldn't take long to hit the dorms and change for the ski slopes. The place was small, but beautiful with stained glass windows and polished woodwork. Very different from the austere Quaker meetinghouses I had known. The service was in Latin with the exception of the sermon, which was in French. I understood that this was a recent change – kind of a liberalization of the traditional, to make it more accessible to the people. Well, that didn't help me. Actually some of the Latin words seemed almost comprehensible, but the modulated French was so different that, without context, I didn't understand a word. But the movements of the priest and his helpers were like some elegant and exquisite, but very formal, dance. I was enthralled as the dancers moved back and forth, swinging incense burners, lighting candles, and whatever else was happening. You could really see how in medieval times the priest going through those motions soothed and fortified the peasants, who, like me, likely didn't understand a word of what was going on. Oh, and I was always a step behind the crowd at dropping to my knees, standing, or sitting. Try as I might, I never figured out how people knew when to move.

As we walked back to the main after the service, I talked to Kaeti about my observations. She had trouble with them because she had been raised with this, or something like it, being the true way to worship. I had only seen a performance like this once or twice before in my life. It was so unlike my faith, which involved a group of individuals sharing their pieces of God with others, in silence, often outside of a formal setting, like sitting in the grass on a hilltop watching the sunrise.

When I think back to boarding school maybe it wasn't so surprising that, unlike Tiny, I had no problem with Kaeti's other activities. The Quakers only allowed couples to socialize for a half hour after lunch, an hour after dinner, and during Friday and Saturday evening events. Also, the official definition of socializing only involved holding hands – no hugging or kissing! I did say official – while I got quite skilled and creative at holding hands, the dark areas on the front walk and occasional accidental meetings during off-campus hikes honed my skills at hugging and kissing. Then again, while couples were not allowed to be together as a couple at any other time, smart couples volunteered for lots of coed projects just to spend that time together, and I had some stimulating and educational study hours in the language lab with Jean.

Chapter Twenty Four

The Ski Team

I had tried several times to insinuate myself into the ski team. Kaeti and Gil were on my side, but Bernd pretty much ignored me. At best, you could call me the team mascot, but there never seemed to be enough room to take me to the meets. When Bernd set up training courses, Kaeti would show me the ropes after everyone else was done. We'd volunteered to pull the flags and get them back to the school so I could run the courses.

Kaeti's specialty, slalom, was tough. The turns were so quick and sharp that I just couldn't get my skis around more than a couple of gates before I lost it and sailed off the course. Kaeti tried to make me feel better by saying that it was the length of my skis, – they were just too long for me to maneuver. Giant slalom was better; the gates were spaced further apart, and I could get through them; I just wasn't fast at it. Kaeti claimed that I needed to stay off my edges and that my turns were slowing me, but she didn't know what I needed to do to fix it.

Gil finally came up with the solution and a plan. Downhill was a race where I didn't have to turn a lot and the gates were spaced so far that clearing them was no problem. The only real problem was holding my tuck to reduce wind resistance and staying on my skis at one hundred K's, about sixty mph. A multi-area race was coming up, and the downhill event was on the Berneuse – my mountain! At Gil's suggestion, I borrowed Robert's spare motorcycle helmet just in case, and we began *schussing* the slopes. I didn't like the helmet. It made my head feel heavy, and the wind whistled, which made me feel off-balance somehow.

I hadn't told Kaeti my plans because I wanted it to be a surprise. When she asked about the helmet one day as we linked up on the mountain, I just told her I was *schussing* and trying something new. She bought it, gave me a kiss, skated quickly away from me, and dropped into a tuck. *It's a challenge!* We flew down the mountain, but she was always a turn ahead. When we hit the field of moguls near the bottom, where I usually stopped, she flew through it, finding a relatively open area on the near side. I saw her hit a depression near the bottom and almost sit on her skis from the Gs. *What a skier! – She held it!* I had slowed in anticipation of stopping before the mogul field, so it was tough picking up speed again, and I was way behind when I got to the lift.

"Nice run!" Kaeti said, but I could tell she was just being kind.

"Yeah, I slowed when I got to the last moguls. They make me nervous; besides that depression at the bottom is pretty extreme."

"You know it! Want to run it from the top?"

The next run was great! Kaeti led, and I followed. We took an intermediate trail and had to dodge other skiers, but it was fun. I even managed to follow her on the left of the bottom field of moguls and hold the depression. I ended the run only seconds behind her. That won me a hug and a heady kiss. Hard to do for two people standing on skis… We went our own ways after that, and I searched for Gil to get some more pointers.

The week before the race Gil took me to Bernd to ask if I could race for the school in the Berneuse downhill.

Bernd gave a frustrated laugh, and, shaking his head, he said, "It's your life, kid!" You'll be in "C" class, the beginners, but you'll probably be the only first-year skier. I won't stop you. See you in the hospital!"

What an ass! But he did just put me on the ski team, whether he knows it or not! I smiled and nodded.

The downhill was the last day of the race. I hadn't pushed my luck. I didn't ask for a ride to watch the other races held on nearby peaks. I waited for the downhill and practiced. The day of the downhill I wore my medium blue pants with the light blue racing stripes that I hadn't worn since I'd bought them at the American high school and carried Robert's helmet. I was up on the course early to register. My name was on the list. I was skiing twelfth in a field of twenty skiers. For some reason, they gave me number sixty-seven. I was having Gil help pin on the number when Kaeti skied over.

"Keeping secrets are we?" she asked.

"I wanted to surprise you. I promised you that I'd make the team before the end of the year!"

"Yeah, but why downhill? This stuff is murder!"

"So I keep hearing. Bernd said he expects me to be carried off the slope."

"Well, if things get out of control, just stand and catch the wind. That'll slow you. Even the "C" course goes right down the advanced trail. This is no bunny run."

"Gil's taken me through the route a lot. I shouldn't have a problem. It'll be fun!" I got a kiss for luck and headed over to the top chair and across to the start.

Watching eleven skiers start was making me nervous. My legs were jumping with the energy. Everyone here was a first-year racer, but all of them had been skiing for years. They were encouraging each other in French, German, and the Swiss dialects of both. No one was speaking English, no one here to relieve my tension. We were way up the Berneuse on the steep area to the right of the moguls. I hadn't started from here during practice. They had three classes of skiers to run today, and ours was the smallest. The run was shifted a bit between each class to make it more difficult for the more advanced skiers. In our level they stacked the skiers to save time. This meant that when a skier was halfway through the course, a second was started. The course was long, and there was no way to catch the person ahead of you. However, if you fell you needed to get off the course quickly, just in case.

It was my turn. I got behind the kick bar and held myself with my ski poles. The top was straight down. The first set of poles was just visible as the run turned to the right below. *Une, deux, trois* and I was off. My original plan was to skate the first portion to pick up speed, but dropping down this slope was almost like falling off a cliff, so I just fell into my tuck. I tried to make my body as small as I could. *Lean back on the skis to raise the tips and reduce friction*, I thought. I was flying when I passed the first set of gates and saw the second in the distance. It seemed only seconds before I soared through the second set. I was traveling faster than I ever had on skis, except possibly when I fell off that cliff following Jean Paul. After the second gate I was in a relatively flat area with no turns. I liked turns because you knew which edge to ride. On the flat, little irregularities in the snow would pop your ski into your other boot, or worse. Worse happened. My right ski popped to the right and up. I was on one ski at speeds faster than I had ever dreamed of going. *I WILL NOT FALL!* my brain screamed. I tightened my leg and slammed the ski back into parallel. Two seconds later, it happened again, but I was ready for it and grabbed it back. *Should I stand up and slow? Not yet...* The next gate took me into a wide left hand turn. I was on the inside edge of my right ski and loving it. I was back in control. The next few gates were turns and drops. I tried to pre-jump the drops to stay on the snow and ski the downhill face instead of flying. Gil had taught me that, but the drops came so quickly I often just sailed and tried to keep from opening up in my tuck.

The next thing I knew, I was flying through the trees in the narrow passage that led to the last field of moguls. The trees were a blur on both sides of me. I was out of line for the next set of gates and took them too wide, almost hitting the right-side poles as I turned to the left. I had made it, but was in the middle of the moguls. The first mogul slammed my knees into my chest, knocking my wind out, but forcing me to remember to breathe. My skis were skittering over the tops of the moguls. The tips were bending strangely, like black noodles. *If I drop into one of these dips, I'm dead! – like slamming into a wall!* – but I continued to skim the tops. The next gate set was probably the last one. *If I can only make it through this and the depression... I can just see that gate!*

Wait! There is someone on the slope ahead! I was catching up with another skier just past the depression. *Has some idiot skied onto the course? – or did the skier ahead of me fall and try to continue?* I was out of the moguls, but at this speed I was going to hit him! I didn't think; I automatically hit a short swing turn to slow myself down as I dropped into the depression. My back and helmet slammed into the snow behind me. Then I was flying! It felt like a front layout off the diving board, head starting down, legs flipping up and the stomach at zero gravity. All I could see was white snow, then a blinding white flash, then blackness… total blackness! No sound, no light, no motion… *Am I dead? Is this what death is like, total blackness – nothingness?* I tried to reach out and couldn't or… didn't have anything to reach with.

Chapter Twenty Five

Recovery

Gray and black dots floating over each other randomly like you see when you can't sleep and stare at the ceiling in the darkness. Then in half-light I see fuzzy mounds of snow in front of my face. *Not snow, sheets – white sheets. I can feel their roughness against my legs and arms. At least I still have legs and arms!* Silhouettes in the distance, but no faces. A face floated over me, someone in a white lab coat with a black thing around his neck. The school's doctor was hanging over me shining a light into my eyes to see if I was awake. He then said in a German accent, punctuating every few words, "You KNOW, if you had NOT had your HELMET on, your HEAD would have been CRUSHED like an EGG!" As he said "crushed," he put one hand in front of my face and pretended to crush an egg as he made a fist.

Everything went black again. No not totally black this time; there was a white oval. I walked toward it. As it got larger, I recognized the doctor. He was in his white coat with his stethoscope. His big belly made him appear round as he sat high on a stone wall. As I neared him, I became him. Rather, I was sitting on the wall looking down at my big stomach covered by the lab coat. As I leaned to see over my stomach, I fell and my body jumped like I was in one of those falling dreams. White lights flashed, and my neck hurt! When the light passed, I was on the ground with cartoon knights in armor riding Disney horses and looking down at me. One, a female knight with long yellow hair hanging beneath her helmet said, "Jim" and something that I didn't understand. I looked around and saw I was in a puddle of clear jelly; then I saw what appeared to be a giant yellow egg yolk. "Jim…" again. *This is a stupid dream*, I thought. *Like some kid's Humpty Dumpty dream.*

What the hell is going on? "Jim, wake up." *Yeah, you're right, I need to wake up! I don't like this dream.*

Wait, someone is touching my right hand. "Jim, wake up," I hear again. My right eye cracked open and slammed shut. White-hot light and pain! Even my eyelids hurt, but I kept trying. Finally I saw cascading tawny hair on the sheets by my side and a hand touching mine. "Jim, wake up," Kaeti said, but she wasn't looking at me. She was just laying her head on the bed repeating those words. I tried to talk but couldn't, so I moved my hand to grip hers but only managed to move it slightly. However, that was enough. Kaeti lifted her head and looked at me worried. The left side of her face was wet as if she had been crying.

"Jim, you're awake!" she said excitedly, wiping her face.

She looked so beautiful! I flashed back to the first time I had seen her. No makeup in the school dining room before the arrival of Prince Paul. I remembered the excitement she had when she talked about skiing and the mountain. "You were right," I croaked softly to her.

She leaned over me to hear me better and asked, "Right about what?"

"Skiing is nothing like standing up on a sled." She laughed and threw a fake punch. My reflexes caused me to jerk my head away from the blow, and white lights went off in my skull; the pain was intense!

I groaned, and she leaned into me, her cool hair spilling onto my neck. "Sorry," she said meekly and kissed me lightly on my lips.

"You can do better than that!" I said as she came back into focus. We kissed this time, longer but gently. "I love you," I said softly.

"I know," she answered with a smile and another kiss.

"What happened?" I asked. "Except for that idiot doctor a minute ago, the last thing I remember is trying to dodge some guy on the course."

"That idiot doctor was yesterday. You've been unconscious for over twelve hours. You really had us worried."

We talked for a long while. The guy ahead of me had fallen at the depression and had not cleared the course. I actually had had a respectable run going and might have placed had I not fallen. Kaeti hadn't seen the fall but heard it was spectacular. She came down when they were *luging* me off the mountain. Luckily I was near the bottom, so it was pretty easy to get me to the doctors. Apparently I had nothing broken, but my neck was badly compressed, and I would have to wear a neck brace for a while. The doc had shot me up with some painkillers, which probably accounted for the weird dreams. As Kaeti left to get some sleep, I asked her to sneak me in a burger and fries. I was starving. I also asked if I could get an ice pack for my neck; it seemed to be on fire.

Gil and Wilds arrived after a while with the burger and fries, but it was tough eating without being able to lift my head. It tasted good anyway. As I ate, Gil apologized for getting me into this, but I told him that he couldn't have stopped me. Wilds, who had been standing quietly while this was going on, led with "Robert is going to be pissed at you!"

"What?" I asked as he pulled out the helmet I had been wearing from behind his back. It looked okay until I noticed that the white interior was hanging out in chunks.

"Man, you destroyed this!"

"Better that than his head," Gil interjected as we examined the destruction.

"Shit!" was all I could say.

Then Wilds added, "I saw the destruction! It was like something out of Wide World of Sports! You flew and cart wheeled, your skis spinning, snow blasting up! It was fantastic... ah... until I realized it was you."

"I am not sure that I need to know this... Any idea when I can get out of this place?"

Wilds responded, "the doc says you'll be up tomorrow with your neck brace but no more skiing for a while"

"That's bullshit!" I said as my emotional response sent spears of pain through my neck. "Kaeti didn't send an ice pack did she? My neck is on fire..." I added, breathing deeply to control the pain.

The next day I awoke as the doctor entered carrying a white plastic neck brace. I tried to sit, but my head felt disconnected from the rest of my body. Between the drugs and the injury, my neck was a mass of rubber with erratic, conflicting messages being sent to my neck muscles. He raised my head gently, slid the brace behind my neck. He then showed me how to lace it up and adjust it, although it didn't seem to be very adjustable. The fit was snug, and it seemed to be made for a much longer neck than mine. As the doctor helped me to the sitting position, the brace bit into my shoulders and under my chin. The device hadn't looked new; perhaps the rubber pads had lost their cushioning. In any case, I was willing to go through anything to get out of this place. He also gave me some pills for the pain: a muscle relaxant and a painkiller.

Wilds showed up shortly afterwards with a change of clothes and my boots. Dressing was an adventure. First the hospital gown that I was wearing... (Don't ask me when or how I got into it. I don't want to know.) Anyway, it was pinned under the neck brace. Once I got it out, I couldn't look down to dress myself and had to do everything by touch. Wilds had to help me straighten the buttons on my shirt and lace my boots. The sun was bright and the air crisp as we stepped outside. Wilds offered me his thin arm for the walk to Hell House. It was good to hear the crunch of the snow under my boots.

I spent the rest of the day in my room. I was a little down and didn't feel like company. I drew the curtains and tried to nap. Wilds showed up with dinner he'd brought from the kitchen. I wasn't really that hungry; my stomach was a little upset, but I ate it to get my strength back. That night's sleep was totally dreamless, and I woke feeling as though I hadn't slept at all. I ached all down one side like I had stayed in the same position too long. I like my dreams and need them and some thrashing at night to wake feeling refreshed. I obviously hadn't gotten that last night. Wilds tried to wake me and take me to breakfast, but I wasn't up to it. I took my pills and went back to dreamless sleep. Gil came in with breakfast, and he, too, tried to get me up, but I just couldn't. As school started, the frat house got very quiet. I got up and tried moving around, but I really felt bad. My stomach, my head, everything felt like crap! I soon found myself lying on the bed in a fetal position. Then I started reliving the accident. I had come close to killing myself. Everyone had warned me, but I did it anyway. Was it worth it?! Nobody cared,... no one liked me... I was just a little shit! I started crying balled up on my bed. I spent most of the day between that state and dozing. A sandwich had appeared during one doze, but I didn't want it.

That afternoon Wilds and Gil came in with the homework they had collected. I sat up for them and pretended to be doing okay. The homework gave me something to focus on besides myself. Gil, at least, took off for the slopes. I am not sure about Wilds. He came in at 5:30 to take me to dinner, but I still wasn't in the mood. I asked him to bring something light back. Besides I still had the sandwich. He came back with chicken soup, bread, and a get-well card from Kaeti. The card and the soup brightened my evening. I even ate the sandwich. I studied a little more, promised myself to get to school tomorrow, took my pills, and crashed shortly afterwards for another dreamless night. I slept like a rock – and for me that's not good. I felt like I had slept under a rock.

The next couple of days went almost exactly the same: I wake to a breakfast roll brought by my friends, take my pills, become inconsolably depressed for most of the day, and my friends return with homework and dinner. I couldn't get out of the room. On the good side, I probably studied more that week than the rest of the year. I liked listening to the adventures of my friends in the afternoon, but it made me all the more depressed the next day while I sat in my room with the curtains drawn.

I am not sure who first put it together. Thursday, Wilds came in with Willie, and he started to quiz me about how I felt during the day. I admitted that I was very down during the mornings and that I was sleeping like crap. He then looked at the pills I was taking and asked when I took them. It turned out that I took them about an hour before the onset of the depression and an hour before going to sleep. The revelation struck like lightning! If I hadn't been going through it, I might have picked out the coincidence. I wanted to stop all medicine, but Willie convinced me to take several aspirins before going to sleep. That night, I slept great! My neck hurt when I turned the wrong way, but I dreamed and thrashed. Kaeti was in my dreams again, flowing over the mountain. I couldn't believe that I had forgotten her; I had been just too caught up in my own problems. I hadn't even written her back! I hoped that I hadn't screwed things up between us.

I woke Friday feeling weak but better. When Wilds came in to invite me to school, I almost joined him until I realized that I hadn't bathed for a week. As everyone headed off, I filled the tub. I'm a shower man. I usually hate tubs. They're just too hot, and you get out feeling dirtier than when you got in. But this morning it felt glorious! When I drained the tub, I sprayed myself down with cool water from the handheld sprayer and felt ready to take on the world. Dressing was another matter. The neck brace still made it difficult to see anything, but I did the best I could. I even found my old *Bass Weejuns* (penny loafers) that I had retired when the snow started falling. I could slip into these without having to tie them. Then I realized that walking outside in them would be taking my life into my own hands: no traction! I had homework to finish from yesterday, so I decided to take one more day off. This day I opened the curtains to my balcony and pushed my desk around so I could look out while I worked. *Switzerland is a glorious country! Maybe, some year, I will come back to live here permanently.*

Chapter Twenty Six

Jean Claude and the GS

To my surprise that evening, the knock on my door that I thought was Wilds bringing supper was from Kaeti. She walked into my room. A week was too long to go without seeing her. I just stood there staring for a minute. *Beautiful!* This was the first time she had been in my room since I had walked in on her and Tiny, I realized. "Hey, I thought you said it was too dangerous coming to my room?"

"I think I can handle you in that collar."

"Promise!" I joked with a predatory smile. To my surprise, Kaeti blinked and looked a little embarrassed by my joke. "Sorry!" I apologized. "I'm also sorry about not writing you back."

"That's okay; you weren't feeling well," she said as she gave me a once over. I wondered nervously if my shirt was buttoned correctly and my fly was closed. As if reading my mind, she corrected a couple of buttons on my shirt. I instinctively checked my fly. It was closed. She had spotted my hands though and smiled knowingly. I felt like a little kid. I didn't like feeling like that in front of her. Once I was presentable, she added, "We have a surprise for you." Gil and Wilds, who had been hiding just outside the door, came in as if on cue. They helped me with my coat and lacing my boots. The three of them did everything but bodily carry me up to the main and into the snack bar.

A small group had gathered, including Tiny, Willie, Baby John and Alice, Colleen, Bennie, and a couple of others from his advanced ski classes. They showed me to a chair that faced the group while Kaeti began: "Last fall, on the steps up from the lobby a student who had never been on skis before announced that he would be on the ski team by the end of the year. At first, I had my doubts until I saw his raw determination." She looked at me, smiled, and looked back at the group. "After the first weekend, I knew that if anyone could do it, Jim would." At that comment, I saw Tiny, standing tall at the back of the group, look away with a hurt expression on his face. Some shorter blonde, perhaps Debbie, was leaning against him, but she didn't seem to notice his response.

"Well, Jim, you made it!" Gil announced as he came up and presented me with the school's racing team sweater, black with gold stripes down the arms.

"Congratulations!" Kaeti said; and with a teasing look in her eyes, she gently held my neck brace and gave me a formal kiss on both cheeks. The group applauded. I was stunned. I felt more like running from the room than standing and accepting the acknowledgement of my success. I never know what to do at times like this.

As I looked around, I realized that they expected me to say something. I also noticed that no one else from the ski team, including the captain, Bernd, was there, and suspected that Gil and Kaeti had cooked this up on their own, but I loved them for it.

Finally I stuttered, "W...what c...can I say? Ahh... If I'd... ah... nn...known that b...breaking my neck would g...get me on the t...team, I w...would have done this much earlier." Several people chuckled uncertainly; not Kaeti, she looked worried. Then, focusing on Kaeti because I could talk to her and pretend the others weren't around, "No, maybe not. Anyway I'm really not sure that I deserve this since I didn't even finish my first race... But I will make you a promise: when I get this thing off my neck, I'll find a way to earn it... Maybe downhill isn't my thing!"

Wilds chimed in, drawing my attention back to the crowd, "You can say that again! Hey, what about ski gymnastics? That was a great flip – but you need to work on the landing. We'll form a committee to begin work on making it an Olympic sport!" The group actually laughed and really cheered at that.

"Thanks, everyone!" *Man, am I embarrassed. I really don't know how to deal with compliments.*

After the group left, I cornered Gil and Kaeti. "Is this for real?" I asked.

"Sure!" Kaeti said. "Bernd agreed."

"With a little arm twisting from Kaeti!" Gil added.

Kaeti snapped, "Like you weren't there at all!"

"Guys, I really appreciate your support. I guess I should have listened to someone about downhill."

Kaeti said, "It was that other clown's fault! He should have cleared the run. One lesson though, don't try to turn quickly in downhill. It doesn't work!"

I chuckled. "You don't have to worry. No more downhill for this guy. What about giant slalom?!"

Gil laughed, "Give it a break! No one's going to help you put your ski boots on until you get out of that neck brace."

"Hey, I won't need help then!"

He left Kaeti and me alone. "Forgive me for being such a... whatever," I said.

"Nothing to forgive. I'd be depressed too. I'm just glad you're back." We kissed. It was good that she was my height. It would have been tough to have to bend over with my neck brace. She added, "I should have come over before. I just didn't know what to do." We sat in silence together for a while. Kaeti looked like she had something else to say. "You kind of scared me when you said you... loved me." She swallowed and appeared to search for the right words. "This is... We are..."

Realizing where she was going, I said, "Wait a minute. That was... there are all kinds of love. I loved you for being there for me. I know that we're just good friends, and I wouldn't have it any other way," I lied.

We hugged, and she added, "Maybe I should come to your room sometimes."

That fantasy whirled through my head for a while, but I said, "I like the idea of the two of us relaxing together. I could even have used a lap to rest my head on when I was down, but... I can't believe that I am saying this... You might be right about the temptation. Maybe... if we pick our times and conditions."

"Sounds good," she said as she laid her head on my shoulder against my neck brace.

"Be careful; that's holding my head on!" Kaeti jumped back startled, laughed, started a swing, and then thought better of it. "Hey, I won't break."

"Glad you're getting your sense of humor back – even if it is strange!"

"That's me!" I joked, then more gently, "You're the medicine I need! That and to get back on the slopes."

That brought a dreamy smile to Kaeti's face. Then a thoughtful look. "I don't know if I could stand being injured and not being able to ski."

"Yeah, although it does wonders for your grades!"

I actually made high honors on the dean's list that term. Studying instead of skiing and drinking really did do wonders. I also got more excited by my classes when I understood what was going on before the teacher talked about it.

One week later, neck brace still on, I asked Willie to help me talk to Bennie. I knew that he hung out at the Vagabond in the upper village on weekends. The students were put off limits at the Vag for a fight early in the year, but Willie said he had some connections there, something to do with being student body president. Kaeti was busy at the snack bar that Friday, so Willie and I went on our own. The Vag was a quiet little bar in the basement of a youth hostel of sorts. It was amazing to see the collection of people there. There were a couple of Aussies who were fascinated with my neck brace and asked how I had earned it. My story bought me a couple of beers while I waited for Bennie. I liked their accents. It was different from the Brits, more masculine. It was kind of fun the way they used the word "bloody." I had picked it up from movies and the Beetles, but these guys used it every other word. I found that it was an adverb, as well as an adjective – and sometimes it might have been used as a verb or a noun. Hard to tell after a couple of beers.

I was also amazed to find a couple of our coeds here whom I hadn't seen at the local hangouts in town. Willie explained that this was a safe haven for them from some of the crap at school – both the studs and the upper-crust coeds who like to rule everyone's lives. Colleen and Yves were there. *Man, is she a dark-haired beauty – and those green eyes glow like jade in this dim light! If it weren't for Kaeti, well... Hell, Colleen is a goddess. She probably wouldn't give me a second look... Yves is a lucky guy! – So am I, for that matter. I have to get back before Kaeti closes up.*

After a couple of hours, Bennie arrived. He was greeted by all as he walked in and scanned the room. He immediately spotted me and came over. "Monsieur Jeem, 'ow are you? Surprise to see you 'ere."

"I was looking for you. Can I buy you a beer?"

"Certainly! 'Ow can I 'elp?" I got him a beer, and we retired to a quiet corner. Before I could say anything, he asked, "Why deed you try zee down'eell? – ees so dangeroous!"

"I'm stupid, I know. I want to be on the racing team."

"Why? Skiing ees fun. Enjoy!"

"Call it a promise to my girl."

"Mademoiselle Kaeti?"

"*Oui!*"

"*Bon!*" After sipping his beer for a moment while focusing across the room, "I 'ave a thought. You recover, keep legs strong, and I weel see what I can do."

"Can you give me a hint?"

"Well, giant slalom is no' so dangeroous... 'ave you 'eard of a French skier, Jean Claude Killy?"

The name sounded familiar, but maybe I was just thinking of Jean Paul. "I don't think so."

"Zee FRENCH national champion! Zee World Cup! NO? *Mon Dieu!*"

"Before I came to school here I wasn't into skiing. What about him?"

"'e skis GS differently zan others... more like zee down'eell position – 'e seets back in 'is skis and keecks zem forward through zee turns. I can promise nothing, but I weel see if I can find films to show you. Maybe you can learn through zee films."

I got back to Kaeti before she closed up, and we enjoyed each other's company for a while – even with a neck brace – although, while necking, I had to turn my head with my shoulders and felt kinda like

Frankenstein's monster! As we sat, I told her about Bennie's idea, and she looked worried again. "Jim, are you sure?"

"Yes! I'm not a kid! I don't need..." I responded with an edge that I didn't know was there. *Maybe it's the beer, I really don't like feeling like Kaeti's kid brother.* "Sorry! God, I'm sorry. Hey, I need my coach again. – kick my butt!"

"Alright, tiger," she said quietly looking down.

Kaeti and I both went up to Bennies to watch the movies. She knew who Jean Claude was. She said he was winning all the events, downhill, GS and slalom, in the world's skiing competitions. Bennie had pulled down a picture of Paris and the Eiffel tower from the living room wall that he used as a screen. The movies were eight-millimeter black and white. Jean Claude was tall and lanky with an arrogant air. He reminded me too much of Bernd, both in body and attitude. The shots of his skiing were hard to focus on, but I could see what Bennie was saying. Kaeti and the ski team leaned well forward on their skis and attacked the gates. Killy seemed to be standing more upright and kicking his skis forward through the gates. We each wondered how he was getting enough edge to turn. Bennie felt that he entered the gates wider and smoother. This meant that he didn't need to edge as strongly inside the gate and he didn't slow down as much. When the movie was over, both Bennie and Kaeti promised to experiment so when I was out of my brace they could demonstrate the technique for me. I promised to be out of the brace in a week – doctor's permission or not!

Two days later and I took off the brace for good. My neck was weak; my head felt very heavy and had a permanent click on the left side when I turned it to the right, but it didn't hurt too much. At Stallone's suggestion, I began isometrics to strengthen my neck. I pushed my head forward, backwards, and to each side into my hands. I'd hold each pose for about thirty seconds and did that about ten times a day. I wanted to be back in shape as soon as I could.

With the brace off, I started skiing again. At first I just went up the Riondaz and skied the simple intermediate trails. I wanted to get my balance and not look stupid in front of my friends. I also didn't think that

I could afford a major fall with my neck in its weakened condition. The slopes were easy, like I was back running the bunny hill. The snow had changed some. It was wetter and heavier. Spring was coming. One day the morning sun caused a cloud to form near the bottom of the trail. Skiing into it was like skiing blind. I knew the trail well enough that I could time my turns and get to the bottom in one piece, but I came dangerously close to colliding with my fellow skiers several times. I did that a couple of times before they closed the lifts. When I asked why they were closed, the answer was it was too dangerous. That evening around the dinner table I heard that a woman had skied into the cloud and struck a pylon for the chair lift. She wasn't expected to live. I was pretty sure that I knew where that had happened. If you didn't make the first turn after running into the cloud and continued across the slope, the logical extension of the trail took you to a pylon. I had skied around it a couple of times on clear days just for fun.

The next day I decided to return to the Berneuse. I wouldn't have to worry about clouds until the last run back to school. Spring hadn't affected the snow on the top – at least not on the Berneuse. The Chaux de Mont was positively slushy. I saw more falls on that slope than I had all season. I actually saw my first runaway ski come sailing down the slope at the people in the lift line at the bottom. One skier actually managed to intercept it before it speared some unsuspecting skier. He skied across its path, causing it to flip sideways and slow. That was some skiing! – assuming that he did it on purpose.

I met Kaeti up top. She welcomed me back to the slopes like she hadn't seen me at school every day that week. Our relationship was different on the slopes – kindred spirits. She warned me about avalanche hazards. As the spring warms the snow, areas become too dangerous to ski. She pointed out crescent-shaped openings in the snow on the Chaux de Mont and explained that these usually preceded an avalanche. The snow had slipped down a little bit and revealed a section of the rock below. They had blocked off the secondary bowl, making the trip down longer and slower; so we planned to ski the top bowl until we had to head down when the lifts closed.

Later on the mountain, Kaeti caught me off-guard with "What are your plans for spring break?" I had forgotten it was coming up.

"Home to Germany, I guess... Unless you've got a better idea?"

"We could stay here. There's only a month or so of good snow left now."

"Whoa, would the school let us? That would be cool!"

"Sure, lots of kids don't have any place to go during the holidays."

I drifted back on my skis then slid forward toward Kaeti, causing my left ski to slide between Kaeti's. "That sounds like a lot of fun," I said with a joking leer as I slid up next to her.

"Henderson, if you cause us to fall down this slope, I'll make sure you're on the bottom!"

"Promise!"

She pushed me back, and I let myself go. When I cleared her skis, I faked a fall down the slope, rolled over, and popped back up on my skis. "Your neck seems better!" she called down to me.

"Yeah, no thanks to you!"

We laughed and headed over the moguls and down to the lift. *Let me see*, I thought, *Spring break with Kaeti, on our mountain, with no school, or home to gray, soggy Germany with my parents – tough decision!* I had to get on the horn quick; it was just over a week away! They didn't know about my being on the ski team – or my accident for that matter – I could claim that I had to stay for team practice. If I could catch up with Bennie, it would kinda be the truth!

That Friday, I got Willie to take Kaeti and me to the Vag. When Bennie showed up I proposed that we start working on the GS. Both looked at me protectively but agreed to start Monday during spring break. That next day, I hit the first lift up the mountain. I wanted to get my legs back in shape. I wanted to run the whole mountain, not just the top, but found the snow so slow that I ignored the warning about avalanches in the secondary bowl. I skied under the crossed sticks and through the bowl but stayed very quiet, just in case. The snow through the bowl was called "corn snow"– basically refrozen slush. The stuff was the size and consistency of gravel and very heavy on the skis.

On my second run through the bowl, I caught an edge and fell face first. Man that scared me. On the way down I thought about reinjuring my neck; then the pain on the side of my face as I plowed through the gravel-like snow almost caused me to scream until I realized that a scream might trigger an avalanche. I stood and walked out of the bowl quietly with the right side of my face stinging with pain. As I arrived at the line for the telecabine, I noticed everyone staring at me. One older Swiss skier I saw frequently on the slopes said something in French about blood on my face. Instead of going straight into the lift, I went into the toilets in the base. I looked like Two-Face from Dick Tracy. The right half of my face was red with spots of frozen blood from several dozen punctures. The injuries stung when I washed off the blood, but they didn't start to bleed again, so I grabbed my skis and headed for the top. *Lesson number 246 – don't fall in corn snow!* I got some ribbing from my schoolmates for the face scrubbing, but Kaeti managed to control her usual jibe.

Sunday, I saw my first avalanche – or, rather, heard it. It was on the Chaux de Mont in an area that was too steep to ski. There was a loud crack and rumble. I looked across to that side and it was over, just a smoke-like cloud above a new pile of snow and a bare area on the mountain face. *James Bond couldn't have outrun that one!* I took that as a lesson to stay clear of the secondary bowl and skied the slower route when I left the top.

Chapter Twenty Seven

Spring Break With Kaeti

School that next week went slow as hell, but it was finally over. I continued to ski each day until the lifts closed. That Friday most students departed, leaving Kaeti and me alone. We spent the whole day on the Berneuse and returned to our dorms to change after the lift stopped running. Then, since she didn't have to work the snack bar, we headed into the village for fun. We hit the Chasseur for their thin pepper steaks and a half carafe of red wine. That gave us only a glass and a half each – actually I had two. The meal was delicious; especially the *pomme frites* (french fries). From there we went to the bowling alley. Kaeti whipped me as usual. Finally we returned to my room. I could tell she was nervous about this, but I reassured her that I would be a gentleman – no, seriously! We spent most of the time wrapped up in my poof standing on the balcony watching the stars and holding each other close. We saw several shooting stars and made wishes. Mine weren't going to come true – or were coming true as we stood there – it's hard to say…

I broke the revelry and suggested that we get her back to the dorm so we could be on the first lift up the mountain. She curled in and looked into my eyes for some direction. I brushed the hair back along the side of her face and kissed her. Her lips were soft and yielding. Her cheeks were warm against mine, in spite of the cold on the balcony, when we snuggled into each other's neck and inhaled our mingled scents. We walked quietly inside and didn't say a word all the way back to the main. Kissing goodnight alone on the stairs to the girls' dorm was tough. It was like we didn't want to separate. I wondered briefly what would happen if I walked her back to her room. It almost seemed like she wanted to take me up. It was nice not having dozens of people around making you feel uncomfortable just standing and holding each other. I felt more comfortable with Kaeti than I could remember. Finally, I decided to ask her something that had been on my mind, "If we can build enough trust this week, I would like to share something with you."

"What's that?"

"I love sleeping out on my balcony at night under that stars. I'd love to share that with you."

Kaeti's pupils flared and slowly contracted. "I'd love that," she said, initially. Then, after thinking a moment, a worried look came over her face, "but I don't know…"

"I understand. That's why I said if we can build enough trust. No pressure."

She smiled and pulled me close. We kissed one more time, and she went up the stairs. I followed her with my eyes – each step was measured as if she was tempted to return. Then as usual when she turned the corner, she flicked her hair over her shoulder and looked down at me. But this time she stopped, turned into the banister, and held my eyes for a long time. So long that some errant satyr caught me and took me up the stairs to give her one last mischievous kiss. It didn't work the way I planned. She was a step up from me and towered over me, but she caught the mood and joined me on mine. We held another long embrace and kiss. Longer than I had planned, but she held me close and I wasn't protesting. Finally we broke, and I patted her on the butt and shooed her up the stairs. "See you bright and early tomorrow!" The pat drew a teasing glare over her shoulder – at least I hoped I saw a bit of a smile before she turned back to go up the stairs.

We hadn't made plans to meet the next morning. She wasn't in the lobby when I grabbed my skis, but her skis were still there. So I grabbed a quick croissant and cup of hot tea at Le Parisienne and watched for her. After a bit, I gave up and headed up to catch the lift. Maybe she was sleeping in. I'd meet her up top. I skied for about an hour before I first saw her as I was riding up the chair lift. She was skiing sluggishly and looked like she hadn't slept. I waved down, but she didn't see me.

I skied quickly but hadn't managed to catch up with her on the chair lifts. In fact, I began to wonder if she was avoiding me. Finally we hit the bottom at the same time and caught a chair together. "Are you feeling all right?" I asked concerned.

"Yes, I just didn't sleep well."

"I slept like a baby! Did you get breakfast?"

"No," she said quietly, not looking at me. *Something was wrong!*

"Let's grab something up top. Hot chocolate would give you some energy."

"I guess," she said passively.

The little snack bar in the lift had a hot ham-and-cheese croissant that I proposed to split as I brought back two cups of hot chocolate. Except for the Swiss teen behind the counter we were alone inside. We sat on a bench at a table by the windows where we could watch the skiers come out of the lift and don their equipment. Instead of enjoying the view, Kaeti sat with her back to the window and was staring down into her cup. Something was definitely wrong. My mind was roiling! I must have said or done something wrong last night, but what was it? Had I said that I loved her again on my balcony? I didn't remember it – but I was getting the same kind of signs from her that I did last time. Maybe she had finally seen through me. *God, don't let this be the end!* I prayed.

After a while Kaeti looked up sadly and said, "I think we made a mistake."

I sat in stunned silence for a while waiting for the axe. When she didn't say anything else, I gave in to my fears. Pleading I said, "Kaeti, I love you." She looked up at that surprised, put a hand toward me for a second then drew it back. I continued, "I have since..." *since when? Saas Fee? before that?* "– for a very long time." She was back looking into her cup but glanced up for an instant. I tried unsuccessfully to capture her eyes with mine.

I was trembling but managed to keep my voice controlled. "I know that we agreed to be friends but... and I know that this will end sometime soon, but I don't care. I enjoy the time we spend together and... I am going to be hurt if it ends now or at the end of the school year. That's life! In fact, as an army brat, if I weren't willing to fall in love until I found that… someone-who-I-could-spend-the-rest-of-my-life-with… I wouldn't ever know love."

Kaeti was looking up at me now and seemed to be listening intently, but she frowned and said, "I know, or… I knew how you felt. You were safe and fun to be with. I… guess I used that." *Please, go on using me!* I thought. Then she continued, "This isn't about you, it's about me."

About her? What can I say to convince her it will be all right – I will be all right? "Listen, I can't believe that there's only one person you will love in your life. Hopefully, there will be lots of them! You can learn from each of them. You… I… will hurt when we break up, but I will know that… but I will hold you in my heart! The things I love about you… like your independence, your strength, your… joy of life… your love of this mountain! – I will carry them with me forever… and I will look for them when I find that person I will marry. This isn't about marriage; this is about now." *God, what else could I say!*

She was back to looking at me intently as if deciding something. Then clarity came into her eyes, and she slid down the bench toward me; we embraced; she nuzzled into my neck. *Hugging is good*, I thought. Then she quietly asked in my ear, "How do you do that?"

How do I do what? I wondered but stayed quiet. *Be careful! Do nothing to dispel this mood!* Staying close to me, she reached for her now warm chocolate and took a bite of the croissant. *I don't know what just happened, but it's good,* I thought. Trying to bring up something funny but harmless, I said, "Hey, we have another lover out there who's beginning to feel ignored."

Kaeti, slowly, as if coming up from a dream, turned and looked at me, "What?"

"Our mountain. You remember Bennie's speech, 'treat her gentle at times and rough…' Actually she's been a little rough with me lately," I said, rubbing the side of my face where she had taken off some of my skin.

Kaeti laughed and added, "Well, let's not keep a lady waiting!"

The rest of the day we skied somehow closer. We took the same or parallel paths down the slopes. Each time we got on the chair lift Kaeti slid over close to me, and we huddled together on the way up. This was good! I tried to remember what I had said in my desperation. Obviously, it was something good. I had admitted I loved her, and we were still together. I had been so sure admitting that would be the end. I missed something. What had she meant by asking how I did something? How had I talked my way out of being crushed? – pure desperation!

When the lifts closed, we returned to our rooms to change and promised to meet at the foot of her dorm stairs. As I walked back up the cowpath to the main, I brainstormed for ideas. I was on borrowed time here. I had to make the right impression. Not too desperate, but not too ordinary. I had a great idea! Kaeti was coming down from the dorm as I ran up from the lobby. As she stepped off the last step I caught her hand and said, "Come here a minute." I started to direct her to the library, but she was already heading that way. Next thing you knew, we were giggling and racing inside. There was a lot more light coming in from outside than the last time, but it didn't matter – no one was around. We curled into each other's arms and held a kiss forever.

"Great minds think alike," she finally said, as we broke apart.

"Even a blind squirrel finds a nut sometimes," I added, still giddy from the exchange.

She started to push me away smiling quizzically then pulled me back with a sharp look. "Which of us is the blind squirrel, and who is the nut!"

"Damn, it's just something my cousin used to say. I got lucky!"

"Yes, you did," she said with her mischievous gleam.

"The Messange next?" I asked.

"What is it about you guys and your stomachs?"

"No rush tonight. I could easily stay right her," I said as I pulled her close.

"Mmmm," she purred.

We did stay a while longer just embracing. I waited a long time for her to break it off, but I finally had to do it. "Okay, this guy's stomach is taking command, sorry!" I joked. The walk to the Messange was much as I remembered it from that first time, except for the snow; it was wet and slushy, and Kaeti was huddling closer. There weren't many people inside the restaurant. A waitress seated us, but Herr Dietrick greeted us at the table. "My favorite couple! What can I get for you tonight? *Tournedos?*" We declined and settled for his veal. He had a great German recipe with paprika gravy, spaetsel noodles, and tiny white asparagus. He offered to give me a bottle of Mosel wine at cost, Piesporter Goldtropfchen. I couldn't refuse, although a full bottle was more than we usually drank. Kaeti and I split the bill. She insisted that her parents gave her money, too.

We took what was left of the wine downstairs to the bar. Dancing that night was a dream. We couldn't keep our eyes off each other. My secret was out, and I didn't have to pretend anymore. It was great! It wasn't that late when we walked back down the road. I thought about going back to my balcony; but as we passed the main, Kaeti led us inside. We made our way into the snack bar. Kaeti turned on one of the small lamps by the couch where we had spent so many wonderful hours. She opened the jukebox and selected several records. We just sat there huddled together, kissing gently for hours. I suspect that I drifted off to sleep for a few minutes because I awoke in silence with Kaeti looking lovingly at me. "Another big day tomorrow. We need some sleep," she said as she helped me up.

Again, the steps to the dorm were quiet and dark as we stood snuggling, kissing, and delaying saying good night. Kaeti finally started her walk up but turned and looked back at me with a resolute look in her eyes. Then she came back to me, took my hands, and said, like she had memorized the right words, "I will always remember... your determination, your sense of humor,... but most of all the way you seem to look inside me and know what I need to hear. I just wish that I had listened before." She kissed me warmly and walked quickly up the stairs. She didn't turn back this time. She may have looked through her hair to see if I was still standing there, but it was too dark to tell. I was there, frozen – frozen and yet vibrating again. Did that mean what I thought it meant?

I walked slowly down the hill toward our frat house and stopped to look back at the girls' balconies, wondering if I understood. *She could have been politely writing me off,* I thought. *'I will always remember… goodbye!' But then why the kiss? Why the time in the lounge? No, that wasn't it. Wait!* I spotted someone walking out onto a balcony – her long, light brown hair illuminated by the light coming from her room. I waved from the darkness. She waved back. *It must be Kaeti; she's looking for me. I'm just a dark spot on the snow. No one else would have spotted me here. Has she fallen in love with me? When? How? What would that mean for us?* I actually felt a little afraid. *I haven't told her the whole truth. I don't think that I have ever felt this strongly about another girl – at least not since Jean, my high school sweetheart, and we beat each other up before the end. The end of school is going to be very painful for me! – and now maybe for her…* As I walked on I realized something else. *I wasn't looking inside her today; I was talking about me, trying to save my own skin. Why did she think that I saw something inside her? What had I said? And after she saved Saundra – I just listened. I didn't do anything special. If she thought that I could read her mind then I am in trouble! I'm not going to tell her – hopefully there won't be any other tests!*

Sunday was much the same as after our talk on Saturday. Fun skiing – maybe not as many close parallel runs on the slopes and back to some old teasing and challenging, but the night was close again. Dancing, talking, necking, and back to our rooms. Monday, GS lessons began in earnest. Kaeti hadn't figured out the trick. She had spent too many years with her forward-leaning style. Bennie showed me some of the techniques I would need to use. I had to try to position myself as I entered each gate so I could almost see the next gate. This meant long swinging turns preparing for the next gate before I entered the first. Kaeti thought that was crazy because it made the skier take a longer path, therefore, slower; but Bennie felt that the downhill position on the skis and the reduced edging would make up the difference by increasing the speed and reducing the friction. *The only thing I know is I am slow using Kaeti's style and have nothing to lose with Jean Claude's.* As I got more comfortable, my speed was increasing and I started making a believer out of Kaeti.

Also each night we used the quietness of the school to grow closer and closer together. Saturday, a few students started to return. We made that evening special walking through the village and holding each other. The Grand Hotel had a band that was playing slow music. We danced for hours before we walked back to the school. We ended the evening by hiding in the dark in the snack bar. We feared that any light or music would draw unwelcome company. The darkness started to arouse me as Kaeti curled up in my arms with her back to me. In spite of the time alone, we hadn't teased each other the entire week. Thinking back, our time together was comfortable but not sexual. I started to tease Kaeti as she was curled in my arms. It was interesting reaching around her like that. At first she didn't help, but she didn't resist either. As she started getting aroused, she turned her head around to kiss me over her shoulder but stayed facing away. *This is pretty cool; I have open access to everything – like a kid in a candy shop!* Then, when she climaxed, I climaxed behind her as her hips pulsed into me. But after climaxing, she rolled over to face me, then nuzzled into my neck like a kitten suckling her mom. She was so quiet in the dark that I began to get concerned. I couldn't see her eyes. "Something wrong?"

"Nothing…" she mumbled as she burrowed closer into my neck.

"Are you sure?"

"Yes. It was different, stronger. I don't know." This was one time that I wished I could read her mind. She insisted that I didn't do anything wrong, but she continued to hold me in a tight embrace for what could have been hours, especially since I hadn't cleaned up and was pretty sticky – but it didn't seem right to remind her wherever she was. Something was going on that I wasn't part of – or maybe I was but just didn't understand. When she went up the stairs that night, she walked hurriedly and didn't look back. I was worried until I looked up while walking down the slope and saw her on the balcony; we exchanged a distant good night.

That Sunday, we were back to normal – skiing our mountain. I didn't ask her about last night. She might have been a step ahead of me. I only now realized that people coming back would be the end of our private time together. A positive effect of the week was that we were more at ease together around others at school. People had known we were dating before, but the feelings between us were more visible now. Maybe that was because there were real feelings between us now.

Wilds was the first to say anything. One evening, he caught me in the hallway going into my room and followed me in. "Did you have a good time over spring break?" he started.

"Yes, Kaeti and I stayed here and worked on my GS."

"I'll bet that wasn't all you worked on!" he said with a smirk.

Warily, "Okay... What do you mean?"

"You and Kaeti seem to be a lot... closer."

"Okay, so...?"

"You two get it on?"

"No!" *He's never asked anything personal like that before. What's this about?* "Why would you ask that? Is it any of your business?"

"You two are kinda inseparable, now – and... well... there's a rumor going around that you did."

"No! Shit! Who started that? Tiny? It didn't happen! We're not going to. We've got to stop this somehow!" My words tumbled over each other.

"I'll try, but you've got to admit something's changed"

"I... We... Nothing happened. We just had a really good time together! It was nice, kinda like..."

"Playing house?"

I wouldn't use that expression but..."I guess – but no sex! Get that straight, okay? Man!"

"Okay! Hey, cool it! I didn't start the rumor!"

I caught Kaeti in the snack bar that evening. We sat together when no one was ordering anything. Things really had changed I thought. Kaeti had tended to stay behind the snack bar before until we were alone. Here we were, curled in each other's arms in front of everyone. Then, after the last few people walked out, I whispered to her. "We may have some trouble. There's a rumor going around the frat house that we… ah… slept together. I'm letting everyone know that's a lie, but it could spread."

"Jim, don't worry," she whispered back. "I already heard it from one girl – and she isn't going to spread it anymore, –" *It would be interesting to know what that meant. I'm not sure that I would want to face Kaeti's wrath!* "– but we should have expected it. The girls' dorm is a rumor mill."

"So is the guys'."

"Don't worry, it'll die out. The people who count know the truth," she said, looking deeply into my eyes.

"Yeah, but it's so unfair!"

"Hey, they already think I'm strange. What else is new? But thanks for caring about my rep. I love that about you, too," she said as she kissed me, then added, "You don't want to know about what some of the other guys would have done."

"Oh, I can guess!" *Did she just say 'love?' Wow!*

Then, with a sweet smile and gently touching my cheek, she said, "I guess that it's good we didn't sleep out under the stars. That would have clinched it!"

"I guess you're right. But it would have been great!"

Her right eyebrow arched high, "Not that great!"

"You know what I mean… I hope…"

"Yeah, it would have been nice. My brother and I used to camp out under the stars. It is great!"

With the tension off, I lay down, rested my head on her lap, and looked up into her eyes as she leaned over me, letting her long hair surround my face. I mused, *it would've been wonderful watching the stars with her and waking next to her, but if she'd asked me to make love with her, I doubt that I could've turned her down. Would that have been so bad if we were in love? Hadn't dad said that making love was the greatest way of physically expressing your love?*

Looking into my eyes and smiling she asked, "A penny for your thoughts?"

How to explain that? "Just thinking about us... wishing that spring break was longer, I guess."

"Mmmm." She nodded and brushed my hair back over my ear. *We hadn't made love, and school starting again would make it nearly impossible. Perhaps it's for the best. I've no experience to guide me, but my gut says that would have made the eventual separation even more painful.*

As class started on Monday, several guys hadn't returned to school. Prince Paul, of course... Let's see; this was his... sixth engagement... in London, I think. But the real news came when I was waiting for breakfast. I overheard two upper-crust girls talking about a car wreck in Spain, and I thought I overheard the name "Stallone." They were two snoots, so I felt a little awkward walking up behind them to eavesdrop, but they didn't give me a second glance. *Am I more accepted or still invisible to them? Hmmm...* It seems that a couple of sophomores had rented a Volkswagen van and headed to Spain for the break. None of them had returned yet. One girl had just talked on the phone to our Spanish flamenco beauty, Miriam, who had met the guys in Barcelona. She said that she was worried one day when they didn't return and the next morning she started searching the hospitals. She found Al in a local hospital, lying in bed crusted in his own blood. Both of his legs had been crushed in a head-on collision with a Mercedes. It seems the locals hadn't wanted to deal with him, so they left him in the bed to die. She cleaned him up, contacted his parents, and found a local specialist to treat him. He wasn't expected to walk again. She hadn't found the others.

I didn't know Al well. Not in my league, I guess, or rather, I wasn't in his. Tallish, slicked back hair and glasses came to mind. – but Stallone was in the car! No one seemed to know what had happened to him?

Stallone showed up at school a couple of days later uninjured. Wilds told me Stallone's story. It seems that they had just returned from shopping in Andorra where they had bought some tax-free Toledo steel swords. They were wrapped in paper, tied with string, and sitting behind his seat. He was catnapping in the back seat when he was thrown onto the floor, and the swords sailed over his head, clattered into back of the front seat, and landed on top of him. The swords had cut through their wrappings and lay gleaming on his chest. When he came to his senses, he got out of the van, but he didn't know enough Spanish to understand what was going on. All he could do was stand there when the ambulance took Al away. Other than that he didn't know what had happened. Then, with very little money and a couple of swords, he had to make it back to school on his own. The school didn't make any formal announcements about this, and I never found out who else was involved, nor did I notice anyone missing.

Chapter Twenty Eight

War Games

The week following spring break brought a new diversion to our mountain. On Wednesday afternoon, dozens of Swiss men started showing up with rifles and backpacks. Several apparently had climbed the winding road up the mountain in the snow on their mopeds with their rifles sitting across their laps. The general rumor was that the Swiss army was staging war games between our *canton*, Vaud, and a *canton* up the valley from us. No one officially told us what was going on, but the town was suddenly overrun with young guys with weapons. The uniforms did not appear until lunch break the next day. Then we saw several teams of uniformed men with rifles walking purposefully up the road in front of the main toward the upper village. Wilds had apparently missed their arrival the night before because he was the first to react: "Geez, have we been invaded?"

"Haven't you heard? They're having some kind of war games here," I responded.

"Ooookay, strange!" he said as he watched yet another group hustle past.

That afternoon while running down to Hell House to get into my ski clothes for the GS practice with Kaeti I ran into a group of soldiers all dressed in white parkas and pants standing together in the parking area in front of our frat house. A couple were helping each other hold their weapons while the others were strapping into skinny white skis that had to be for cross-country because they didn't look anything like downhill skis. As I watched I noticed that white gators covered their boots and a sleeve of white material also covered their rifles up to their metal barrels. White mittens completed their camouflage for the snow. *Pretty cool!* I thought. I slipped past the group and headed up to my room, then out onto my balcony to see what would happen next. From that height the soldiers were already hard to see. Then they filed out in twos into the field where I had first learned to ski. From the back they proceeded to disappear two at a time. Since I knew where they were headed and could see the trails that their skis made in the snow, I could follow the dark barrels of their weapons as they moved out into the distant fields. I could even spot a couple who had taken up a position near a snow mound that likely hid a large boulder near the high part of our field – anyway I thought the two dark sticks were rifle barrels. They didn't move much… maybe I was imagining it… *Cool!*

I talked to Willie about the Swiss army that evening in the snack bar while Kaeti was working. It seems that every male between the ages of eighteen and forty-five was in the army, no exceptions. And everyone has his own rifle at home just in case.

"What about conscientious objectors?" I asked, thinking about my own status.

"There aren't any. Either you're in or you go to jail."

"Seriously?"

"Yep."

"Damn!" Somewhere along the year I had gotten the idea that Switzerland might be a good place to escape Vietnam; that was until I learned it took twelve years to become a citizen. This had just dealt another blow to my pipe dream.

"What's it matter, Jim? The Swiss haven't been at war for what… five hundred years!"

That's true, I thought. "What about 4Fs? – if you're not physically able to serve?"

"I've heard they have to pay additional tax, but I don't know if that's true."

"I don't get it! Why's the entire nation in the army if they've never been at war?"

Willie shrugged his shoulders and smiled knowingly. "Maybe that's why. I understand even Hitler said that he thought he'd leave Switzerland alone to give everyone a place to vacation."

"Really? Interesting!"

"You know this country is a fortress, don't you?"

"What do you mean?"

"All the roads run through mountain valleys, and if you look closely, you'll see tank traps across the fields near the borders. Some of those concrete traps can also be dragged across the road during war to block the entire valley. And have you noticed that rock wall across from the Château de Chillon on Lac Léman?"

"Huh? What about it?"

"It's fake! Train tracks lead into a big door there. It's a hollow mountain with big guns."

"Yeah, right!" I looked at Willie with a big grin, but he didn't smile back.

"Seriously?"

"I've seen them open. Never seen what's inside, but there are huge doors there."

"Spooky!"

"And have you ever seen the Swiss air force fly these peaks?"

I flashed back to the beginning of school and my hike up the Tour D'Ai. "OH, YES! Man, they are unreal! You know, I think you're right."

That evening, after Kaeti and I said our goodnight on the steps, I walked out the front door to find a soldier in brown fatigues sitting on the steps with his rifle across his lap. He wasn't much older than me and had dark hair falling in his eyes. I nervously said "Hi!" and went on my way. The guy waved and continued to watch down the street. I wondered what he was waiting for. I also wondered what it would be like to know you had to go into the army. I guess that you wouldn't know any different if everybody did it. Besides, the Swiss government wasn't about to go out and attack some other country. This was just preparation for that defensive war I had thought about in Paris – people shooting my family and my neighbors...

The next morning another soldier was sitting on the steps in front of the main, a middle-aged man with light brown hair and a reddish mustache. He ignored me as I went inside. At breakfast, the story passing from table to table was that Mr. Van Vuuren, our art teacher and former-South African commando, had happened on a sleeping soldier on our steps, perhaps the kid I saw. He proceeded to slip the rifle off the guy's lap, unload the clip, put the rifle back, and wake the soldier. As the soldier snapped to attention, Van Vuuren handed him his bullets and walked into the main. One guy even claimed that they were real bullets! That seemed crazy! Live ammo in our village – they must have been blanks – or maybe Van Vuuren just popped the rifle's empty clip and returned that to the soldier. That made more sense!

My guess was that this was Van Vuuren's idea of a lesson for the solder, but it started something all together different. The students started picking on soldiers they caught walking or sitting alone someplace. An occasional snowball knocked off a hat or hit them in the back. Then a couple of soldiers were "accidentally" knocked down, rifles and all, when they passed between groups of our guys. Things really got out of hand when a group of our guys who were coming back from drinking at the Messange caught one of the soldiers walking up the road and bodily flipped him over the railing and down the steep snowy slope beside the restaurant. I was amazed that the soldier managed to keep his cool after that. In fact, it was amazing that there had been no retaliation on the Swiss' part. I reflected that those stunts would be unbelievably dangerous if those rifles really were loaded.

The following morning, classes were delayed, and everyone was asked to stay in the dining room after breakfast. President Arnold, the Gut, got up on the stage and was joined by rat-faced Dean Zagier. Both wore very serious expressions. They stood silently waiting for everyone to quiet. Then President Arnold said simply and forcefully, "I don't care who is doing what with the Swiss troops in our village. I want it stopped, NOW! It is time we declared peace." That statement drew a couple of chuckles until Dean Zagier stepped forward and scanned the room with a searing expression as he tried to identify the individuals who found that funny. The laughter died in mid breath. "These people are here for very serious business, and there is no place for your foolishness. IS THAT CLEAR?" I and the guys on either side of me started reflexively nodding our heads. Some of the girls looked a little puzzled, especially those who hid in the dorm. I wondered if they even knew about the invasion. The soldiers were pointedly ignored after that, and the guys went back to their usual amusements – drinking, *zim-zim*, and... more drinking.

Chapter Twenty Nine

LAS Governor's Cup

Kaeti and I had continued our giant slalom practice after school each evening. By the end of the second week after spring break I was matching if not beating Kaeti through the same course. Bernd even stopped to watch our progress one afternoon but didn't offer any advice. Kaeti mentioned that he had asked about me later and she told him that Bennie had shown me the new style and it seemed to be working for me. My next surprise came from Bernd. He actually came up to talk to me. He explained that there was one last race on our mountain: the LAS Governor's Cup, which the American schools sponsored each year. He wanted me to begin training with the team. At first I was thrilled. He had finally recognized me as being on the team, and I felt like I could wear my sweater without any ribbing. But then he laid his cards on the table. He wanted me to show everyone on the team what Bennie had been showing me. This concerned me because I'd lose any advantage that I had gained from this new style. However, I talked it over with Gil and Kaeti, and they reminded me that I would still be skiing in "C" class so I wouldn't be competing against anyone else on the school's team. Then it was fun! I was really making some good runs, and I had a style that none of the others were able to mimic. Each had spent too long in the old style. Bernd was the first to start understanding the theory behind it; but in spite of the stopwatch, the style wasn't as aggressive and it just didn't give him the same adrenal rush as the old style; so he stayed with what he knew. With me, it didn't matter. I was getting the rush just running the courses with the team.

Finally, the day of the LAS Governor's Cup Race came. It was cloudy and warm – not good for skiing! The snow was crap! – more slush than real snow. This day the more advanced classes started first while the snow was still cold. By the time the "C" class was ready, the slopes were torn up. I was wearing my team sweater, but it was wet enough that I wore it under my ski jacket. The race consisted of two runs on slightly different courses. The racing order would be reversed after the first run to make up for the fact that the course would get more torn up as more skiers ran it. I would be skiing next to last in the first run; twenty-three of the twenty-five other skiers in my class would go before me. My number for this race was lucky thirteen! I wasn't that nervous as I waited for my first run. The course was set up on a slope that I knew like the back of my hand. Kaeti had placed second in her heat, and she had given me a kiss for luck. I had blocked her last good luck kiss from my mind...

The start was steep but not as steep as the downhill. I got in a couple of skates for speed before I began a wide turn for the gate. I was outside the tracks of the other skiers on cleaner snow as I leaned back and kicked my legs out to increase my speed. A deep trench in the gate caused me to slam down in my tuck as I cleared the first gate. The trench had been dug in the slushy snow by the turns of the twenty-three other skiers ahead of me. My long swinging turn took me to the next gate and into a second trench. The impact was hard on my thighs in that position, but I held it. But by the sixth gate, I was starting to feel sharp pain in my thighs as I crashed into the trench; and by the seventh, I had rocked forward to ski the gates like everyone else. I just couldn't hold the tuck that long taking that kind of a beating. I finished with a respectable time, but I was in the middle of the field and nowhere near a medal.

The second run was different because I was the second skier. I could see the path of the person who had skied first, but I took my own route. I skied long turns, leaning back and kicking my skis forward through each gate. There was no trench to trash my thighs. I was running smooth and strong. Lord knows what the skiers behind me would think of my path, but it didn't matter to me – I was flying! God, this was fun! The wind was ripping across my face, I was holding my tuck, what could go wrong! I found out in the last two gates and the finish line.

They were set up in a long gooseneck to the left across the face of the slope. The first one was easy, but I didn't have enough pressure on my edge to get to the right spot on the second gate. I took that one a little wide and knew that centrifugal force, and the fall line of the hill were going to carry me to the right of the finish line and outside the course. I stood and tried to throw my weight forward on my edges but lost my balance in the process. As I started to fall, I leaned uphill on the wrong ski and spun around backwards. I remained upright but passed across the finish line backwards then flopped onto my side in a jumble.

I was sick when I took off my skis and walked into the crowd. Several were laughing – at me. What a fool I was for even trying! Kaeti came up and gave me a hug. I tried to shrug her off, but she held on. "What's wrong?" she asked.

"I screwed up again! Yeah, I know, at least I didn't end up in a hospital… Shit!"

"You went across the finish line backwards… so what! You still finished!"

"Does that count? Am I still in the race?"

Gil came running up, and he heard my question. "Sure as shit! You're in first place!"

"What? How the hell could I be?"

Kaeti explained, "Your combined times are great! Now we just have to wait to see how the others do, but remember the course is going to get rougher and rougher as more skiers run it."

We waited. The next skier wiped out in almost the same spot where I had started to loose it. The following skier beat me and put me into second. The next skier knocked me into third, but that was the last good run. The remaining skiers either skied slower through the trenches or were tossed out one side or the other. I held third place. I had earned my sweater!

That evening I was positively strutting in my ski team sweater as I walked into the high school dining room, where they were to hold the awards ceremony. Kaeti and Gil had their sweaters on, too. Each of them had a gold medal won during another race pinned in the center of their chest. The dining room was long and narrow with an elevated stage set up at one end and row upon row of chairs facing it. The wall that faced the street was lined with windows. Kaeti, Gil, Wilds, and I found seats about midway to the front and near the window side because three of us would have to walk to the stage. I was initially worried about that, but Kaeti assured me that I wouldn't have to speak. We'd just walk up, grab our trophies, and return to our seats. I made Kaeti promise not to do anything that would embarrass me during the ceremony. She turned it back on me. Not that I was even considering it; I was really excited!

I examined Kaeti's gold medal as we waited for things to begin. It was engraved on the back with her name and the event, Slalom. She explained that she had a couple sweater medals, but loved this one because she beat one of the female Swiss junior national team members in that race.

The event started pretty much as we expected. The first-, second-, and third-place skiers in each race and category were brought up as a group. Plaques were handed out, and we returned to our seats. Kaeti and I sat close and exchanged brief kisses as we returned from the stage. No one noticed us. I asked the group if we would get sweater medals. Gil said that he didn't think they were going to have any. I was really disappointed. I loved the way Kaeti's gold medal looked between her breasts on her team sweater. I knew that mine would only be bronze, but what the hell!

Gil said, "You know, I almost forgot. I've got a competitor pin for you from the *Semaine de Ski*. It's bronze color, I think. You could wear it as a reminder of both races!"

"Gee thanks, Gil… Wait! That might not be such a bad idea! I could even get it engraved on the back like Kaeti's. Interesting…"

I thought the show was over when the next stage started. It seems that this was the last race of the year and the annual ski awards were to be handed out to both the American high school and college. The event started to turn dull and boring as they went through a dozen or so high schoolers: best downhiller, best all-around, best... *Snooze City* until Bennie got up on the stage.

"As always, ees my privilege to award zee skier 'oo made zee most advancemoont thees year. Thees year one young lady showed enormous skeell and determination *dans* zee class. She was always weeling to try new theengs and to learn from 'er mistake. Mademoiselle Louise Sherman" *Hey cool*, I thought. *I could have a shot at this award for the college. I might get two awards tonight!* Louise walked up to the podium. She was short, nicely rounded, especially her cute derriere, and her cowl of dark hair made her look like a younger sister of Spyder's girlfriend, Carole. I caught a sharp elbow in my ribs. "Oooof, what?" Kaeti was giving me a dirty look. *I guess I paid too much attention...*"Its Bennie" I blurted.

"Uh huh." She replied sarcastically. *Kaeti jealous? I've never... She's never reacted like that before. Maybe I did watch too long, but that high schooler is no competition – she should know that! – shouldn't she?* As I returned my attention to the stage Bennie was kissing Louise on both cheeks.

When the college awards started, I fell back into boredom as Bernd was called to the stage for more than half the guys' awards. But when the girls' turn came Kaeti began running to and from the stage. It was great! She deserved it! I gave her hand a squeeze each time. But when she was called up for "Best All-Around Female Skier," I couldn't contain myself. I hopped up as she returned, grabbed her, and kissed her in front of everyone. I was so proud! She, on the other hand, was bright red and pulled me down into the seat.

"We promised no messing around!" she said harshly under her breath.

"I'm sorry, I just lost it!"

When Bennie approached the podium for the second time, I was both excited and afraid. Afraid that I had my hopes up too high..."Again, ees my pleaseur to make thees next award to zee skier who made zee most advancemoont thees year *dans l'*college. Thees gentleman ees truly a pleaseur to 'ave known. 'e is so strong and courage zat I suspect FRRRENCH blood flows in 'is veins." *Cool compliment!* "Many of you 'ave train weeth me and know my favorite espression, 'You are no' learning eef you are no' falling!''e 'as some grrreat falls!" The crowd started laughing. Kaeti and Gil were glancing over at me. Wilds was staring with a silly grin. *This can't be happening!* He continued, "I did no' see but 'e rrreadily a'mits to ending up in zee top of a tree when 'e first start skiing." *The top of a tree! That wasn't me. Who talked about that? Was that the Turk?* "But my favorite ees when 'e falls and slides 'ead first down zee slope ending up at my feet, and 'e says 'Still learning!'" Everyone was in stitches! *Damn! It is me. I'll never live this down.* "You weel all know 'im by 'is spectacular *fini* to *le Semaine du Ski* down'eell. We thought zat we 'ad lost 'im." The crowd quieted with that. "But 'e come to me with neck in brrrace and 'e ask me to teach 'im to RRRACE! When I say 'why?''e say 'I promise a woman.'" Kaeti gave me a shocked but delighted smile. "'e ees a Frenchman in 'eart! 'e 'as grrreat promise and I 'ope zat 'e continues to learn, Monsieur Jeem 'enderson!"

I walked to the podium among laughs and cheers. Even the high schoolers had joined in the merriment. I spotted the dark-haired Louise staring at me as I passed. She was probably happy that she hadn't gotten the same embarrassing introduction. *Well, if you can't beat them, join them!* I thought as I walked onto the stage, threw my hands over my head and bowed deeply. As I approached Bennie an errant thought raced through my mind, *if he tries to kiss me on both cheeks, I am going to punch him!* Maybe he sensed my concern because he put out his hand instead. *Thank God!*

The crowd quieted as I walked back toward my seat. Kaeti stood as if to let me pass. But as I did she grabbed me with one arm at my waist and the other behind my head, planted a lip-lock on me, and tried to bend me over backwards! I resisted, grabbed her, and pressed back against her. We end up wrestling back and forth for a few seconds until we blew the kiss apart as we erupted in laughter! The audience was back in stitches, and we sat down hiding our faces in our hands and laughing so hard that we were crying! Without thinking, I raised my hand over Kaeti's head, perhaps to push her head down or muss her hair; but, as if reading my mind, she shot me a glare that said 'do that and I'll break your arm.' My arm jumped back of it own volition, and we broke out laughing again. Wilds had seen the whole exchange and had fallen off his chair and was laughing and pounding a fist into the chair ahead of him as he sat wedged between the two rows of chairs. I quietly took Kaeti's hand into mine and caressed it. She squeezed mine back. *So much for no embarrassing stunts!*

Chapter Thirty

Le Palais Montreux

The weeks after the awards ceremony were amazing! Everyone seemed to know my name. I was invited to sit with Bernd and the studs at Le Nord. They picked me to join their *zim-zim* competition. People I hardly spoke with let me use their left over pinball games as they headed to get another beer. And when I was waiting for Kaeti to close up, the girls in the snack bar would call me by name and invite me to join them. However, our rich southern princess, Nonni, apparently thought my name was Jeem and was surprised to learn that I was just an American army brat named Jim. For the most part, it was nice. Kaeti was busy, and I had new people to talk with. What could be better! I will admit that I had missed Kaeti's snack bar close up one evening as Stallone and I challenged Bernd and Cliff to a grudge match. I was only minutes behind her, but she was gone. I paid for that one the next evening. She didn't need my help until I begged.

That weekend brought another rude surprise when she asked me if I knew there was a formal dance the following weekend in Montreux.

"Wow, you're right!" I said. "I forgot! We are going to have such a great time!" *It would be awesome! The dance was to be in the ballroom of a palace or something.*

Kaeti looked at me with a questioning frown. "We are? Are WE going?"

"Of course!"

"Have you forgotten something?"

Oh no! Mind reading test! What did I forget? It's formal – Flowers? "I haven't been to many formals – any formals! What am I forgetting, a corsage? Yes, what color is your dress? Do you have a favorite flower?"

She smiled at that but kept a serious look. *Okay, I'm squirming!* "I'm sorry! What am I forgetting?" I asked.

"Have you asked me?"

Whoa! No I hadn't, but I hadn't remembered until you reminded me. But we're a couple now. Who else would I ask? Almost pleading, "Please, Kaeti, will you be my date to the formal?"

"I'll have to think about it…"

Oh, no! Kaeti wasn't like this when we were friends – was she? Is this a test? How do I…? What should I…? My mind roiled while my body was frozen in shock.

Then she added, "Blue."

Blue? BLUE!! "Geez! Okay a white corsage or pink?"

"Not pink! White… maybe…– No, white will be great!"

"True love," I blurted.

"What?!" Kaeti responded with a shocked look and a questioning smile.

"Oh sorry!" I smiled, embarrassed. "I told you about that character in the flower shop in Germany 'red roses for passion and white for true love' didn't I?"

"Oh, okay, yes, and you got some off-color rose. Maybe you should be looking for that here…"

"No, white's good, or red?" I popped my predator smile.

Shaking her head, "White definitely, for a while."

I turned, kicked my heel against the floor like some spoiled kid, and started to walk away slumped over with my hands in my pockets. I got about two steps before I looked back over my shoulder to gauge the effect. I got the smile I had hoped for.

I went back for a kiss, which I got, with some fained reluctance. Then as if she just remembered it, "Jim, don't worry, I'll wear flats."

Ouch! That hurt! What could I say? – do? I noticed the step down into the snack bar behind her. I grabbed her hand and walked around her, then I stepped down onto the lower level. I reached up and took her face in my hands. I brought her head down to me for a lingering kiss. "I think I can handle you in heels. I love you, remember. Wear what you like."

That drew a big smile. "Okay."

That week on the ski slopes was sloppy! The snow was too wet by the time we got off school, and the further down the trails we went, the more rocks and grass was showing up. We continued to ski the top, but we skied carefully down each evening. Then the Saturday of the formal was warm – slightly above zero C on the top – and the sun was intense. Luckily the sun didn't reach the snow on the north face or it would have been gone. The remaining areas of snow on the Chaux de Mont that had not been destroyed by landslides were melting to the stones. Kaeti and I had to strip to our nylon turtlenecks to stay cool. I wished I wasn't wearing my thermals. Cliff showed up on his skis in a tux that I assumed he had rented for the formal. *That's pretty cool!* – then Spyder and Carole showed up in shorts and t-shirts. *Unbelievable! Spyder doesn't have the legs for shorts. He looks like a stork! – but Carole in really short shorts isn't bad looking... Good thing Kaeti isn't around to catch me staring. I don't need another elbow in the ribs.* I had taken a couple in the ribs or sharp warning glares earlier this week in the snack bar for no reason that I could identify. After all, I was only killing time talking to people while I waited for her to close up.

As I caught up with Kaeti, it hit me – *I haven't rented a tux!* I shouted, "Troubles!"

"What?"

"I haven't rented a tux. I thought you could wear a suit to the dance!"

"You don't need one. Cliff's just showing off. Besides, I doubt that you could rent a tux anywhere on this mountain."

"Then where...?"

"He probably owns that."

"He owns a tux! Who owns a tux?"

"More money than good sense!" she said with a smirk, and I laughed.

"You can say that again, Man! I thought I was in trouble. How does this place keep doing that to me?"

"Don't ask me. Maybe you're just too innocent! Let's get back to our mountain while she still has her white dress on!"

"What? Oh, I get it. Let's go!" *A little slow on that one – trying to come up with a response to the innocent crack.* Kaeti headed down the mountain early that afternoon – she needed time to get ready. I skied until I barely had time to shower.

That evening I wore my shiny black mohair suit with pegged legs from my high school graduation, a white oxford-cloth button-down shirt, and an inch-wide dark blue tie with a tiny gold and iridescent blue Roman Legionnaire cameo tie tack, and I carried a small white corsage box. Kaeti came down the upper part of dorm steps in the gossamer blue dress with short puffy, almost transparent, sleeves that she had worn to the Association party. Her hair was fanned out and flowing down her back like a veil. *She is extraordinary! It's like there are three Kaeti's: my girlfriend, a ski buddy, and this goddess. I'm not sure that I deserve this one...* As she turned and came down the stairs toward me I noticed that she had decided to wear flats. I blocked her on the last step and started to reach up to her with my free hand, but she caught it and stepped down. "Don't be silly!"

"Just trying to say you still can go up and put on your heels!"

That brought a crooked smile. "I'm more comfortable in these. You just want to see if I can walk in heels without tripping."

"Yeah!" I said quickly like I knew what she meant. *I hadn't thought about that. Heels must be a pain to walk in. Dancing can't be that much fun either. Maybe her first comment wasn't a put down on my size.*

Having never done it before, I found pinning the corsage with the three white sweetheart roses a little awkward. Not that I hadn't been there before, but we were in front of everyone, and I didn't want to stick her. Kaeti acted very trusting as she held her chest forward, but I could sense a little nervousness at my clumsy attempts. Her putting on my white carnation was a breeze, like she'd done it many times before. *Oh, well! I wasn't her first and won't be her last.* My brain said that, but my stomach turned over. Anyway, my lapel was several layers away from my skin, so I wasn't in quite the same peril.

As we walked down to the bus, I said, "I love that dress!"

"Thanks!"

"I loved it when you first wore it."

"You remember?"

"How could I forget?" I flashed back to that moment. "I guess that I hadn't really thought about you as a girl – or woman until I saw you come down in that dress."

"Really? You didn't think I was a girl? What did you think?" Then teasing, "Are you in the habit of dating people who aren't girls?"

"God, no! Sorry! I thought about you as a friend – a... a tomboy, I guess."

"A tomboy?!" she replied with a hurt look.

"Hold it! I've always liked tomboys! They understand guys better, and they like to do the same kind of things! How many other girls here could have taught me what you did?"

With a rye smile she asked, "Just what are we talking about here?"

With an embarrassed laugh, "Skiing... mostly! How many other girls are on the ski team – and can outrun half the other guys?"

"Half! Hah! Three-quarters, at the very least! Yeah, I guess I am a tomboy, but not tonight!"

I scanned her from head to toe. "Definitely, not tonight! You're beautiful! How do you get your hair to look like that?"

"It's not easy, let me tell you! It takes hours to dry, and then brush!"

Climbing into the bus and sitting in formals seemed a little strange. *We should have been riding in a limo or maybe a sleigh, if there were enough snow.* As we pulled off down the mountain, Kaeti whispered, "Don't say anything about my wearing this dress before. It's a real 'faux pas.' Formals are to be worn only once, but I don't have that kind of wardrobe, and, unlike most of these girls, my folks aren't rich."

"Neither are mine. Besides, it's really pretty, and being practical is very Quakerly!"

"Oh? Would the Quaker church approve this dress?"

"It's called a meeting. – but – yes, it comes below your knees, nothing shocking is showing... The color's bright, but I've seen pale blue skies like that, very natural! This Quaker approves!" That brought a shy glance from under the sweep of her hair.

The Palais Montreux wasn't a palace – or if it was generations ago, it wasn't anymore. It was a grand, old hotel built with massive stones. The bus couldn't get in the drive, so we had to walk from the road. As we approached the main entrance, several cars were pulling in the drive. Prince Paul and his latest fiancé stepped out of the embassy limo – body guards first, of course! The next limo held Cliff, Stallone, and their two dates. Cliff's tux didn't appear wet. *Maybe he owns two – one for skiing!* Stallone just had on a black suit, like me. In fact, with a few notable exceptions, like Cliff, most of us were wearing suits. Issa and his wife showed up in his MGB MkII. Finally, Willie drove up with his date in a black sedan. Kaeti caught me staring enviously. "Don't worry about it!"

"How'd they get cars?"

"Rented, probably, but it's okay!"

It isn't okay.

I caught Willie in the line to get into the ballroom. "How'd you get the car?"

"I rented it for the day."

"Where? How?"

"Here in Montreux. I took the train down this morning and will return it tomorrow." Kaeti was giving me a little disgusted look like I was making a big deal out of nothing. *This isn't nothing – this is pretty cool! I'll know better next time,* I thought. *I heard about another formal just before the end of school on a boat. Maybe I should ask Kaeti tonight so I don't forget!*

The line into the ballroom was taking forever, and I didn't know why until I neared the front. President Arnold and someone I assumed was his wife, Dean Zagier without his wife because Dr. Zagier had already committed herself – *probably due to living with him* – and several other faculty were in a line greeting everyone as they entered the ballroom. I flashed back to seventh grade cotillion. Our parents dressed us up in white sport coats and bow ties, and forced us through this kind of reception line, then forced us to dance with strange girls in party dresses! *Holy crap, that's a memory I'd just as soon forget!* To gain admission to the ballroom we mumbled pleasantries to the President. His powerful grip reminded me of his athletic prowess – in spite of his tubby looks. I even found something nice to say to the dean as I asked about his wife.

The ballroom was impressive! High ceilings with chandeliers, heavy curtains hiding portions of the walls, sconces, a large wooden dance floor with a raised stage, and instruments ready for the appearance of a band. Tables complete with white linen tablecloths, silver, and stemware. Each had a bouquet of flowers in the center. After the reception, the line took us to a small bar set in an alcove. "Aperitifs" were offered. I had no clue what that meant, but we were offered a choice of red or white Martini and Rossi vermouth. Kaeti took red, and I took white. She won! Hers was tasty and sweet, mine was nasty! – but I drank it without – verbal – complaint. Kaeti shared hers so I could get the taste of mine out of my mouth, but she wouldn't try mine, especially when she saw my expression at each sip.

The meal had several courses, from soup to dessert, and each course had a different glass of wine. Kaeti tried each wine but left most of her glass for me – if I wanted it. Most of the wines were nice, but a couple were too dry for my taste, and the desert wine almost curdled my teeth with its sweetness. I was so glad they brought that out in a special tiny glass! Oh, the main course was some local fish. Now, I'm not a big fish eater. I worry too much about the bones, but this stuff had a creamy white dill sauce that made me forget my fears. Unfortunately, that's when they brought out the driest white wine – and they had stolen the glass that held the last of Kaeti's former wine... Dessert was a flan – or custard with burnt sugar on top. I'm not much of a dessert-eater, but liked the bite of the burnt sugar with the cool, bland custard. It made a neat combination of flavors.

As the dinner ended, the band – or orchestra – started to tune up. I say orchestra because the musicians were in tuxes and looked rather like they had just come from a concert hall. Then the music they played wasn't anything that a teenager usually listened to. Most of the students just sat around and complained about the music, but a few of the couples, like Kaeti and me, made the best of it. The fastest thing

they played was a cha-cha, which I was pleasantly surprised to find that
Kaeti also knew. We both fumbled over the fox trot and a few other old
dances, but it was fun! Waltzing with Kaeti was always fun – but some
of these tunes demanded long flowing, ballroom steps – like Cinderella,
and occasionally I held Kaeti tightly and swung her off her feet. She
smiled and laughed like a little kid when I did that! It had probably been
eight years since I had tried any of this stuff, but we sailed over the dance
floor like we took on the ski slopes! *Who cares if we aren't perfect! This is
fun!*

The evening ended too early, and it was back into the ignominious
bus. As we drove out of town, I spotted Lac Léman and remembered
my earlier mistake. "Hey, Kaeti, before I forget. Will you be my date to
the formal on the boat?"

"Aren't we getting a little ahead of ourselves? That's almost two
months away. A lot can happen during that time." That turned out to be
prophetic…

"I don't want to forget again! Besides there's no one else I want to be
with."

"Let me think about it."

"Dress color?"

"Let me think about that too. I can't wear this again…"

"It wouldn't bother me."

"The society police would get me! I noticed one of the girls was
looking at me like I had two heads. I suspect she knows."

"Who cares? I had fun!"

"Me, too!" On the way up the mountain, we sat cuddling and
necking in our seat. *Maybe a bus isn't so bad!*

Chapter Thirty One

The Stones

Near the end of the following week I ran into Wilds. He popped his head out of his room when I came in after school. He called to me, "Hey, haven't seen much of you lately!"

An odd comment. I've been here. "You know… Kaeti and I…"

"Yeah, want to get together for *zim-zim* later?"

"Sure!" *I guess that we haven't gotten together much lately what with all the attention I've been getting after the awards.* "Damn, you're right! Let's go get a beer right now and play a game or two, my treat!"

"Sounds great!"

On the walk to Le Nord, Wilds asked, "Have you heard about the Rolling Stone's concert?"

"No! What about it?"

"They're coming to Zurich in a couple of weeks, and Jolie's checking with his dad to see if he can score tickets."

"Serious! What kinda pull would Al Jolsen have with the Stones?"

"No idea. Maybe they have the same manager. I just know he's going to try to get a bunch of them, and it's first come - first serve. I've already reserved a ticket!"

"Cool! How much? I need to find Jolie!"

"They might be free. I think Jolie was headed for Le Nord."

"Outstanding! Let's get there before everyone else has one."

As we entered Le Nord, we saw a group of guys surrounding Jolie. Everyone was talking about the concert. After a bit I managed to catch his eye. "Hey, Jolie, I need a couple of tickets to the concert, too!"

Jolie waved his hand at me. It held a lit cigarette and a shot glass, but he didn't spill a drop! "Sure, Jim! I'll put you down." *Wow! A few weeks ago, I'm not sure that Jolie would've remembered my name – in spite of rooming next to me. That ski award really did buy me some recognition, cool!*

Wilds and I teamed up to be beaten soundly in our first game of zim-zim. A couple of beers later and we were heading to dinner. Plus, I needed to find Kaeti and tell her about the concert. We met at our usual table, and the news poured out, "Kaeti, Jolie's going to get tickets to the Stones concert and he promised me a couple." Then I added with a cautious smile, "Will you be my date?"

"I just heard about it! Of course!" *Oh, now she says 'of course!'* "You got tickets!"

"Well, he promised me a couple."

"I'll pay for mine. How much?"

"Don't worry about it. I don't know. They might be free!"

"You don't have them yet?"

"No, but he promised.

Kaeti shook her head. "Keep reminding him. It's in Zurich, right? How would we get there?"

I hadn't thought about that! "We'll figure something out. Maybe I can rent a car."

Wilds interrupted, "I'll go in with ya!"

"Great, it's the three of us!"

Jolie managed to score almost three dozen tickets for the school. Either Wilds or I stood at his door constantly for the week we were in limbo. We got our three. They weren't cheap, but it was for THE STONES! Willie somehow got the school involved in the transportation and scored a bus for our group. April 14, seemed like it would never come. When it did, thirty of us piled into the bus, rowdy and ready to ROCK 'N ROLL!! The usual cases of beer were piled in the back, and a mere request would send one forward. Kaeti and I were in one row with Wilds across the isle – and we were psyched! THE STONES!

The trip seemed longer than we all had planned, and soon, in spite of my drinking only a single beer, all our bladders were bursting! We appealed to the driver for relief, and he pulled into a rest area along the highway. Unfortunately, on close examination, the facilities appeared to be a narrow stand of trees and bushes beyond a bent-over fence. I and the rest of the males leapt the fence and scattered into the brush. I came back to find Kaeti and the rest of the girls standing and staring enviously. "Come on Kaeti!" I called. "I've an idea." She stepped toward me timidly and looked at the other girls. A few started to walk forward so she joined me. "You said you used to camp with your brother, right?"

"Yeah, but we had a toilet nearby. What's your idea?"

"I'll show you." We walked back into the woods while I scanned for a likely dead fall. I spotted a small tree that was laying sideways about a foot or so above the ground. I lead Kaeti to it, tested it for sturdiness, and then demonstrated how, as a scout, we use to brace our knees against the tree to steady ourselves while taking a dump. Kaeti looked desperate but skeptical.

"I need some... paper." I reached in my back pocket and came out with the Kleenexes I kept for emergencies. Kaeti's eyes popped! "What? How did you...?"

"I was a boy scout, remember? Actually, it's a habit. I have hay fever in the States and never know when I am going to erupt! It's pretty cool here..." I was about to explain about not having any symptoms in Europe, but Kaeti grabbed the Kleenexes and headed for the fallen tree. I turned my back and waited.

A couple of other girls returned from the woods relieved, but most didn't even try. As we reentered the bus, the girls staged a mutiny and forced the bus driver to turn into the nearest village. The place was an old walled city. The bus driver looked nervous as we passed through the narrow passage in the walls. Traveling through the windy interior streets was a challenge. They were built for carriages, and this bus filled both lanes and threatened thousand-year-old walls as it rounded the bends. After a couple of turns we found a hotel, and the girls abandoned ship. Then the bus driver got out leaving the bus blocking the main roadway, and went in search of a place to turn around. Luckily, he found that the road passed through the village and out a gate at the back. The road back to the highway wound through a narrow valley, but we managed to make the whole detour without meeting a single other moving vehicle.

The noise as we entered the concert hall was deafening and electric! French, German, Italian, and English speakers shouted for attention and for the sheer excitement of the event! Our tickets took us to a stage-height platform that was between the lower and upper rows of seats. Joined sets of folding chairs had been set on this wide platform for our group and several other VIPs. We were about halfway back from the stage, so we obviously weren't the prime visitors, but the wide platform offered an unobstructed view of the stage and unlimited legroom!

The noise in the auditorium rose another ten decibels when the warm-up group took the stage. It was so loud that you couldn't hear the band, and it didn't sound happy. Everyone wanted the Stones – not these pretenders – whoever they were. At first the crowd's shouting thundered off the walls and then it became more unified into some kind of chant. The cacophony was focused in two loud blasts that I had to assume was an international version of "We WANT the STONES!" But it sounded like a frightening rendition of "ZEIG HEIL!" from some Nazi war film. Kaeti and I were more that a little spooked at the anger in the crowd. Then the crowd below and on the sides of the stage began hurling cups and trash at the pretenders. Their performance didn't last long, but this crowd really didn't need any warm up – it just needed the STONES!

The stagehands took only minutes moving the equipment around, and then the Stones came out with THUNDER AND LIGHTENING! Mick Jagger, Keith Richards, Brian Jones, Bill Wyman, and Charlie Watts on drums!!! No, I didn't know anyone except Jagger, but Wilds had them all down. He was dancing and floating even before they started playing. The show went something like this. I might have added or missed a few:

The Last Time

Paint It Black

By *19th Nervous Breakdown* the crowd was insane! People on the floor had pushed the chairs out of the way and were dancing in a mob. Again the crowd was so loud you almost couldn't hear the band! Our group was standing on our fold-up seats dancing and singing! From the floor beneath the stage one nut in the dancing crowd stood on another guy's shoulders, jumped up and grabbed the banner hanging from the stage, then started crawling up the banner toward the front ledge. It was a wonder the banner hadn't torn! As the climber neared the top, two bouncers on the back of the stage ran up and looked down at him. Apparently noting the distraction of the bouncers, someone on a platform like ours at the far side of the hall jumped to the stage, ran across, and grabbed Mick Jagger by the long tails on his yellow jacket. I'm not sure what he was trying to do. Probably get the jacket as a souvenir. But he succeeded in lifting Mick up by his coat tails and throwing him face-first into the stage. You could hear the "OOOFFF" in the mike as Mick landed! He wasn't lip-synching! One of the two bouncers ran back, threw the attacker to the floor, pinned his hands behind his back with a knee, and took out handcuffs or a rope or something. At the same time, the climber had just poked his head above the stage floor only to be pushed off by the other waiting bouncer. His fall into the crowd had to be almost two stories, and he wasn't going down feet first! Hopefully someone broke his fall! Both bouncers joined together to drag Jagger's attacker off the stage into a back entrance and returned only a minute later. Mick had hardly missed a beat!

Lady Jane

At *Get Off Of My Cloud* someone from the row behind us got angry at our standing on our seats, came up, and started pushing people. Wilds, Kaeti, and I got down, but I was kinda pissed! Then he caught tiny Ting around the waist and pulled her bodily off the chair. I missed the next song as I launched myself over the row of chairs into the isle where he was holding struggling Ting! I almost cleared the chairs, but my trailing foot toppled the set of four and sent them crashing to the floor. I landed fine, but some of my steam was gone. The tubby, middle-aged guy who held Ting had released her by then, but I moved toward him, fists clenched, unsure what to do next! Stallone had also vaulted the chairs, successfully, and he pinned the now frightened little man's arms behind his back, waiting my arrival. Now, steam almost gone, I cussed-him-out in German, French, Spanish, English, and a few languages that I made up on the spur of the moment, then motioned for Stallone to release him. Upon release the poor little guy shuffled quickly back to his seat.

The song that I missed had just finished by the time Stallone and I set up my row of chairs.

Ruby Tuesday followed.

Let's Spend The Night Together

By the finale, *Satisfaction*, we were back on our chairs singing and dancing like nothing had happened.

It was dark, and we were fatigued as we crawled into the bus and curled up in our seats. Kaeti was unusually quiet, but so was I. I relived the incident with the little man several times. I wondered what had happened to my pacifism. *If I hadn't knocked over the seats, would I have hit him? Probably! What he did was bad, but not enough to deck him. How did I loose my control?* I suspected it had something to do with the crowd and the noise. *Crowds push people to do things they wouldn't otherwise do, like lynch mobs.* Suddenly Kaeti interrupted my self-examination. "Why did you do that?"

"I don't know. I just lost control…"

"Why her?"

Why her? Why who? "Huh?"

"Why'd you protect Ting?"

Okay, I'm on a different page here… "I don't know. She seemed so small and helpless. That guy just picked her off the chair. I don't know…"

"Why not me?" she asked with a touch of resentment.

Oh, God, I'm lost! "You what?"

Getting angry now, "Why didn't you come to my defense?"

"When? Why?"

"That same man pushed me off my chair! Why didn't you care about that?"

"What?! When?"

"Right before that! He knocked me right off, and you ignored it!"

"I didn't…" *He had kinda pushed us both a minute or two before, but we got down on our own, I thought. Besides, Kaeti could have decked that little guy on her own.* "I didn't see that. Sorry!"

"You like her, don't you?"

"Who, Ting? She's nice, but she's dating Robert."

"And if she wasn't? Besides, you sit with her all the time at the snack bar while I'm working!"

Now that is exaggerating. She calls me over occasionally when no one else was around. "A couple of times maybe, but I'm killing time waiting for you."

"And you can't come up and sit at the counter with me."

I'd been doing that before the awards thing…"But you're busy." *Dumb, not a good time to justify myself!*

"NOT THAT BUSY!" *Damn, I think that she just woke half the bus!* We lapsed into a smoldering silence after that – I was smoldering ashes, she was smoking! – I squeaked out, "I'm sorry" two or three times on the remainder of the trip, but I might have been sitting alone for all the response I got.

When the bus stopped in front of the school, Kaeti pushed her way over me and moved quickly out the door and up into the dorm before I could follow.

Chapter Thirty Two

In Hell!

The next day, Kaeti sat with other girl friends at a full table each meal. That evening I waited patiently at the snack bar counter for her arrival, but she ignored me and went straight to work. I stayed there like a lost pup for the evening and ignored the others who invited me to join them. She didn't talk to me all evening. She did put a glass of coke in front of me, but I hardly touched it. At closing, it was obvious that "everybody out!" included me. As everyone left I suggested, "We should talk."

"Not now! Time for me to clean up!" *No subtle hint that!*

The next day was worse. Kaeti had a circle of friends guarding her from me. That evening she didn't show at the snack bar. I had no clue what I had done wrong! *How can I fix something without understanding or talking?* I went to Le Nord and had a few too many beers, then staggered to Hell House and stood on the balcony in the cold staring at the stars – hoping for a miracle, a shooting star, or something. Nothing happened. I began to think I wouldn't have a chance to make it right and that it was finally over. I cried myself to sleep.

My dream that night was frustrating. I was crawling through internal windows in some maze-like building. I didn't know where I was coming from or going. I just wanted out. When I escaped the building, I fell out a second-story window and got hung up in the brambles that surrounded it. I couldn't move. I woke the next morning with an understanding that I couldn't do anything about whatever had happened. I couldn't even figure out why I was to blame. Whatever was going to happen had to come from Kaeti. I joined Wilds for breakfast and went through my day like Kaeti didn't exist. I drank too much at Le Nord and actually lost my way back to the frat house five blocks away. I found myself on a dark street that didn't look familiar in a village where

I had just spent the last six or seven months. After a while I saw the bowling alley where Kaeti and I had spent so may happy hours, went in, and had another beer that I didn't need.

The next day I woke with a miserable hangover. I had not had one like this for months. I took a couple of aspirins and tried to drink some tea before going to class. While in my first class, history I think, the sunlight from the window behind me crossed my back. At other times it might have felt warm and comforting. In this case, I broke out in a sweat, my stomach flipped, and I ran from the room without permission. Luckily the toilet was just across the hall. I held myself over the toilet for a couple of minutes but didn't loose it. I was a little light-headed, so I sat on the floor and tried to keep from passing out. The room was on the back of the building, so it was underground and very cool. I started feeling better fairly quickly. I went to the sink, splashed cold water on my face but stayed inside until I heard people changing classes. I joined the crowd and went to my next class. In the French room, I traded seats with someone so I could stay out of the sunlight. Instead of going to lunch I sat out on the steps in front of the main in the cool, fresh air, thinking. *I may be going through hell, but I need to watch how much I drink. Why the hell is Kaeti doing this?*

After a long while Kaeti walked up behind me. "Are you okay?"

"Yes!" I snapped. *No thanks to you! Why are you doing this to me?* "Can I help you?" I asked with even more edge.

Kaeti looked stung. "I think that we need to talk."

"I said that a couple of days ago!" I spit out venomously, got up, and walked down the hill toward the frat house. Half way down the cow path, I wondered why I was so angry. I went up to my room, skipped classes, and spent the rest of the day on my balcony watching the sun change the shadows on les Dents du Midi. For dinner, I grabbed a couple of croissants and hot tea at the Parisienne. My stomach still didn't feel right. *No beer tonight!* As the sun set I returned to my room and sat in the dark.

After a while a knock at the door roused me. Through the door Wilds asked, "Jim, are you in there?"

"Yes."

"Can I come in?"

"Sure."

Wilds walked in, "Damn, you got any light in here?"

"Sorry!" I flicked on the light by my bed and asked, "What's going on?"

"That's what I was going to ask you. What's happening?"

"Kaeti."

"What about her?"

"If I knew, I could fix it but I don't."

"Should you talk to her?"

"I tried. She ignored me."

"She wants to talk now."

"Did she send you?"

"Yes."

"Why didn't you say so?! Where is she?"

"She said you'd know."

The snack bar, I guess. "I'd know, huh?!" being obtuse. "Where is that?"

"God, don't get me into this. The snack bar, probably!"

"Yeah, I know. Sorry! It's just... I don't understand."

"Well, Jim. Skiing's over now. Maybe it's just withdrawal symptoms, or her time of the month! What do I know about women? I should be so unlucky as you!"

"I'm sorry, Jim. You're a good friend! We don't need you messed up in this. I guess I'll go see what she wants. Thanks for coming."

I walked quickly up to the main but entered an obviously closed, dark snack bar not knowing what to expect. I was beginning to wonder if she was even there when she spoke softly from our couch in the shadows. "I'm keeping it dark, so we aren't interrupted."

"Okay," I said cautiously as my eyes adjusted to the light coming from the jukebox. I sat timidly on the couch beside her. She slid away a bit. *Bad sign!* As she started speaking I realized that I couldn't see her eyes. I wondered if she had done that on purpose.

"I'm having troubles with this – us." *Oh, no! Not a good start.* "I need to get my head on straight. I didn't think it would be this hard." I stopped listening. *It was over!* Her sentences rang hollowly around my head. "I don't know how you do it! How can you be so sure? – Sometimes, I can't stand being with you!" *Damn, I don't need this. I'm glad it's dark.* My eyes were starting to well. "I don't mean that! It's me… my problems. It's just that I worry… I can't explain it." *I need to leave before she sees me crying.* "Can we take a little break so I can figure it out!"

"Sure! I gotta go!" I said hurriedly. "Let me know, okay." *That's crap! She's trying to make me feel better by blaming herself, and she's giving me some hope so I won't do something drastic. No woman is worth that!* I wiped the tears clinging on the corners of my eyes and walked out into the hall, leaving her in darkness.

When I returned to my room Wilds was waiting. *I really don't want company now, but…*

"How'd it go?" he asked concerned.

"She dumped me! I hate her!" *God, my eyes are starting to fill again!*

"She wanted to talk to you just to dump you? Does that make sense?"

"How the hell should I know?! Fuck'n girls!" I kicked my chair into the desk. *PAIN! My foot!* "SHIT!! OOoow! DAMMIT!!"

"Geez, Jim, cool down! Hey, if you don't want her anymore, can I have her?" *He's joking to cool me down. That shit isn't working on me tonight!* My body got hot, and flames shot from my eyes toward him. "Maybe I better go!"

"Good idea!"

"Yeah, you really hate her," he mumbled to himself as he walked out the door.

I do hate her! No, I don't… I… Shit! Make up your mind! I walked out into the cold on the balcony and started searching the skies for a miracle. *I don't hate Kaeti. I love her, but I have to get over her. Hatred has worked before… But, somehow I want to still be friends. Impossible! NO, its not! What's that political theory? Shoot to the opposite extreme and return to the middle, 'dialectic' something. Why in hell am I thinking about politics now?! Jean and I were friends by the end of high school. How did that work? Time,*

I guess... Is there enough time left here? I can't wait five minutes! I returned to my room and got into bed. It was hours before my mind stopped arguing with itself, and I fell back into the same building I had crawled through in my dreams the night before – or was that two nights ago. Dreaming wasn't providing any relief or solutions!

I spent the rest of the week in a coma – eating meals, sitting in class, grabbing a tea at the Parisienne after school, and retiring to my room. I couldn't focus on anything. Class and homework were not getting done. My grades were crashing from my Dean's list honors of last term, but I didn't care. Wilds checked in each night to be sure I was alive and to talk about something funny that had happened during the day. He helped a little. *He's a good friend...* I began to dread the approach of the weekend. *Skiing is done; I have nothing to do – except catch up on homework – Fat Chance! It would be a void!*

I got up late on Saturday and walked to the Parisienne for tea and a croissant. I sat on the second floor looking out and up the mountain. A couple of other students were there, but they were giving me my space. The sun got higher, and I traded a tea for one of the small beers they served there and another croissant – just watching the wind blow through the trees. I reminded myself not to have too many beers today. *No hangovers tomorrow!* A patch of dark hair blocked part of my view. I drew my focus inside on a dark head silhouetted against the window. My eyes adjusted to the dimness inside. "Like some company?" The face was cute, young with too much eye makeup – although the eyes had kind-of a Cleopatra look. Her hair was black and cut in a short cowl, like Spyder's Carole. *She looks familiar...*

"Hi. Do I know you?"

"I don't think so. I'm Louise. I'm a senior at the American high school. Can I sit?" she asked quickly as she moved to sit on the window-ledge bench.

"Sure." *Louise? How do I know that name?*

"You were at the ski awards. You got the highest achievement award for the college," she said and added brightly, "I got it for the high school!"

The memory flooded back to me, complete with watching Louise's cute derriere and Kaeti's elbow in the ribs. "Louise, of course! Hi! Can I buy you a –" I looked down at my beer. "– a coke?"

"A beer would be good."

"Are you sure? Is that allowed?"

"Sure, besides no one comes down here."

"Ah… Okay."

I hopped up and ran downstairs for another small beer and croissant. When I returned, my chair had been moved around to the side of the table closer to Louise. Her dark eyes were watching me walk toward her. *There's something more. I remember seeing her around the village lately at odd times in unusual places.* "I took the liberty of getting you a croissant. They're good, and it helps to have something in your stomach when you drink beer. Have I seen you down here lately?"

Her eyes flashed and she smiled, "Yes, did I say I was a senior? I'm thinking about coming to college here next year. I just wanted to see what it was like." *Oh, damn! A new innocent for the slaughter,* I thought as she took a big pull on her beer. *She seems to know what she's doing.*

"Stateside schools are better for academics. This place has a library the size of a coat closet."

"My parents work for the State department in the Netherlands."

Figures! "Well, you know the skiing's great. But watch out for the guys…"

"Oh, I can handle the guys!" she said with a sly smile. Her dark eyes sparkled with mischief. *Nice eyes!*

"I'll just bet you can. But these aren't high school guys. In fact some of these guys are…" *What do I say? – experienced? – studs? – turds?* "Well, just be careful! A word of advice. Don't try to be the most popular; just be yourself. If you can find a friend, someone to ski with, maybe – who doesn't pressure you to do things you don't want." *God, where am I going with this?! I don't know this girl!*

"Are you coming back next year?" she asked with an expectant look in her eyes!

That question brought me back to reality; sadly I said, "I don't think so."

"Are you all right? Why not?"

"Oh,… I'm a… sophomore. I… graduate this year."

"But aren't they planning on making it a four-year school soon?"

"They're talking about offering junior courses next year, but I need to get back to a real college."

"What's wrong with this one?"

"Academics…"

"Enough about that," she said suddenly and took another big gulp. "That's so depressing. What attracts you to a girl?" *Holy crap! That's scary! Where'd that come from?* "I like a guy's chest – well, not his chest exactly – sort of here." She reached over and ran her hand down my right side from just under my pec almost to my hip. *Whoa! That wasn't a tickle exactly, more like a caress, and it was certainly stimulating!* "Do you have the small muscles here on your ribs?" she asked as her hand again brushed across my lower ribs.

Gulp! She's coming on to me! "I guess, ss…sure!" I stuttered. Her eyes were too dark for me to see what the pupils were doing, but the sparks in her dark eyes flared as they opened wide. Her tongue peaked out for just an instant to moisten her rose-pink lips. I gazed at her neck under her ear, then scanned down to her round breasts. *Much fuller than Kaeti's. – God! Kaeti! I can't do this! Besides, she's a high schooler – senior or not.*

I stood quickly, "Sorry, I've got homework to get to. Nice meeting you! Remember, make a friend first!" *Not that this girl is going to have any problems!*

Before I could get to the stairs, she slugged the rest of her beer and called, "Wait, I'll go with you."

To Hell House? Man, she's brave! "Sorry, no girls allowed in… the men's' dorm." I lied. *Maybe that isn't a lie. Rumor was early in the year a couple of guys were kicked out for having girls from the English finishing school in their rooms. I could see being caught with a kid from the American high school. What am I thinking!*

"Well then, walk with me back up to my school."

"Ah… I really need to get to my…" furiously trying to come up with an excuse "– history! I have a research paper due Monday."

She tilted her head forward and looked under her dark bangs, her rosy lips pursed, "Please."

Damn! "Okay. But I need to get right back."

On the way past the main, Louise asked, "What are you researching?"

Damn! "Ah… the…" *What the hell are we studying in history now? The European Economic Community – no that's my audit course – Well, okay.* "I'm comparing the EEC to the ah… U.S. during the confederation!" *Quick thinking!*

"Really? I thought you said the library was small. Where are you getting your information?"

Holy crap! She's no dummy! Lucky I have an answer. "My econ professor has his own library. He's really into it."

"Interesting! Do you do lots of research papers for your courses?"

"No, this is my first."

"Bad luck it's this weekend."

"Yeah, I was kind of putting off getting back to it. I guess I should thank you for giving me a shove." *Whoa, that's a stupid thing to say!*

"Mmmm…Just let me know if you need another shove," she said, moving against my side and pushing gently against her favorite area of my ribs again. "I'll be around until June." *Pheeww! This little lady is trouble!* The remainder of the walk, we talked about skiing. She had almost as many stories as I did. It surprised me that we hadn't met in the top of a tree one day. My story about my downhill crash, the doctor, and the humpty-dumpty dream had her laughing so hard that she was tearing. *I don't remember it being that funny.*

When I dropped her off at the high school she turned, leaned into me, and looked up for a kiss. My arms automatically went around her waist. It was interesting looking down into her dark eyes and rosy lips. There was something kind of small and vulnerable about her like this. *With Kaeti I would be looking straight into her eyes. Kaeti!* I brought a hand up and touched the tip of her nose. "Sorry, I have a girlfriend!"

"I know," she said with a mischievous but very sexy smile. My body started to react, so I held her away, but she slid back in running her hands over my butt and pressing her hips, solid stomach, and full chest against me without embarrassment. *I'm embarrassed!* "I can tell you like me!"

Wow! This is a high school girl? I need to back out! "Sorry, but I have to run! Nice getting close to you – I mean, ah… getting to know you, ah… Louise! Later!"

"Nice getting close to you, too. Any time! I'll be around." Luckily I didn't run into anyone I knew on the way back down to Hell House because I wasn't able to get control over myself until I got there, if you know what I mean. That fantasy stayed with me for a while, too!

THE AMERICAN COLLEGE OF SWITZERLAND ZOO

Chapter Thirty Three

The Princess and the Dwarf

After the episode with Louise, I really did study. She had done wonders for my ego! Then after studying I vowed to find a way back into Kaeti's heart! I needed advice, but who could I turn to? Wandering the streets that evening thinking – trying to come up with a plan – I found myself within a few blocks of the Vagabond. *What about Bennie?* I wondered. *He's a Frenchman. He's got a cute wife! He should know about women!*

I was nervous as I entered the Vag since I wasn't escorted by Willie, but no one challenged me. I guess that I had been here enough that I was recognized, and they knew that I wasn't a troublemaker. Bennie was at the bar talking to a couple of guys in French. He spotted me as I walked to the bar and ordered a beer. "Monsieur Jeem! 'ow are you?"

"Good! I see you have a beer. Can we talk?"

"Certainly!" He made excuses to his friends and we retired to a booth. "But skiing ees over! 'ow can I 'elp?"

"Its Kaeti."

"Your girl?"

"Yes, she dumped me!"

He shrugged, "Eet 'appens!" *Man, I don't need that!* Reacting to my expression he said, "But you two were so good together! 'Ow can I 'elp?"

"I don't know… I need her."

"Love, she ees no always so simple. Tell me."

I described as much as I could remember of the night she dumped me. "Was she angry or sad?"

"Sad… and angry, too!"

"Thees ees good. She 'as feelings! Did she cry?"

"I couldn't tell. It was dark." *I was crying.*

"She meet you in zee dark so you no could see 'er face?"

"Yes, is that important?"

"I think, maybe! And before zat, 'ad you done something bad to 'er?"

"No! – Well... she thought I did." I described her jealous rage on the bus back from the Stones concert. "But I hadn't... I couldn't even think about anyone else."

"Jealousy, thees ees very good!"

"How can that be good?"

"She would no burn eef she were no een love!"

"But why dump me?"

"Maybe, she no dump you."

"I was there!"

"Maybe she 'urts inside. Maybe she knows no where thees ees going." Then looking carefully at me. "Where ees thees going? Weel you marry 'er?"

Marriage! Marriage? "No, I can't... I'm not old enough! I mean, I need to finish college and get a job and... why marriage?"

"Woman think a lot of thees."

"Can't you be in love without thinking about marriage?" Bennie shrugged. *Maybe I'm a nut! I move too much! I know things just have to end!* "If things were right,... If I were ten, maybe even five years older... with a good job, yes, I'd marry her. We fit! But not now, I can't."

"'ave you two made love?"

"No..."

A bit of astonishment escaped Bennie's face. "No? Why no?"

"We plan to save that for marriage."

"Oh, I see!" shaking his head in disbelief. "Zen maybe ees good it ends now. You weel only be sad later. School ends soon."

I won't accept that! "No, I don't care! If we can just be together, even as only friends! Don't you know some way?"

"Zen fight for 'er! Woman love thees! Be 'er prince! Sweep 'er from 'er feet!"

Yeah, right, I sweep Kaeti from her feet! Almost shouting in my frustration, "I can't! She's Cinderella! I'm not the prince! I'm... one of the seven dwarfs!"

"Seven what?"

"Nothing!" *God, I'm even mixing up my fairy tales!* "Thanks for trying, Bennie." I shout back over my shoulder as I walk toward the door.

Bennie calls to me, "Jeem, zee way you ski together say more zan zat!" *Whatever that means!*

Walking toward the steps to the lower village, I passed the dark window of the flower shop where I had bought Kaeti's corsage. *Flowers! – Kaeti had said something about flowers when she was with Tiny. Tiny forgot to get her flowers or...– No, he helped me with flowers for the twins over Christmas, and she got upset – that's it! I forgot that. Women love flowers, and I never got her flowers! I should have thought of that. Would that do the trick? – couldn't hurt! I'll try that tomorrow...*

Sunday after breakfast I had a mission! The stairs behind the school were the quickest way to the upper village. I started to walk, but... *I hate walking steps – boring! In fact, I'd rather run!* I started a slow jog and quickly found myself sprinting! *Damn, it feels good getting some exercise again! – stretch it out and breathe!* The top came quicker than I remembered from last fall. *I must be used to the altitude by now.* Everything seemed closed as I walked into the upper village. The same was true of the flower shop; its door was locked. *Damn!* I found an open patisserie just up the road, ordered tea and a croissant, and sat down to wait. I walked back at 9:30, and the shop was still closed, so I went back into the patisserie and asked the owner. The flower shop wasn't open on Sunday. It was open through the week and Saturday from 8 to 4:30. With school out at 4, I'd have to sprint up to make it after school. Walking back down the steps, I wondered, *how would I deliver the flowers? I don't want to take the chance of rejection, and I don't want to embarrass Kaeti. Best bet is to leave them like a secret admirer would, but, short of leaving them in the snack bar, I need to find someone to sneak them into the dorm. Who'd do that for me? I know a couple of girls from the snack bar, but I'd have to find someone who won't make Kaeti more jealous. I'm pretty sure that Colleen would do it for me, and she should be safe. She has a steady guy – then again, so does Ting. No telling what would set Kaeti off! – what had set her off? – Jealously is good according to Bennie. – Geez, I don't know how!*

I hung around the main that afternoon, avoiding being seen by Kaeti and looking for Colleen but had no luck. Shortly before supper I ran into Kathy at the entrance to the hall that led to the classrooms. We'd talked a couple of times at the beginning of the year but not much lately. She was from Richmond, Indiana, and knew of my college there. She had been pretty impressed that I went there because she understood that they had a reputation for high academic standards. However, my mentioning being on academic probation spoiled her first impression. I suspected that Kathy was one of the dorm hiders because I hadn't seen her at any of the hangouts for several months, if ever. She was at the snack bar occasionally and seemed to be friends with Kaeti, although she hadn't said much to me when I was there. Kathy held herself like a snoot, but that might have been a defense mechanism for the upper crust coeds because she had been friendly at the beginning of school. She had shoulder length dark hair, intense blue eyes, and a round face. In fact she was round all over – not fat but definitely not athletic. In fact, while I believed that she was in the beginner ski class last fall, I hadn't seen her the slopes since then.

I caught her eye as she walked toward the hall. I started to ask about Colleen, but she beat me by asking about Kaeti and me. She was concerned. I told her that I was determined to win her back and asked for a girl's impression of my plan. "You want to secretly give her flowers? That sounds wonderful! Can I help?"

"Sure! I was…" I almost asked her if she knew where Colleen was, but you could see the excitement building up her round body to her eyes! "– hoping that you'd offer!"

"I'd LOVE to do it!" She looked around furtively and led me into an unoccupied classroom. Inside came a torrent of questions. "What kind of flowers? How many? Do you have a vase? Where are you getting them? When will you get them to me?"

I just stood there with my mouth open. *I hadn't thought of any of this. Flowers were the plan!* "Whoa! Slow down! Roses – Ah… the flower shop in the upper village is the only one I know. I'll have to run up after school."

"Run up?"

"Yes!"

"Ooookay?!" She looked skeptically at me. "Have you thought about how many?"

"A dozen of whatever they have, I guess. What would you suggest?"

"Well, not that a dozen is bad, but you don't want to overwhelm her. Then again, you don't want to be too cheap! Hmmm... Why not try this – three flowers a day for a few days instead of one large bouquet. That way it will surprise her each night, and she'll wonder what's coming next."

Laughing, I said, "Perfect!" I went forward to hug her, but she backed away a bit.

"Now, the problem is when," she went on. "If you get them after school we could meet by the front door just before supper. I'll sneak them up to my room. Hmmm..." Her eyes brightened with excitement! "Oh, this is perfect! My room is just up the hall from Kaeti's. I can watch until she passes headed for dinner and sneak them into her room, then go down before supper starts. Good plan?"

"Great plan!" *Cool! Someone is smiling on me today!*

Monday after school I sprinted up the stairs and caught the florist getting ready to close up. We talked for a while. The only large roses he had were red. I wasn't sure about that symbolism just yet. He did have a collection of sweetheart roses in red, white, and pink. I had hoped for some other colors, but beggars can't be choosers! We worked out a plan. I'd get three white today, then pink tomorrow. I knew that Kaeti wasn't really into pink, but I didn't want to push the red right now. I wanted friendship first... The florist said he'd try to find some other colors by Wednesday.

I hopped down the steps with the three white roses and some greenery in a bud vase. It was the closest I'd come to skiing for weeks, and the excitement added spring to my legs! I had a plan! Kathy was waiting in the front lobby as I peaked in the door. She spotted me and rushed out. She was as excited as I was! She grabbed the vase and scooted back inside.

Immediately after dinner I caught Kathy by the stairs up to the dorm. "What'd she think?"

"Are you kidding? I took it up right before dinner. I don't know if she's seen them yet."

"You're right. I can't wait! Let me know tomorrow, okay, when I bring the next batch!"

"Okay."

The next day I bounced down with the three pink sweetheart roses and transferred them to Kathy. "What'd she think?"

"I don't know. She hasn't talked to anyone about them."

That was a little disappointing. "Okay… See what you can find out tonight."

"Okay, but I don't want to get caught. I think its better to surprise her!"

"You're right."

After supper I didn't spot Kathy outside the dining room, so I started to head back to the dorm. However, by the main door I heard "Psst, Jim!" come from the alcove that had the phone. Kathy peaked out and motioned me inside.

I checked up the stairs and walked into the alcove. "What? Did you find out anything?"

"Well, she didn't throw the first ones out!"

"That's good, I guess…"

"Better than good! I put them on the desk, and she moved them next to her bed!"

"Nice! That's good, right?"

"You bet! Tomorrow we'll need a larger vase."

"I'll see what I can do."

"No, I'll get it. There's a lot of them around the dorm." I gave Kathy a hug that she didn't resist and snuck out of the alcove. *It's working!*

Wednesday, the florist hadn't found any other color roses. Red it was – I prayed it wouldn't send the wrong message! As I met Kathy she sighed, "Those are beautiful!" *Maybe red isn't so bad – after all they are just roses!*

After supper, Kathy caught me by the phone alcove again. This time she was standing outside looking a little down. "She caught me. She knew the roses were from you but didn't know who was delivering them. She really likes them but asked me to give you a message. She wants more time."

More time! "Damn!"

"No Jim, I don't think it has anything to do with you. I think she really likes you. She just needs time. Just be patient with her, okay?"

"Have I got a choice? Should we stick with the plan?"

She bit her thumbnail and looked up the stairs. "I think so. She really loved the red sweethearts!"

Thursday, as I entered the flower shop, the florist was beaming. A shop at the bottom of the mountain in Aigle had a new variety of sweetheart rose. He went to the cooler and brought out three amazing roses. The petals were white with deep red edges. "Wow! I'll take them!" They were almost double the cost of the others, but they were worth it!

I hid them behind my back when Kathy approached and brought them out with a flourish. "Ewww, Nice!" She said with a kind of confused look on her face. I expected a bigger response! *Maybe she's seen these before. I sure haven't!*

As she took them, I asked her to take a message to Kaeti. "Tell her that she has all the time she needs. The flowers are just to remind her that I'm here and don't want to loose her friendship. – Does that sound good?"

Kathy hugged me. "Perfect!"

Friday and the florist had sold the other variegated roses, so I bought three more red. Kathy took them up, but no messages came down…

That evening I caught up with Wilds at Le Nord. We teamed up for *zim-zim* and beat a couple of teams before getting trounced by Bernd and Stallone. As we headed toward the bar I caught Wilds. "Hey, lets go find a good beer! My treat."

Wilds looked around questioningly. "Have they got a Scottish pub nearby?"

"No! German beer, it's the best! Do the Scots make beer?"

"Yeah, there's a brewery in Glasgow that puts out some great swill!"

"Well German beer isn't swill, and I know where we can find some."

We hiked up the road past the main to the Messange and went into the bar. I ordered a couple of German beers from the bartender as we sat down. "This stuff is export beer, like the stuff we got in Paris, so it isn't as good as you'll find in Germany but it is great compared to Feldschlösschen!" As I turned, I found that Herr Dietrick had brought the beers personally. He usually stops by later to see who ordered the beer, but I guess he was pretty bored, too, after ski season. He shook my hand and slowly asked, emphasizing keeping the verb in the English order rather than the German, as I taught him, "Vere IS Kaeti?"

Kaeti? He knows her first name. I wonder if he knows mine... "She's not here... to...tonight."

He must have read my expression, or maybe he just overheard my conversation with Wilds about export beer because he put the bottles he brought down behind the bar and said. *"Bitte!* COME with me upstairs. I a real *Deutscher bier g' ah...* have!" Looking at Wilds, "Your *freund?"*

"Yes, this is Jim."

"Jim? *Ach,* but you ARE Jim, *ja?"*

Cool! He knows my name! "We both... are Jim."

"*Ach, Gūt!* Heinrich." He introduced himself as he shook hands with Wilds. *Heinrick Dietrick! Someone had a sense of humor. Not that I understand the German sense of humor.* "COME!" he ordered.

We went upstairs, and behind the restaurant entryway a door led to another set of stairs and an apartment above the restaurant. Herr Dietrick went into a small compartment in the wall that didn't look refrigerated and pulled out three full-sized bottles of beer. Keeping one for himself, he handed the other two to us. I was amazed to see the label. Bellheimer Silber Pils! "I know this beer! It's made near Landstuhl, where I live! How did you get it?"

"I remember! The military hospital vere you're *Vater* works, *Ja?"*

"*Ja.*"

"I HAVE a *freund* who near there... lives. With him this *bier* he... ah... come."

"Great! Wilds, you won't believe this beer. It is soooo smooth!"

"Vwileds?"

"Oh, I'm talking to Jim. Wilds is his last name, sorry!"

"*Gūt*! Vwileds, you will this *bier* like!"

We flipped the tops and took a drink. It was cool, like the apartment, but smooth.

I said, "This is the closest beer to root beer I have ever had!"

"*Rōt bier*? Red, ja?"

"*Nein*, its an American soda, like Coke. Roots, like the bottom of a tree." I stuck my fingers down attempting to imitate the roots. "The soda is made with sassafras ROOTS."

Wilds exclaimed, "Jim, this is good! Does all German beer taste like this?"

"*Nein*, in my home *besser*... IS better!"

"Jim, we need to visit his home!"

"*Fasching* IS soon coming. In *Fasching*, I... go."

Wilds asked, "*Fasching*?"

"I've heard of it," I said. "Its like October Fest except in the spring."

"Cool!"

"*Ja*, Spring! Many girls to *Fasching* come... COME to *Fasching, ja*?"

"I'm ready!" Wilds announced holding his beer high.

Many girls, I thought. *I only want one girl...*

"Come, music!" Herr Dietrick announced as he went to an old boxy record player and searched a stack of 45-rpm records. "Here, I have HEARD you play this many times."

"Love me, Please Love me!" comes belting out of the single speaker. *Damn! Not now*! Looking at me, Herr Dietrick asked, "You no *g'* ah... like?"

Wilds explained, "He's having some girl problems."

"No, no it's fine..."

"This *besser* is... and in German!" He put on a second record, and the Beatles singing *"Komm gib mir deine Hand"* (*I Want to Hold Your Hand*) came belting out.

Wilds said, "Whoa! I heard that the Beatles played over here someplace. I haven't heard them in German before!"

"*Ja*, German!"

I added, "Tony at my boarding school somehow got a copy of this back in '64 before the Beetles were anybody! This is great!" We nursed our beer and listened to some interesting music, most of which I didn't know and probably wouldn't want to hear again; but it was pretty cool being invited into Herr Dietrick's apartment. He didn't offer a second beer. We shook hands and headed off after about an hour.

As we walked down toward the main, Wilds asked, "What's happening with Kaeti?"

I explained talking to Bennie and getting Kathy to take flowers up. "I don't know what else to do."

We were in sight of the girls' balconies by then. Wilds looked up and suggested, "What about a serenade?"

"Can't sing! Besides, she's way up there on the fourth floor. I'd wake the entire dorm before she'd hear – and embarrass the crap out of both of us! Besides, she wants me to wait."

"I wasn't serious. Wait for what?"

"No clue... You know that song Dietrick played is our song."

"Kinda guessed that."

I realized that I wasn't going to ever hear that again when I headed back to the states. *Herr Dietrick's collection... How could I get a copy of that record?* "Hey, I need to run back to the Messange!"

"Why?"

"I need to get a copy of our song for Kaeti! That way she'll have a copy and can listen to it and remember me."

"Does she have a record player?"

"I'm talking about later, after we're back in the States."

"Are you sure that's such a good idea?"

"Sure!"

"Well, I've heard of a big department store in Montreux that has everything."

"Man! Maybe Herr Dietrick knows someplace closer." We went back. He didn't – Montreux was it.

I needed to find a ride to Montreux, but only Issa had a car, and he was hard to find. Robert had just rolled his motorcycle out from wherever he had hid it for the winter. "Let's try Robert!"

"I'm not sure he'll let you after destroying his helmet. Besides, you'll freeze your butt off getting off the mountain!"

"Hey, I've got ski clothes!"

"Then you'll melt in the valley!"

"Forget you! I'm asking!" *Maybe Wilds is being contrary because he wants to go along.*

Wilds went up to his room. I found Robert studying in his room. *I need to do some of that this weekend, too.* "Robert, can I ask a favor?"

He turned from his desk with his big black-rimmed glasses. "Ask!"

"I need to get to Montreux tomorrow to buy something. I wondered if I could hitch a ride."

"Don't know – don't have a spare helmet anymore!"

I hope he's kidding! "Yeah, sorry about that. I'll buy you another as soon as I get some money from my parents."

"Kidd'n. Kinda feel like I saved your butt!"

"You did!"

"Sure, tomorrow I was planning on taking it out and loosening it up. Dress warm!"

"Sure thing! Thanks! What time?"

"How about after breakfast?"

"Great! Thanks again!"

The trip off the mountain was COLD and fast. Robert's Matchless had four gears, and he ratcheted back and forth through all of them as we sped down the curvy road off the mountain. The valley was warmer, but the ski jacket helped break the wind. When we hit the highway north of Lac Léman, he opened it up. We were tooling! As we passed Château de Chillon, I saw the steel tracks that seemingly led into a rock wall. The surface of the wall was smooth and looked like the side of the Matterhorn at Disneyland, where I rode the bobsleds. *I guess Willie wasn't kidding. Something is going on inside this hollow mountain.* I thought to ask Robert about it, but we went by so fast and the cycle was making too much noise.

Robert dropped me at the department store and said that he was going for a ride. He'd be back in an hour, maybe. He suggested, "If I don't make it back, the train is just down this road."

"Hey, I've got enough money for the one-way fare. You take off and have fun!" The sun was intense down here, so I took off my jacket and tied it around my waist. It was like summer! I pushed up the sleeves on my shirt and still felt hot.

The record department was great! I found our song and got two copies, one for me and one for Kaeti. Then I found a half dozen other records that I had to have. Unfortunately, I had only enough money for three more. I picked my favorites, paid, and asked for directions to the train station. I got almost three blocks when I realized that I had spent my train money on the records! *Now what? Well, I hitchhiked in the States between my college and my boarding school. Besides, Willie had hitchhiked from Geneva to Paris in the snow. It's a glorious day! How hard could this be?*

I started walking east out of town on a city street with lots of parked cars but not many moving ones. I figured that I'd have to walk to the highway before I'd get picked up. I did walk on the road, just inside the parked cars, and kept checking back, just in case. I heard a noise and turned to stick out my thumb when I realized it was just a moped, or motorized bicycle. I waved, and we both got a laugh! By the second moped, I was pretending that I really wanted a ride just to see what they would do and to get a laugh. One lesson I learned in the States was that people would give a happy hitchhiker a ride a lot faster than a passive one. When I thought I saw a third moped coming over the rise, I stuck out my thumb only half looking while trying to dodge a parked car. The thing that thundered by wasn't a moped! I followed the growling motorcycle with my eyes as it rolled to a stop about a half block down the road. The rider turned on his bike and motioned me forward. Cool!

I sprinted up to the bike, stuffed my records inside my T-shirt, and hopped on. Only slightly cautious, I told him I was going to the next town, Villeneuve. I didn't know the guy well enough to put my hands on his waist so I grabbed onto the seat. The motorcycle was different from Robert's. It had a tiny sweptback windscreen that the driver couldn't get behind unless he laid on the gas tank. It also had short handlebars that didn't go outside the windscreen. I was looking for a marking that would identify the type of bike when the driver popped it in gear and sped off. Sliding backwards, I grabbed his waist to stay on the bike! We cruised out of the city at fairly high speed then hit the highway. He dropped it to second when we entered the highway. He wound that out, then third screaming, then fourth! We were flying. I was a bit scared, but it was terrific! Suddenly something hit my left foot and clattered to the ground. The driver hit the brakes and squealed to a stop in the middle of the highway, throwing me into his back. He looked back down the road, spun around, and sped back to whatever had dropped. He picked up what appeared to be a chrome electronic horn, stuffed it into the pocket of his leather jacket, and then spun back around.

This time from a stop he lay down on his gas tank and burned rubber, leaving me choking in the stink for about a millisecond before we flew forward. My hands clutched his leather jacket since I couldn't reach around his waist anymore. He caught rubber in second and screamed into third. By fourth I was ready to scream! He wound up fourth so tight that I thought that he was going to blow his engine, when he did the unthinkable, he hit fifth! I was screaming! Not that it was doing any good because my screams were only audible a half mile behind us! We were flying! I lay against his back. My world narrowed to the thin red "X" he had across the back of his white helmet. My ski glasses were floating on my face, and I was sure that I would loose them but didn't dare release my grip on his jacket. My jacket, tied around my waist, was snapping in the wind so loudly that it sounded like it was going to tear. My jeans were flapping so hard against my legs that I was certain they were going to be bruised. I couldn't feel my records under my shirt. *They must be lost! It doesn't matter; all that matters is survival!* We started to hit traffic, which, I prayed, meant he had to slow! Instead, he pulled onto the double yellow line in the center between the east and westbound lanes and started passing everything! We roared by a red sports car, something I had never done or seen done in Europe before! The seam in the middle of the highway made our tires squirm sideways occasionally, but the driver didn't seem to notice or care.

The trip to Villeneuve only took a couple of minutes, but I aged a lifetime. My legs were shaky and I was trembling when he dropped me at the side of the road. I checked my clothes and found the records had migrated to the small of my back. My legs and face stung! Staggering backwards, checking to see if I had all my clothes while trying futilely to straighten them, I noticed the red sports car coming up and half-heartedly stuck up a thumb. I heard it purr to a stop on the road behind me. *Damn!* I spun around. *It doesn't have a driver! There's a shock of blonde curly hair in the passenger's seat.* The passenger turned and waved me forward.

The car was an older Triumph with the top down. It had British right hand drive, but I automatically walked to the right side. "Hop in!" came from Brigitte Bardot! – *No seriously! Blonde, cloudy blue eyes, pouty pink lips, in a pink sundress that I could see right... down... the front... and she wasn't wearing a bra! Damn!* "Hop in, please! – Do you need a lift? – Are you feeling well? – Do you need help?"

I swallowed and shook my head like a dog sprayed with a hose! *Damn!* The accent was French, but she was speaking English like Brit. "I'm sorry! Yes, I need a lift, please!" I ran around the car to what should have been the driver's side.

"You had me a bit frightened for a moment. Are you certain that you are feeling well?"

"Yes, just a little dazed. I just got off a motorcycle."

"Yes, I saw you. That was quite dangerous. You should tell your friend to drive with more care."

"Not my friend! I needed a ride, and he picked me up. I don't even know the guy."

"Goodness! That must have been quite exhilarating!" she said with a pixie gleam in her eyes!

"You can say that again! Nice wheels!"

"It's my... friend's. He's from London but has a chalet up the Rhone Valley from here."

I reassessed her as she pulled back into traffic and continued to talk. She was thirty-something but very cute. She had nice smile wrinkles starting at her eyes and beside her lips. She didn't seem to mind her curly hair blowing in her face as she sped forward, and she obviously knew how to run through the gears. It was strange seeing her shift with her left hand. Her dress was so light that it seemed it would blow away with the next gust of wind coming into the car, although she occasionally tucked the bottom of the dress under her legs against the seat as it started to blow up. Intently watching the action, I suddenly realized that she was asking me something. "I'm sorry! What did you say?"

She smiled knowingly, as if I had just complimented her. "Where are you going?"

"Oh, sorry!" *I was saying that a lot!* "Leysin, up top from Aigle."

"I know it, yes. You're American, yes?"

"Yes, how...?"

"Well, your accent, of course, your clothes, and Europeans don't stick their thumb up when seeking a lift. They wave." She demonstrated a side-to-side wave with her hand.

"And that will get you a ride... a lift?"

"Yes, if they are willing. Leysin? Are you from the American School there?"

"The college, yes." *Make sure she hears that!*

"College, of course. Do you know Roark? I believe he is your climbing instructor."

Roark! Of course she would know Roark. Blew that fantasy! "Yes, but Roark's not..." *oh, wait!* "– climbing, yes! He's the head instructor. I worked with Bernd."

"Do you know if he is at school today?"

"I left early. No, but he could be." *Maybe I can get a ride to the top!*

"Let's see, shall we."

"Okay with me!"

The ride up was amazing. She wasn't a particularly fast driver, but she handled the car well. She was talkative, which gave me a reason to stare. She lived in the English guy's chalet year round, but he was rarely there – a couple of months of holiday here and there throughout the year. The car was his, but she used that year round, too. And, if she knew Roark as well as I expected, she had plenty of freedom when the sugar daddy wasn't around. *Interesting arrangement!* It got cooler on the way up, so she cranked up the heater. It kept our feet warm, but you could tell she was starting to get chilled.

We hit the turn across to Leysin before I realized it. I told her to pull to the side and gave her my ski coat. Also, I began to make plans. *This could be a real coup with the guys!* I had her pull up outside Le Nord, and I ran in to check for Roark. Unfortunately no one was in there from the school. Next stop, the Parisienne. A couple of people were there, mostly girls; but they were all upstairs and I wasn't sure they could see anything. When I returned to the car, "Sorry no Roark! Let's try Hell House."

"Hell House?"

"Oh no, the dorm."

"The dorm?"

"Yes,… No,… Ahhh…" *I'm not good at this lying thing!* "He… he's our dorm resident. Makes sure we don't get into trouble, you know!"

"Oh, I see."

We pulled up at Hell House. Several guys were on the balconies to witness our arrival. More came out as we walked inside. *Me in a sports car with a cool blonde who is wearing my ski jacket. Major coup!*

"We should go up the stairs," I urged. "No telling where Roark will be."

We walked into the parlor, where a couple of guys were working out half dressed. "Hey, guys!" I stood aside so they could see who I was with. As we got out of earshot, "No Roark there. Lets try his room. It's right next to mine." We got to the fourth floor and knocked on his door. I peaked in when no one answered, but no one was there. "Sorry!" My knocking brought Wilds out his door. Puffed up, I said, "Jim, meet Bridget...!" *Oh, no!* "I'm sorry I don't know..."

"Collette, pleased to meet you!" She offered her hand.

That was stupid! I didn't ask her name! Idiot! "We're looking for Roark, our... climbing instructor and dorm resident." *Wilds will play along. Besides I'll tell him the truth later.*

"Climbing...? Oh, yes... No! No! Haven't seen him today. Nice to meet you, Collette," he said with a big smile!

We took the elevator down. It should have been exciting closed in that small box with her, but that was when I first noticed her perfume. It had a heavy, musky smell, and my sinuses were starting to burn. *If I don't get fresh air soon I'll be sneezing for the next hour!* I held my breath and began pressing my tongue into the back of my teeth. My eyes started tearing. In desperation, I pushed down hard on the tip of my nose. "Are you feeling well?"

The door opened at that question, and I rushed out smashing my nose into my face and gasping for air! *That did the trick!* "Fine, just allergies." *Stupid thing to admit!* I wiped the tears from my eyes and grabbed a Kleenex from my back pocket for my nose as it started to run.

"Oh, you're allergic to me?"

Oh, that smile! "No, just your perfume. I'm fine. Let's try the main." I regretted it as soon as I said it. *Kaeti's in the main. I'm not here to make her more jealous! Damn!* I pocketed the Kleenex and ran up to check the main on my own. I didn't find Roark and didn't run into Kaeti. As I returned, I helped Collette put up the top of her car, and she returned my jacket. She then left me with a kiss on both cheeks as she sped off into my dreams.

That evening a group of us were standing around on the street in front of the main waiting for dinner. Stallone was passing a football to a couple of guys up the street. I was standing on the sidewalk by the railing talking to Wilds, who was leaning on the railing. I could see the mountains behind him. Les Dents du Midi still had snow on its peaks. Wilds and I had been trying to come up with something interesting

to do after dinner, but nothing novel was coming to mind. Suddenly
Wilds froze with this strange, amazed look over my shoulder. I noticed
the same look on a several other faces as they all pushed off the railing
and stood more erect. At first, I passed it off as Stallone showing off
until Wilds, without looking at me, barked a laugh and said excitedly,
"Jim, I think that someone's looking for you!" I turned to see what
he was talking about and spotted LEGS, long legs, then a blue, maybe
turquoise, hip-hugging mini skirt and a flowered blouse with frills up
the middle to the collar. The blouse had turquoise flowers on a cream
background with swirls of green and light brown. Light brown hair
resting on the puffy sleeves was blowing slightly back with the forward
motion of the wearer. My eyes kept popping back to the legs as I looked
at each new feature until I recognized Kaeti's tan face. Kaeti was in a
mini skirt shorter than I had ever seen before – It was slung low on her
hips and just barely covered her crotch! My jaw was on the pavement!
My brain was stuck in a loop! *What the hell!* flashed over and over in my
mind at each stride. She was pacing toward me, sure and confident on
beige colored heels; each step brought the echo of the heel contacting
the cobblestones. Everyone seemed to be frozen in place staring, just
like me. *What the hell!*

As she stopped inches from my face, I managed to get my mouth
shut and swallowed, but was incapable of speaking. She smelled
wondrously of "Ambush." The mountains behind me were reflected in
her eyes. She was so close that my automatic response was to kiss her,
but my mind warned me, *we aren't a couple anymore. Is this some kind of
cruel game?* Then she leaned in and down, looking at my lips. She turned
her head slightly to the side, as she did when we kissed. Instincts won
out, and I leaned in for a kiss. She joined me, and I crushed her to me.
She then leaned back, as if she were doing a back dip in dancing. This
almost caught me off guard, and I had to step well forward and behind
her to take her weight. The kiss continued. I thought that I heard Wilds
clapping, maybe a couple of others, but the blood was roaring in my
ears, drowning out most sound. I lifted Kaeti upright, and she turned,
took my elbow, moved close against my right side, and started walking

up the hill, away from the main. I followed robotically. My brain still echoed, *What the hell!*

About twenty paces up the hill, she intruded into my confusion, "Dinner? My treat!"

"Sure" was all I could get out.

She continued to walk powerfully on those heels, no slip, no wobble – like she's in a pair of hiking boots. I looked down at the legs, then the heels, and finally back up to her eyes. They were perhaps an inch above mine, but I wasn't really measuring – just trying to comprehend – to read her mind..."Not stumbling on my heels, am I?"

"Nope." My eyes flashed back to her long legs and up to her face. I must have looked like I felt, totally confused. Kaeti just smiled, basking in my stupor. I found myself closing my mouth once again and licking my lips, which seemed unusually dry. My brain started to function again as we went into the Messange. "What's going on? I thought you said this – we were over."

"That's not what I said, but... anyway, a girl can change her mind," she said with a smile.

"Okay..." *I am starting to sound retarded, and she's loving this. I need to find some kind of control.* "I'll pay for dinner."

"No, it's arranged. I'm paying and that's that!" *She wants me off balance!*

As we sat I asked. "Where did you get that skirt?"

"In Paris over Christmas, but I haven't had the nerve to wear it before. Like my legs?"

I chuckled and then exhaled loudly, blowing off some of my tension. "Like them! I think that half the guys in school are going to be dreaming about those legs tonight, and the other half weren't even there! – unfortunate for them!"

"You remember what I asked on our first date?"

"At the Association party or here?"

"Our first real date, here."

"We talked about a lot. What?"

"What attracted you to a girl."

Spooky! "Okay, ah… yes, eyes. Why?"

"I was hoping that you would say legs. I think they're my best feature."

I stared down in the shadows under the table. The way she was sitting I could just see her smooth, strong thighs; and where they came together, I could just make out some white frill on her panties peaking out from beneath her skirt. My eyes jumped quickly back to her eyes. I closed my mouth again. "Whoa! Okay, beautiful legs! And eyes! What can I say?"

The waitress came in with a couple of glasses of sweet vermouth. Starting to find my brain, I toasted her legs, which drew a laugh! A few minutes later Herr Dietrick arrived with the preparations for *Tournedos*, and the waitress began opening a bottle of Moulin à Vent. "Had this planned, huh?"

"Yes, like it?"

"Brings back memories!"

She smiled sweetly. We ate mostly in silence. I didn't want to take my eyes off her for fear she would disappear as I woke alone in my bed. After the steaks, Kaeti finished her second full glass of wine – a first for her in my experience. Then she started softly, "I think that I owe you an explanation."

That brought a broad smile to my face. "Do you think?"

My smile was contagious. "Yes!"

"Okay, I'm listening!"

Her smile faded as she lowered her head. "My boyfriend back home wrote me and–"

"Boyfriend? I…" *Boyfriend! Of course, what had I been thinking!*

"– he wanted me to stop dating…"

Hanging my head "Oh, I see." *No I don't! What's this about? – my last meal! – SHI…*

"Shhhh, please let me finish!"

Okay, just listen. It's worked before. At least I can see her eyes. If only she would look at me.

Almost mumbling while looking down, "I didn't like it. I mean we have something special –" *We who? – me or him?* "– but he shouldn't try to control me."

She looked up at me for an instant. "Besides, we have something special, too." *Me now, I think!?* "It was making me nuts. So I had to take a break – a step back. I didn't know what else to do."

She took a deep breath and sighed before she looked at me again and continued. "But it wasn't..." She searched my eyes. "I wasn't having as much fun... without you. I loved your flowers and wanted to do something, but I was stuck. I didn't know how to make everyone happy – but I figured that life is too short for someone to tell me what I can and can't do when I am thousands of miles away. Jim, I love the fun we have together! I... I wanted to talk to you about it, but I didn't know how to start. I was worried that I'd loose you... your friendship, I mean. I was afraid you'd get mad again. Then today, when you showed up in that sports car with that blonde... well, I knew that I had to do something drastic!"

The blonde in the sports car! That's what this is all about! Should I tell her the truth? That would be stupid! "I have a confession." *I'm stupid!* "I was hitchhiking back from Montreux, and she just gave me a ride back up the mountain. I don't know her. In fact, she's one of Roark's conquests. We went looking for him but couldn't find him. She left. It was nothing."

"Oh, and what about the brunette from the high school?"

God! Did she have spies? "Nothing happened!" *That sounded guilty!* "I hate to tell you this, but there is only one girl on my mind here."

"Who's that?"

"You shouldn't have to ask Kaeti; you've been my friend, my teacher, my... love, – I... there is no way anyone can compete with that!"

The smile on her face seemed to brighten the room for a second. "Thank you for being so patient with me!" *Patient? If only she knew!* "I love the flowers! Can I ask one thing?"

"Anything!"

"Can we take it easier – not so intense..."

Searching her eyes to understand what she meant. *My feelings have stayed the same. She's been the one who's... what?... taken me on this roller coaster!* "What? Do you want to start back as friends?"

"How about right here – last January – the first time. It was such fun then!"

"You've got it!" That brought a smile and a kiss.

Then she pulled back with sparks dancing in her eyes. "Oh, and your not one of my seven dwarfs!"

Seven dwarfs! I drew a sharp breath and pulled back. "How did you...?" *Who was around me at the Vag?*

"Bennie and I are friends. He thinks a lot of you! In fact, you have a lot of friends around here! I was getting all kinds of pressure to get us back together."

Wow! I wonder who else? Do I have friends I don't know about? Then chuckling she said, "You know I got the prince and Cinderella image quickly, but the 'seven dwarfs' thing took a while! Bennie hadn't quite understood what you said."

I started laughing, "Yeah, I was so frustrated that I was screwing up my fairy tales – and in English to a Frenchman!" Kaeti joined in my laughter. "I'm surprised you got there at all!"

She quieted, put her hand on mine, looked deeply in my eyes and said, "You're my Prince Charming!"

"Yeah, right!" *I really can't handle compliments.* I flipped my hand and squeezed hers gently. "I'm no prince. You'll have to find Paul if you want that."

"Yeah, right! I could be his what... sixth fiancée!"

"Tenth, at the very least! But just think what you could tell your grandkids – and you'll get a ring!"

"You're nuts! But I love it!"

"Love!" *Got to be careful here...* "Why don't we just talk about friendship?"

"Cloooose friends!" She slurred a little, tipping her head forward and looking through her lashes toward me.

I smiled, "I was hoping that was still on the menu!"

She leaned in very close my face. I could smell the Beaujolais on her breath. "That was part of what I was missing," she whispered.

That started to get my body's attention. "Control yourself! I think you've had one too many wines!"

"I'll try!" she said as she straightened up and brushed what little there was of her skirt, then added, "Let's see if they're playing our song downstairs!" We headed down the stairs toward the bar.

On the way down, I asked, "How long is this skirt anyway?" Kaeti smiled as I measured it across her hipbone with the span of my hand. *Exactly eight inches, the distance from the tip of my thumb to the tip of my little finger.* "Eight inches! How do you...? Aren't you worried that someone will see your...?"

"The trick is to wear pretty panties!"

"They are!"

"What?" she said, laughing.

"Sorry, but it's hard not to notice!" Instead of talking she leaned in for a kiss in the privacy of the stairwell and pushed one of my hands down to the back of her skirt.

When we broke, she asked, "Are we still on for the formal on the lake?"

"Oh! Yes! – Wait! Now I know the real reason for tonight! Needed a date, huh?"

The punch caught me off guard, and I had to grab the railing to keep from falling down the stairs! Kaeti, realizing what she had done, tried to catch me but stumbled and lost one of her heels. I ended up having to catch her before she fell past me down the stairs. Her lost heel clattered down to the bar level. We ended up laughing in a huddle sitting on the stairs. "Kaeti, you need to learn your own strength!"

With her head on my shoulder, Kaeti said, "This is what I missed!"

I thought of another joke about her pushing me down the stairs but said, "If you will, I can think of a way to keep us... to keep me out of trouble."

"What's that?"

"Will you be my date to anything and everything between now and the end of school? Say 'yes'– and I am not getting ahead of myself. We'll keep it fun!"

Kaeti sobered a bit at that. "I don't like to think about the end of school."

Someone started coming down the stairs behind us, so Kaeti pulled off her other heel; we stood and headed on down. *Maybe Wilds was right. It might not be a good time to give her the record, at least not yet.* I retrieved the heel at the bottom of the stairwell, but Kaeti decided not to put them on and carried them into the bar.

It was almost empty. *The end of ski season did really take the life out of this village! – not that I'm complaining.* We had the dance floor to ourselves and could pick our music. "Love me! Please Love me!" was soon belting from the jukebox. As we went out to dance, we left her heels sitting on the table next to the two untouched glasses and half empty wine bottle that Herr Dietrick had thoughtfully brought down from upstairs. Before the song ended, Kaeti broke into a shocked smile and said, "It would have been funny if we'd both broken our legs falling down the stairs together after ski season!" We were laughing, foreheads touching as we continued moving in each other arms across the floor. Then later, back in the dark snack bar... well, it may not have been as intense as the first time – but it was close and there was less fumbling – no instructions were needed! As we broke apart on the stairs to the girls' dorm, Kaeti said 'yes' to my earlier suggestion about events from now to the end of school. She warned that we needed to keep it light, like tonight, and languorously walked up the stairs knowing that I could see everything from behind – and so could every other date saying goodnight near us. As she turned the corner, she leaned over the railing, let her long hair fall over her shoulders, and held my eyes for an eternity. Then she quickly scanned the other couples, raised her eyebrows with delight, winked at me, and continued her delightful walk up out of sight.

On the way back to the dorm, Gil, who had obviously been half of one of the couples, caught my arm and said, "Jesus, Henderson! That was some show!" I couldn't agree more! I doubt that day surpassed my skiing adventures, but it came close as it circled the rumor mill. I was a God! – for a short while…

Chapter Thirty Four

The Race

Things between Kaeti and me did slow some after that evening. I don't know if it was intentional. Actually, the whole town seemed to start shuttering up after the ski season. It was nice being able to go out without heavy clothes, but it was hard finding fun things to do. At the same time, I was getting more and more excited about the upcoming formal in the boat on Lac Léman, and I wanted to do it right this time! I started making plans for getting a rental car. A bonus of the slowdown was that Wilds and I were hanging out more, playing *zim-zim* and tossing back a beer or two. One evening with Kaeti I asked about finding a date for Wilds to the formal, and we started making plans. A couple of days later Kaeti said that she had overheard Kathy, the girl who had helped me sneak flowers into the dorm, say that she wished she could go to the formal.

"Great, you check with her, and I'll check with Jim. Wait!" I said chuckling. "Wilds is tall and skinny, and Kathy is short and round, won't they look a little funny together?"

That brought a fiery look from Kaeti. "What's wrong with that?! They're just going to the dance together!"

Holding my hands up defensively, I said, "Whoa! Nothing, sorry!" *What set that off?*

Hugging me and leaning on my shoulder, she said, "Sorry, Jim, you just hit a nerve. I went with a guy in junior high until the beginning of high school who was short and round while I was tall and skinny. The teasing we took probably caused us to break up. Ronnie's a really nice guy. We're still friends. He's in the Navy now. He's even written me a couple of times since I got here. You kinda remind me of him."

Short maybe, but not chubby! "I'm the one who should be sorry." Hugging her back. *Hard to think of Kaeti as ever being teased for her looks...* "Wilds and Kathy are both nice. Besides it's just for fun! Let's do it!"

So we started playing matchmaker. It didn't take much convincing to get Wilds to ask Kathy and Kathy to accept. The results were two, if not three fold. The two could enjoy the dance, even if they weren't a couple, and I would get some financial help renting a car.

As the weekend for the formal approached, we got another surprise; the school was invited to send a team to an intercollegiate track meet in Fribourg on the morning of the formal. Kaeti was psyched about participating; she had run sprints in high school. I thought briefly about distance running, but without chasing a soccer ball, I wasn't sure how I would maintain my focus. I decided just to watch and root for Kaeti. A dozen other students expressed interest, so the school accepted the invitation. The next problem was getting the students to Fribourg. Wilds and I had a plan. We'd rent the car we'd planned to use for the formal on Friday and have it ready for the following morning. The other students would have to fend for themselves.

To be sure we had enough time, Wilds and I slipped out of classes early on the Friday before the track meet and the formal. We started hiking out of town, hoping to catch a ride off the mountain. One of the local delivery trucks with a young guy who seemed to know me stopped to pick us up. He had Wilds sit on a metal box in the back and invited me up front. "You ski with the long blonde?" He drew a hand down from behind his head to near his waist.

Known by association! Kaeti's hair is light brown, but the Swiss tend to call anything lighter than medium brown, blonde. But Kaeti hates being called a blonde! "Yes, you mean Kaeti?"

He shrugged. *"Tres beau!"*

"Yes. Thanks!" *I wonder how I know him? Was he the guy who ran the snack bar on top the Berneuse? Had he witnessed our scene up there last month?*

"Where are you going?" he asked.

"Montreux. You?"

"No, Gstaad." He was heading north, so he only took us to the turn to go down to Aigle.

It didn't pay to try walking down the narrow road off the mountain. It was too dangerous and would take us until after dark to get down, so we sat at the intersection for a few minutes waiting for a ride. The first driver sailing down from the north saw us waving, slammed on his brakes, and came to a brake-ringing stop. The car was a tiny gray Citroen Deux Chevaux, the cheapest car that Citroen makes. From the side it was shaped like a hay mound with bulging headlights. The kid inside leaned across and popped open the door. *"Allez!"*

"Sorry?"

"You American? Come!"

"Okay, we - go - to Montreux."

"Bon, I go! Come!" The driver flipped the front seat forward onto the dashboard and Wilds crawled into the back with a thump! "What the...?"

"Sorry, I have no... buy the seats yet." I looked inside to see Wilds sitting on the floor tangled up in what appeared to be the frame of an aluminum lawn chair without the strapping. Wilds straightened around and clung to the sidebars of the frame that I noticed was bolted to the floor. I flopped my seat down. It wasn't much more sturdy, but it did have some strapping to sit on. I reached for a seat belt and found none as the driver sped off. He apparently had 'no buy' those either!

The car had a Spartan dash: a speedometer, a couple of gauges, and a few idiot lights all in one little cluster. The gearshift was also strange as it popped out of the middle of the dash. The car engine sang metallic as the driver ran through the gears. As we picked up speed, the lower half of the door windows started flapping. The windows were divided in half and hinged so the bottom half could be raised to let air in. But it didn't look like they had latches to hold them down. There we were, sailing down the mountain, windows flapping, with Wilds and me hanging onto the seat frames; at least I wasn't sitting on the floor. We shared stories with our driver in pigeon French and English. He was heading to a midget racer show in Montreux. From his description, it sounded like fun!

When we pulled into the city, he headed straight to the waterfront. A small racing oval had been set up in a large parking lot next to Lac Léman, and formula one midget racing cars were spinning around it. They had tubular little bodies with extended wheels at each corner and a little roll bar behind each driver's head. We watched for a short time. It looked pretty cool! It would be fun being able to see your tires as you slide into the curves. "Hey, Jim, check this out!" Wilds shouted from the front of what looked like a small arcade booth. Inside was a guy sitting next to a mock-up of a driver's seat with a stoplight above the steering wheel. There was no back on the booth. You could see out over the parking lot.

"What's this?"

"It's a reflex test. If your reflexes are good enough, you can get a job as a race car driver!"

"Outstanding! Let's try it!"

Wilds went first while I watched. The object was to press the gas pedal to the floor until the lights switched from green to red. Then you hit the brake and clutch as quickly as you could. *No big deal!* After Wilds jumped on the pedals a card came out of the side of the machine next to the attendant. He looked at the card, thanked Wilds for trying, and invited me to the seat. *Okay, let's see how fast I can do this! My ski racing couldn't hurt my foot speed!*

"English?"

"Yes."

"Hold the gas until the light is red; then you must hit both brake and clutch!"

"Okay!" No sooner than I put my foot on the gas pedal the light went red. I slammed my feet onto the other pedals. "Hey, I wasn't ready!"

The attendant shrugged, pulled the card out, and looked at it. He got a puzzled expression on his face, looked at me, then my feet and tossed the card in trash. "Encore!"

"Sure, Great! Thanks!" *He's giving me a fair chance!* I pressed down on the gas again and waited... and waited... and waited – RED! I slammed my feet onto the other pedals, and looked at the attendant with a smile. *I nailed that one, ha!*

He ignored me again and waited for the card. When he examined this one, his eyes opened wide, and he got an amazed expression on his face. Then he dug into the trash for my last card. I started to get up because a couple of other people had lined up for the test. "Wait!" he ordered and held up his hand. I dropped back into the seat. He compared my two cards and shouted, "Monsieur Jarden!" over his shoulder out the back of the booth.

A man back by the parked cars alerted, walked toward us, and through the back of the booth. They exchanged a few quick phrases in French, and Monsieur Jarden asked me to try again. As the test began, he watched my feet like a hawk. This time I waited fairly long, again. *Red light – slam feet! What's the deal?* I wondered as we waited for the card to appear. This time Monsieur Jarden jerked the card out and compared it with the earlier two.

Peaking back into the booth, Wilds asked, "Hey, what's taking you so long, Henderson? We need to find the car rental place."

"No clue, but they had me do this a couple of times. I don't think the machine is working right."

"Well we need to get going!"

"Okay!" I got up and turned to join Wilds.

"Monsieur, please come."

"Huh? Okay." I turned and followed Monsieur Jarden out of the back of the booth. He had all three of my cards in his hand.

"English, yes? You have very interesting results – very fast!"

Very fast! Cool! "Ah... Okay..."

"My assistant had not seen this before – quite amazing, really!"

Amazing! "Ah... Okay..."

Wilds had walked around the booth and joined us. "What's amazing?"

Looking at Wilds, Monsieur Jarden said, "His reflex are very fast! His first two tests are nearly fifty percent of normal. This last was only slightly slower. Quite amazing!" I was stunned!

"Cool! Can he be a race car driver?"

"That is what I wish to talk to him about." Then to me, "Do you live here?"

"No, I'm in school."

"When does the school end?"

"In June, why?"

"You have very fast reflex. It would be interesting to see if you can drive."

"These cars?" I asked, looking at the midget racers.

"Of course."

"Whoa! I don't know. I'd have to ask my parents. When? Where? How long?"

"Our training start anytime. Most finish in a few weeks… a month maybe. Then the circuit travel Europe almost all year. Only… the winter we stop."

"All year!? I'm still in school! Can I just do it like… this summer?"

"What you say?"

"This summer – June through mid September."

"No, is job! We train! You must drive for eight month more."

"Eight months! No, I can't. I'll be back in the States. Sorry!"

"*Bon!* You must know that I no see this reflex before. It should be very… how you say… helpful? – I think."

Helpful skiing, too? Interesting! Although it would've been more interesting if it kept me from crashing and burning! But maybe my reflexes caused the accident by making me turn before I thought…

"Hey, Jim, don't let it go to your head! Besides we need to find a rental car company."

"Sure, I'm… All right! Thanks!"

"Rental car? You need? Just up this rue there is Montreux Louet… rental. Ask for Jacques, tell him Andre Jarden send you. Have you driven the English Mini? He rents! You will enjoy! Is front-wheel drive – it turns fast and accelerate all through the turn."

"Okay... Thanks, again!"

"Here, take my card in case you change your mind."

"Sure! What about those machine cards?"

"Certainly! You can repeat them if I need?"

"I hope!"

Montreux Louet was just two blocks up the road. Jacques showed us a white Mini. It was tiny – not four feet high! Little tiny wheels! The hubs were only eight inches across; I measured them with my hand. The tires were very fat – nearly half as wide as they were high. The car body was shaped like two little boxes glued together; the larger held the passengers, and the other, that held the engine, sat below the windshield and extended only about two feet in front of the car. There was almost no trunk, the car was chopped in back like a station wagon.

Wilds measured the car with his eyes and said, "Cute car, Jim, but I'm not sure about getting in it with formals!"

"Good point! Have you got anything bigger?"

"No. I have! But no now... rented. Now, only Mini."

"Is there another car rental office open near here?"

"No. Is near train station. Not know when close. Soon. Soon I close."

"What ya think, Wilds?"

"A bird in the hand!"

"Yeah, me too! We'll take it!"

After showing Jacques the business card, he gave us a really good deal for the weekend, but we had to come up with a four hundred Suisse Franc deposit. It took everything we had. He gave me the keys, and I opened the door and almost fell down into the seat. It was so low that I felt like my butt was going to be dragging on the ground.

Wilds dropped beside me into the passenger seat and looked around. "This is bigger inside than out! How is that possible?" It did feel good sized. There was plenty of head and leg room. In fact, there was no dash – just a little tray to put things on just below knee height. Like the Spartan Deux Chevaux, the dash had only a speedometer, a couple of gauges, and a few idiot lights. In this case, everything was mounted in the center of the dash. At least the stick shift was on the floor where it should be!

Wilds joked, "Hey, this actually has a back seat."

I turned and looked back. It was tiny. *No backseat parking there!* There were deep buckets in the wall on either side of the small bench seat. I checked the front door and found a similar bucket there.

"Strange!" Wilds exclaimed. "The door's hollow! There's no place for the windows to roll down!" Sure enough the windows were divided in half, in this case divided front to back and they slid one way or the other but didn't open all the way.

"Strange windows!"

"Yeah!" Wilds agreed, then added, "Check it out! No door handles either!"

I looked at my door, and he was right; there was no way to open the door from the inside. "Do you suppose you have to reach out the window to get out?"

Luckily Jacques was still there. "Hey! How do you open the doors?"

"Oh! I show." He reached into the bucket and pulled a wire that I thought might be part of the electrical system that had fallen out of its clip. The latch on the door moved.

"You just pull a wire? Strange!"

Wilds said, "Yes but very practical!"

"If you say so…" I wondered…

I started the engine, and it purred to life. "Not bad sound for a tiny car."

Wilds said, "Wait! Lets see what's under the hood!" He struggled his way up out of the seat. I popped the hood, and we stared inside. The motor was sideways and not much bigger than a large radiator. We spotted its baby radiator facing into the driver's wheel well.

"God! Will this thing even pull a car?" I wondered aloud.

"It should! The car is a 'MINI!' It's starting to get late. Let's get heading back!" As he closed the hood, Wilds commented, "No wonder the Brits call these 'bonnets'! This is a baby bonnet!"

We fell back into our seats, fastened our lap belts, and I put it into gear. As I started to gun the engine, my foot hit something small and slippery. I moved my foot and stared at a shiny metal plate the size of a large postage stamp hanging in midair about where the gas pedal should be. "Wilds, check this out!" He leaned over to see where I was pointing.

"God! That's the gas pedal! Saving money on this thing!"

I revved the engine, dropped it in first, and let out the clutch. The little machine squealed on the concrete floor and sped out of the garage.

"Damn, Jim! He's going to drag us back there and keep our money!"

"Sorry, the clutch is a little touchy! I'll get the hang of it." First gear barely got the car rolling, but second was a little deeper, and third and fourth were positively spunky at high revs! Did I mention cornering? The little bugger went around corners like the wild mouse ride at Ocean City's amusement park! This became increasingly apparent as we climbed back up our mountain. I had to do a lot of down shifting, but the car buzzed around corners without any body sway. Also, in the Mini, the road up the mountain felt wide, and the bridge across the granite face felt like a four-lane highway as we sailed across it! About two curves past the bridge Wilds exclaimed, "Man, Jim, this thing drives like a sports car!" *It really does!*

It was dark as we pulled into the lot behind our frat house. Robert was outside locking up his motorcycle for the night. He stared at us as we climbed out of the car. "Damn, Jim, where'd you get the Cooper?"

I stared around at the car – *Cooper?* "We rented it. It's called a Mini. Pretty cool, huh?"

"I've heard about them. They were made as economy cars in England, but the racing version, called a Mini Cooper, is winning all the mountain rallies in Europe. They're beating the snot out of cars with twice the horsepower! How's it handle?"

"Great! You want to try it?"

"Sure thing!" Wilds flopped the passenger seat forward on the dash, like in the Deux Chevaux, and hopped in the back. I rode shotgun as Robert tooled up through the upper village and buzzed back down. As we pulled back in front of the dorm, Robert said, "Nice! It's the nearest thing to a motorcycle on four wheels! If I ever think about getting a car, I just might consider it."

"Me, too!" *I'll be heading back to the States next school year,* I thought. *Maybe I can convince my dad to send one back with me. I'll need to be able to get around somehow, right?*

We had missed dinner and had no money, so I mooched some snack food and a warm beer out of Wilds' secret stash. I caught up with Kaeti at the snack bar and told her about the car. She sounded excited. "Sounds like fun, Jim! I'll help split the costs."

"Don't worry about the rental. Wilds and I have that covered. But, well… I hate to ask, but we used all our money for a deposit on the car, and unless we can get to the bank tomorrow we may need gas money! It shouldn't take much."

"You got it, and I'll treat you guys to lunch!"

"Great! Thanks! We'll get some money somehow tomorrow – before the formal!"

"Don't worry! We shouldn't need that much." *She's right; I've already paid for the corsage, and we can catch dinner at the school. Everything's free at the formal. But I hate being without some pocket money! And relying on Kaeti…* We hit the sack early. Kaeti needed rest for the meet. Without money, I only spent a couple of minutes watching *zim-zim* at Le Nord before heading to the dorm.

The next morning Wilds banged on my door as I was dressing. "Hey, Jim! I found some money that I hid just in case last fall."

"Great! Kaeti also said she'd pay for gas, if we need it." I didn't mention lunch. I'd rather borrow from Wilds.

"Sounds good!" After dressing, we ran up to get breakfast and met Kaeti. She was psyched for the track meet.

When we finished eating Kaeti ran up to gather a few last minute things from her room, and the three of us hopped down to the car in front of our dorm. Issa had parked his MG beside the Mini and was checking it out. "I have only seen a couple of these strange little things. This looks nicer than its predecessor, the Morris Minor. It's a little more square."

"It handles great! Might give your MG a run for its money!"

"Oh, I doubt that! This is the top of its lineage – short of having a Jaguar, of course!" *He's probably right.* Wilds piled in the back, and Kaeti got in front next to me. She had a copy of the directions to the school in Fribourg and a Swiss road map, just in case. As we started to back up, I spotted Spyder, in black, come running out the front door and join Issa in his MG. We buzzed out with Issa on our tail.

The map took us north toward Gstaad. The roads were curvy, and the little car clung so tight to the curves that I was taking them all out! Issa was actually having trouble keeping up. Wilds started getting excited by our success and began tolling the approximate distance between us each time he spotted Issa. We turned to the left before we got to Gstaad and the road straightened out. Then Issa caught up and blew past us! We went into hot pursuit, but Issa's car had twice the power of ours. However, after a couple of K's, we hit curves again, and we quickly caught up. I started riding Issa's bumper, trying to find enough room to pass, but we couldn't see far enough. Then Issa pulled up behind a slower car as we hit a particularly curvy section of the road. In order to get the Mini running fast enough to pass, I dropped back a ways and accelerated toward the two when I thought I might have a chance to pass. I did this several times before I spotted open road ahead, and I slingshot around the two. Pedal to the metal, I rolled the Mini through a very curvy section. Kaeti kept constant track of our route and made sure we caught each turn. Wilds continued staring out the back of the Mini, waiting for Issa to reappear.

He never did... We pulled into the Fribourg school holding the track meet and got out of the car before Spyder and Issa appeared. As Kaeti warmed up, Wilds and I teased Issa about beating his sports car in this little shoebox of a car.

"Okay, Henderson, the race back is for the cars!"

"Sorry, man, this isn't mine! It's a rental! I don't even own a car!"

"Okay, then I will sell my car if you win!"

There doesn't seem to be any downside to that wager. "Okay, you're on!"

"Also, we'll take the longer route through Montreux."

"Great!" I didn't know the longer route, but it sounded like fun!

The meet was against several other Swiss colleges in the area. Each of the other schools had extensive teams, matching uniforms, and coaches. We were the joke of the day as we arrived in different vehicles, with random T-shirts and shorts or sweats, and no leadership, except possibly Stallone. He rounded up our ten other competitors, asked everyone what events they wanted to try, and took that information to the event coordinators. We didn't have enough people to go around, and we had no organized training so I didn't expect much, except an exciting day away from school. Kaeti was the first one to hit the winner's circle. By a half stride she just edged out the next fastest competitor in the two hundred-meter dash. Wilds, Kaeti, and I joined hands and bounced in a circle beside the track after her win shouting, "U-S-A!"

A couple of freshmen guys placed well in the long jump, but the next big surprise came from a freshman named Ralph! I didn't know Ralph well, but it was obvious that he was a chain smoker. You could tell as he lined up for the fifteen hundred-meter run taking the last couple of drags on his cigarette. He crushed the butt out just before the judge said something in German that we assumed was "Runners take your mark! - get set!" and he fired off the starter pistol! Ralph started off kicking long powerful strides. He moved quickly to the front of the pack, but his pace seemed too fast. I was sure that he would wear himself out trying to run fifteen hundred meters at that pace! By the end of the second lap, the crowd started to drop away. Likely they also believed he would kill himself at that pace, but Ralph kept striding. By the last lap, Ralph still hadn't slowed his pace and was almost a quarter lap ahead of the rest of the field! At this point, the race was for second as the other runners started to their push to the finish. As Ralph broke through the tape, he flipped two birds at the crowd and grabbed a cigarette away from one of the other freshmen smoking next to the track. He took a victory lap with the smoke trailing behind him like some steam locomotive. *Man, if my soccer coach had only seen that one!*

At this point, we didn't have any runners lining up, so we walked in to watch the other field events. One freshman said that Stallone was getting ready to do the shot put. We walked over and watched as several of his competitors lofted their metal balls. Each ball dropped onto the sand, and the distance from the depression in the sand to the pit was measured. Finally it was Stallone's turn. He stepped into the shot-put pit, spun, and hefted the steel ball into the air. The height and arc was tremendous, much further than the other contestants. In fact, the ball landed outside the sand-covered area on the grass beyond. The judges spent several minutes feeling the ground for a depression before measuring the distance; but one thing for certain; no one else was close to Stallone. His second throw was at a different angle, but the steel ball once again landed on the grass. His third was a bit shorter and landed near the edge on the dirt just before the grass. *He cleaned the event without breaking a sweat!* In spite of the small size of our team, we let the Swiss know that we were there; in fact I found out later that our team came in second out of the six competing schools!

As things started to wind up and the awards were presented Wilds spotted Issa and Spyder sneaking back to their car. Kaeti was already wearing her blue ribbon and medal when I grabbed her and explained the wager. We scrambled to the car and buzzed off campus a couple of minutes after Issa. That couple of minutes was a long time for a car race. Kaeti belted in as Wilds unfolded the map. The route toward Montreux started back the same way we had come into town. Kaeti took over the map as we sped through the town. "Jim, this doesn't look good!"

"What?"

"The roads look straighter, less turns!"

"Damn! We'll never catch them!"

We buzzed out of town and into a very curvy valley; the road slid along the side of a small creek. I had floored the gas pedal, and the Mini was squealing around turns as we flew through the valley! We had to catch up! We passed a couple of cars that, at our speed, seemed to be driving to church or something. Luckily, there was little traffic coming toward us! Before we left the valley, we caught Issa and began hugging his bumper. He sped up as we began tailing him, but his car started sliding on the curves that we buzzed easily through. After one hard curve that threw Issa into a fishtail, he slowed dramatically, and I had to brake to keep from tagging him.

As we hit the straight-away, he left us in the dust! It was all I could do to keep him in sight before the next set of curves. Luckily, he once again got stuck behind a slow moving vehicle, in this case a delivery truck, and we caught him – back on his tail and into the curves. In a short straight-away he managed to pass the truck with us hugging his bumper. We were so close that the Mini must have looked like a wagon being towed behind the MG. We followed as the K's clicked away. He was too fast to pass on the straight, and I couldn't find a safe spot on the curves. Damn, it was getting frustrating! Finally, I managed to slingshot him on a curve and began pulling ahead. As I did, a small Fiat spyder came buzzing around Issa, too. A third had joined our race! When we exited the curves, the Fiat hugged my tail, which left Issa trailing two cars. We stayed this way for several K's until the Fiat either came to his turn off or lost interest. Then Issa pulled ahead again! Immediately after he passed me, a Porsche blew the wheels off both our cars! Issa was breathing the Porsche's exhaust for several K's, while I trailed far behind trying to keep the two in sight.

The Porsche turned off in a small town as I caught up with the pair. Suddenly Kaeti announced, "Jim, there's a turn just ahead. It looks like it trails down into the valley just east of Montreux – and it has dozens of hairpin turns." As we hit the middle of the little town, two signs appeared on one post: Lausanne straight ahead and Montreux to the left. Issa flew straight through the intersection as we squealed around the turn!

In the middle of my turn, another car, a red MG Midget that I hadn't seen before, cut diagonally across the turn and squeaked ahead of me. Wilds erupted, "Damn! Where did that asshole come from?" We trailed the midget until I watched his car fishtail dangerously as he pulled out of a turn. I decided to back off – my race wasn't with this nut! In a straightaway just outside of the little town a motorcycle sailed by, and I wondered if I was really going as fast as I could. Wilds complained, "Who invited these guys, anyway?" I tried to keep up with the cycle, but he slowly pulled ahead as the driver leaned steeply to each side, almost brushing his knees on the pavement as he took the turns.

Even with my pedal to the metal, the cycle was soon a full turn ahead and pulling slowly away. I was just thinking about letting him go when we flew around a turn and into a herd of cows! There were a dozen of them across the road. I slammed on the clutch and brakes, like I was back in the reflex test. The Mini skidded to a stop with the bonnet under one cow's udder. *God, the thing looks enormous from this angle! I think this lady needs to be milked.* The hairy light brown wall that was the side of the cow spanned the width of the car! She swung her head around to stare at us. "Moooo!" *Damn! Hopefully she doesn't think we were here to milk her!* I slid back the front half of the window and waved my hand outside –"Shoo!" I thought about beeping the horn but didn't want to panic the herd. She moved slowly out of our way, but another started to take her place. "Shoo! Shoo!" I inched the car forward blocking its path. I could just see the helmet of the motorcycle rider weaving through the herd. Kaeti got the idea and stuck her hand out her window. "Shoo!" Wilds reached forward from the back and beeped the horn. I swept his hand off the wheel. "Cool it! I'd just as soon not have these things stampede! We'd be crushed!" I started weaving slowly through the herd. It took a couple of minutes, but we made it through. I was amazed that there was no farmer around.

As we cleared the herd, I pushed it to the floor and ran through the gears. The motorcycle was long gone! We hit the shoulder of the plateau and looked over the valley below. Lac Léman was at least seven hundred feet nearly straight down. Vineyards covered the steep slope, and our road was hemmed with rock walls as it twisted through countless hairpin turns between fields of grapevines. I downshifted into third on the curve and slammed the accelerator to the floor! The Mini squealed and started to slide through the first hairpin, but the front-wheel drive pulled it through. Then back to fourth as the car raced through the straightaway. After the first couple of hairpins, I got the rhythm. The car squealed through the turns; the speedometer never dropped below sixty K's and popped back past one hundred as I roared through each straightaway.

Six hairpins down and we were entering the seventh. It was a left-hand turn, and like the other left turns, I started wide and cut about halfway into the other lane to shorten the turn. As I did, I spotted the red MG Midget that had cut us off in the last city. It had hit the stone wall on the inside of the curve. Its driver, a young, sandy-haired kid, had one arm up and the car's tail was directly in our path! I jerked the steering wheel to the right to avoid it, but I ended up driving straight at the opposite wall! As I passed the tail of the car, I jerked the wheel back to the left away from the wall, and the left side of the car lifted off the ground! Everything went into slow motion... I looked over at Kaeti – she had fallen against the car door and was pushing against the window to stay upright – her face was pale through her dark tan. Her eyes bulged in terror as she looked up at the wall I could no longer see – only the pavement was visible out her window. Out of the corner of my eye I saw Wilds lying on the car side with his head pushed into the roof. His knees were up against his chest. Gravity and centrifugal force was pulling me to the right. Only my seatbelt and my right hand pushing against the stick shift were holding me in place, but I was loosing the battle. My left hand started to drag the top of the steering wheel to the right. However, as that happened, the car dropped back onto all fours! I straightened our path on the roadway and upshifted to fourth as I sped into the straightaway, then down again to third as we sailed into the next hairpin. The last five seconds were forgotten for now. I had to keep the speed up or risk loosing to Issa. Not once had losing my life crossed my mind. Neither Kaeti nor Wilds said a thing, and the car remained eerily silent, except for the engine sounds, until we reached the highway along Lac Léman.

The highway was the straightaway where I had hitched a ride with the crazed motorcyclist. *No way I could match that speed!* Once we were relaxed and weaving through the normal traffic on the highway, Wilds asked "Did we almost roll?"

Kaeti replied with a muted "Yes."

Wilds exhaled loudly, "Whoa boy!"

I looked over at them both. "That was close! Too close! Sorry."

Wilds added, "Good reflexes!"

"Yeah…" *I doubt reflexes had anything to do with our survival – blind luck – maybe someone looking out for us – but not reflexes!* I wouldn't deal with how close we came to death until two nights later when I would relive that turn in my dream – or my nightmare. We didn't make the turn in my nightmare; I lost my life, my girlfriend, and my best friend in one instant! Everything in my dream went black, and I woke in a sweat, yelling, 'I'm dead!!'

However, at that moment I was concerned only about Issa. Where was he? Had he continued straight believing that he could make up the almost seventy K difference in the length of the two routes on the highways, or had he turned around and come after us through the hairpins? In any case he would be catching up now. I was pegged at about one hundred and ten K's. His car would do one hundred fifty to one hundred seventy K's. Wilds took up a position watching for Issa through the rear window as Kaeti looked over at me.

"Did you see the driver of the little red car? Was he okay?" she asked.

I flashed back to that instant. I pictured the sandy-haired kid. He looked frightened, but unhurt as he held his hand out trying to ward us off. "I think he was okay. His car didn't look bad. I think that he just lost control and spun out."

"He needs to learn how to drive." Wilds added from the back seat.

Kaeti grew quieter and looked lost in thought.

We got to Aigle and started the road up our mountain without seeing Issa, but he couldn't be far behind now, and the Mini didn't have power going up hill, especially with three people. Downshifting and upshifting to keep my torque up and to maneuver the curves – pushing the car as fast as it would go, I flashed back to my first trip up this mountain with my parents. I was now one of those crazy rally drivers racing blindly around the turns and pushing my car to the max! – but I wasn't born on this mountain and didn't know each turn by heart. Wilds had his nose pressed to the back window, still watching for any sign of Issa

When we got back to Leysin, Kaeti said she needed to start getting ready for the evening formal, so we dropped her at the Main. Then we drove through the lower village looking for Issa's car on the chance that he had somehow passed us and was already back. There was no sign of it. I left Wilds at the corner by the Parisienne to keep watch while I raced to the upper village to pick up our corsages; then I drove back down and parked the car by Hell House. I jogged back to the intersection, but Wilds had no news. He had grabbed a roll and a beer at the Parisienne while he waited. I bummed some money so I could do the same as he also headed off to get ready for the formal. I opted for a cup of tea, instead of beer, and several sweet rolls. We had missed lunch, and I was starving! I grabbed a table where I could see the road. I was really beginning to get worried that something had happened. *This race was stupid. Why did I keep doing things like that?*

Almost an hour later a tow truck containing Issa and Spyder stopped at the corner and dropped them off. I ran out. "What happened? Where's your car?" Issa took one look at me a stormed away.

Spyder came up, put his arm around me, and said, "Buy me a beer. I've got a story to tell!"

"Sorry, no money left, but I want to hear what happened!" Spyder's story went something like this – They lost a wheel on the way up our mountain. Luckily it happened on the only straight section of the road up – in the bridge hanging on the side of the cliff. Spyder first saw the spinner fly forward catching the light and wondered what it was. Issa's car had wire wheels with a single knock-off spinner holding each wheel on the axle. Spyder then saw a wheel race ahead of the car, bouncing toward the far end of the bridge. He still didn't realize what was happening until his side of the car dropped down and they skidded to a stop. They got out and checked the car. Their right front wheel was gone. It was lying on the road near the rock wall. The exposed front rotor was worn flat on one edge from sliding on the pavement, and there was a gouge in the roadway. It was shear luck they hadn't gone off the edge! After a few minutes a passing driver helped them put out warning triangles and took them to the local garage in Leysin. The garage sent a truck to tow the car up. They said that it would take several weeks to get parts and repair it. According to Spyder, Issa claimed that the garage had worked on the car the week before and hadn't put the wheels back on correctly. He just had an argument with the owner about that.

(A couple of days later Issa congratulated me for beating them back but claimed that I had cheated by hitting the road to Montreux. I argued that Montreux is where he said we were headed. He hadn't sold the car when the year ended. I didn't press it – it was just a silly bet.)

After listening to Spyder's story, I had to hustle to get a shower before dinner.

I stopped by Wilds' room before heading up for dinner. I knocked, "Wilds, you ready to go?"

"Not going!"

"What? Why?"

"Don't feel like it!"

"What's going on? Can I come in?"

"I guess…" I opened the door and found Wilds in the dark.

"What happened? Are you okay?"

"I just got dumped!"

"Kathy, your date to the formal?"

"Yeah."

"No! She can't! It's too late! What'd she say?"

"She's not feeling well."

"Come to dinner. I'll have Kaeti see what's going on, okay?"

"Nah!"

"I'll be back!" I said as I sprinted down the stairs and up to the main.

I spotted Kaeti getting ready to head in to dinner. "Kaeti! Got a problem."

"I know. Kathy says she's not feeling well," Kaeti said while avoiding my eyes.

"Uh huh! What's the real story?"

Shaking her head, "I don't know. That's what she said."

"But we had plans!"

"I know – what can I say? I'm not sure it's Kathy. She seemed excited just yesterday. Some of the girls are real twits. They like to tell everyone how to live their lives. Wilds is just not…"

"What? Acceptable! – Am I acceptable? Why can't they just leave people alone?"

"I don't give a damn about that – but some girls do…"

"That's a bunch of crap! Can't you talk with her? We have the Mini and everything!"

"I'll try but… I want to talk to you about something else… Would you mind if we didn't take the car?"

"What?! Why? That was the plan!"

"I know, but we're going to be coming back so late"

"Are you worried about today? I know that was stupid. I won't do it tonight. It will be fun in our own wheels! Come on!"

"Please, Jim, think about it. We've been going all day, and this boat trip goes late. We'll be driving back up the mountain after midnight. I'd feel a lot safer on the bus."

"You don't trust me? I would never do anything to…" I flashed back to the race and the close call on the road down to Montreux.

"Besides, Jim, you'll want to be able to have a few drinks on the trip. They will tire you even more. And… the bus ride can be fun, you know that!" Kaeti used her secret weapon as she dipped her head and melted me with her eyes peaking under the sweep of hair that crossed her forehead.

I smiled, "Damn! Okay, we bus it but…"

"I'll make it worth your while!"

"Promises, promises… I can't say no to you. But what about Wilds?"

"He'll understand!"

"No, I mean his date!"

"I… She has to make up her own mind. Can we just make it a threesome?"

"I'm not sure what Wilds would say, but that'd be nice. Why would people do something like this? Don't they give a crap about others? Did you ever get the feeling that we don't belong here?"

"Don't blame Kathy!"

"I'm not. She helped me. I just thought that the two of them would really have fun together. It's just a dance!"

"I know, but it's not that easy."

"You do it!"

"I'm different."

"That's what I mean."

"I know... Ask Wilds – We'll have fun together!"

"Thanks, Kaeti! I gotta go now. Save me some food. I'm starving!"

I ran back down to the dorm. Wilds was still hiding in his room. "Wilds, Kaeti said Kathy really isn't feeling well," I lied. "But we want you to join us! It's near the end of the year – it's for fun! Kaeti is a great dancer! Join us, please!"

"Gawd, Jim, I'd just be a third wheel. You two have fun! I'll be fine..."

"Come on, man, please!"

"Nah, you two have a good time. I'll be fine. Third wheel is not my style."

"Ahh... okay. Oh, we're not taking the Mini. Do you want me to leave the keys?"

"Okay, but why not?"

"Truth? I think Kaeti doesn't trust me after today."

"She might have something!"

"Bullshit!"

"Just pulling your chain!"

Kaeti was a princess coming down the stairs from the dorm. Her dress was cream with lapels, like a suit and a full skirt. She wore matching flats. Her light-brown hair was again a veil down her back. I caught her hand at the base of the stairs. "Beautiful! You know sometimes I have a problem linking up runner Kaeti with this! How do you do it?"

"It isn't easy! I'd rather be the runner! Where's Wilds?"

"Couldn't convince him. He didn't want to be a third wheel."

"I wouldn't let that happen! Let's run down and try together!"

"Wait, your corsage!" Pinning it on this time was much easier. The wide lapels didn't hurt! As I pinned it I noticed her necklace. It was a lattice of gold chains with what appeared to be diamonds at the intersection of each set of chains. "Wow! That's beautiful! Is it real?"

"I don't know. Kathy lent it to me, and she said to be very careful with it – so I guess it might be."

"If those are diamonds, it's got to be worth a couple of hundred bucks!"

"More, I expect. You know, I think that she loaned me the necklace as a way of saying that she was sorry."

"She needs to say that to Wilds."

"I know, lets go down and talk to him."

Kaeti and I talked to Wilds and she convinced him that Kathy was upset about not being able to go. However, even working together we weren't able to convince him to join us, but we seemed to cheer him up enough to think about plans for his evening.

"Hey, there's got to be some girls ticked at not getting to go to this thing. Maybe I can console them!"

Kaeti and I wished him 'good luck' and hurried back up to catch the bus.

We boarded the boat in Montreux in the darkness. The band played good music – modern stuff we all knew and liked. The whole scene was more informal and fun – not fancy like the last one. Kaeti and I danced for a while, but both of us were dragging so we sat out a lot of the dances. The couple of glasses of wine I drank went right to my head, and by midnight I was thinking more about finding a bed than partying. I don't remember leaving the boat or getting on the bus. I was dreaming about seeing Kaeti floating in the sky with her head silhouetted by the Berneuse. She was wearing a brown plaid flannel shirt and smiling at me as she pulled her long hair over her shoulder. The dream was so quiet and peaceful, I wondered if it was some prediction of a future between us. It couldn't be reality. She would have to be floating in the air to have the Berneuse behind her like that, and I'd never seen her in flannel, that is stateside camping clothes. I woke on the bus with my nose buried in Kaeti's hair. She had her head on my shoulder and was breathing deeply in sleep. Her hair smelled of some shampoo, maybe Clairol, and of Kaeti. Something was very comforting in her scent. An errant thought – *we finally slept together – perhaps, not in a bed under the stars, but we shared one more little experience.* Kaeti snorted a little, stirred, and caught me staring at her.

"Sorry!" she said, wiping the side of her mouth.

"Don't be I was sleeping, too."

"No, I promised something special on the trip back…"

"This was something special, trust me!" That drew a gentle nuzzle under my neck, then kisses up my cheek to my ear, where she got my attention with her tongue! *That made the hair stand up on the back of my neck!* The rest of the ride was stimulating, to say the least. Not many of the others were awake – nor did it matter if we were observed.

The next morning, I found that Wilds hadn't used the Mini the night before. He just didn't like mountains and clutches. We rolled off the mountain! The car was like riding a toboggan down the mountain road. Wilds took over on the flat, and we sped back to Montreux. We dropped off the Mini at Montreux and asked the manager how much money it would take to buy one. He said that you could buy one new for about five thousand Swiss francs, or about one thousand, one hundred dollars. I was so in love with the car that when the clerk gave us our deposit back less costs, I didn't bother checking his count. We had hiked several blocks from the shop down to the parking lot where the midget racers had been on Friday. We then divided up the money while looking for a place to get lunch. We were forty francs short! We triple checked to be sure we hadn't screwed up and ran back to the rental company. The clerk just shrugged and told us he gave us the correct change. He wouldn't listen to our arguments, and the manager was at lunch. We left without getting any satisfaction. Later, Willie demonstrated a way of counting money where you folded bills in half and counted them in your own hand. That way you count both ends of the same bill. Likely that's what happened.

Hitchhiking back did not involve motorcycles or blondes in sports cars. The best ride was the one up our mountain. A guy in a Peugeot demonstrated that he knew every inch of the road, and his car had power to spare as it climbed to Leysin. Maybe a Peugeot was now my dream car! But the driver said his car cost over twice what a Mini did. *Oh well, I can dream!*

The weekend after the prom, Kaeti and I walked to the upper village planning to have lunch at our favorite tearoom with the view of *les Dents du Midi*. However, as we approached we spotted Wilds and Kathy sitting in the front window talking together and smiling. We pretended not to notice and walked past like we were headed on up the road.

As we got out of view Kaeti grabbed my hand and said, "So cute. You don't suppose?"

"I don't know. Wilds hasn't said anything to me about it."

"Neither has Kathy, but it would be nice."

"Yeah. Wait a minute! How did they get up here? I can't imagine Wilds hiking it – and Kathy?"

"The girls take the cog train up."

"Isn't that expensive?"

"Not for these girls, especially if you think about the walk." Kaeti's eyes flash and she began laughing to herself.

"What?"

"Nothing. Well, I was just remembering a walk up the stairs with Lynn."

"Lynn?"

"You know her. She's tall, stocky, with short hair about my color. She smokes a lot, too"

"I guess. What about her?"

"I laughed remembering what she said to me afterwards."

"What's that?"

"Well, she was way out of shape and smoked to boot. She had to stop every three or four steps to catch her breath. I thought she was going have a heart attack. And I was so… well I'd be walkin' up and realize that she wasn't with me, so I'd hop back down and encourage her along. I must've done that a hundred times. Anyway, when we finally got to the top, she told me that if she had had the energy she would have thrown me over the railing, just to shut me up."

I laughed. "Yeah, I can see it."

"You know, I never did convince Lynn to take the stairs again."

"Yeah, hey, any ideas for lunch? I'm starving!"

"You guys!"

We didn't see Wilds and Kathy together again. It may have been a chance meeting, but who knows. Kathy was the planner. If anyone could keep it secret, she was the one!

Chapter Thirty Five

Spring Sports

As the snow left the mountain it revealed the fields that we had once hiked across. They became play areas for the informal and only slightly more formal sports of the spring. The first sport was very informal, and, like most of the spring sports, involved a fair amount of beer and, in this case – a boomerang.

It seems that Cliff had bought a real wooden boomerang from some Aussies staying at the Vag. The thing was enormous compared to the Whammo plastic version, almost two and a half feet from tip to tip and three inches wide near its middle. Its inside edge was sharp, and with the exception of the rounded tips, it looked like the wings from a large model jet. Cliff explained that the Aussies kept the edges sharp to use for hunting game in the Outback. Anyway, a half dozen of us grabbed beers from Le Nord and went out to the relatively level area where I had first tried skiing to try our hand at throwing a real boomerang. Cliff took the first toss. It sailed far out over the field and slashed into the soggy earth without turning back. Then Stallone tried. His powerful toss accompanied with a loud "whoop!" sent the boomerang high into the air and far out over the field. At the end of its arch, the boomerang plunged into the earth and stood erect like an upside-down "L." Bernd followed with similar success, then me and the others. No one could get the damn thing to come back. Spyder made a beer run and came back with a dozen other guys and lots of beer. Each of the newcomers claimed to know the trick – and each failed in turn. At this point we had developed a method of dealing with the failures. The group formed a great ring around the thrower and whoever it landed next to would become the next thrower. By this time the beer had hidden any concern that the flying object was a lethal weapon.

We tossed the thing up into the air, down toward the dirt, bent arm forward, and arched back forward. It didn't seem to matter! It would sail up then begin a great curve and come diving into the earth after nearly severing the head of one of the drunken contestants. After the second hour, Roark showed up. He watched from a hill behind me for a while and warned a couple of us near him to not get in the boomerang's way. Then after I made a valiant, if stupid, effort to catch the boomerang as it sailed over my head and impaled itself in the turf behind me, he gave a disgusted grunt, walked over, and retrieved it. Roark tested its weight and looked around as if trying to find a safe direction to throw. Then he pinched one tip between his hand and thumb, holding it bent arm forward and almost vertical, and tossed it off across the field. It sailed in an enormous arc, then turned and spun back to Roark, who caught it and handed it to me.

"How the hell did you do that?!" I said as I stared down at the wooden enigma.

"Practice!" was all he said as he turned and walked away.

"Shit!" I imitated Roark as best I could and threw it. Once again, it buried itself back into the turf some distance away, and we started over again. At least we knew it wasn't defective – we just needed practice! – and maybe a few more beers!

Beerball was the next "competitive" sport! It was announced on the school bulletin board, and competitors were asked to sign up. Not being a baseball player, I invited Kaeti to go with me as a spectator. The event was on a field north of the village. Makeshift bases were set up, and cases of beer were placed at each of the bases and in the field positions. The rules matched baseball, with the exception that everyone playing had to take a large slug of beer at each event – each pitch – each hit – each time a ball was caught and before it could be thrown – each base crossed – and on and on and on. *Man, I thought baseball was boring before!*

It only took about an hour before the contestants were totally snockered. Hits became rare – pitches across the plate almost rarer – players were confused about which way to run, if they happened to hit the damn ball – guys started running around the bases not realizing that they hadn't hit the ball into the field. Then again, it didn't matter – the players in the field had no clue about what happened, anyway! From the bleachers the fans, including Kaeti, me, and a couple of dozen others, were too sober to comprehend the game. Several began booing the disoriented players. Being with Kaeti was keeping me relatively straight, but I began wishing that I were drunk or someplace else. It was then that one of the contestants changed the uniform standard as he mooned the fans. The fans laughed so hard that the entire team on the bench mooned them. The next thing I knew the field was filled with guys standing around with their pants around their knees. Either they had decided to set a new uniform standard or everyone had simply forgotten to pull his pants back up. One guy, who had swung at a ball that hadn't come anywhere close to home plate, had thrown down his bat and was shuffling toward first base with his worm hanging out. As a result, the fielders were tripping around their positions, looking for a ball that had lodged itself underneath the bench that held the opposing team. Needless to say this wasn't doing anything for me, so I turned to tell Kaeti and saw her walking up the road toward the school. "Hey, hold up!" Kaeti looked back and waved me forward. As I caught up, "You just goin' to leave me at that crap?"

"Thought you were enjoying it," she said with a teasing smile. "Wasn't doing anything for me."

"Shit! I'm sorry! And you think it was doing something for me?" She smiled again, threw her arm around me, and we strode off in each other's arms.

The next sport was football. In this case, Stallone initiated the action, and he was determined to make it real! I was down in the parlor working out with the weights when Stallone walked in. "Play football?"

"Ahh, American football? I guess. I was on a midget league in elementary school. Since then only screwing around. Why?"

"Challenged. Freshman dorm." The way he talked, I wasn't sure whether he had challenged the Freshman dorm or they had challenged him, but it sounded like fun!

"Sure! I used to be a pretty good center and love rushing the quarterback!"

He looked at me critically, "You're a little small." At that he turned and started to walk out.

"Wait! Where? When? What equipment?"

"Tomorrow after school on that field they used for that worthless ball game. We'll talk there."

"Okay!" Stallone had apparently liked the beerball game as much as I had.

A batch of us, both freshmen and sophomores, showed up the next afternoon. I brought Gil. Wilds wasn't interested.

Stallone got everyone's attention with a loud whistle, "Here's da thing. I got a football and they got some kinda hockey helmets, but we ain't got nothin' else. We could play flag football…" That was greeted with a round of "boo's.""OR we could play TACKLE!" This was followed by a group cheer. "Tackle it is! Pad up your shoulders with an extra sweatshirt. Oh an' the helmets ain't got ear protection. We'll divide up the days for the practices. My team is here today. Freshmen get lost!" Stallone put a smile on that, but it had a definite crocodile look.

We spent the rest of the time talking about experience and what positions we wanted to play. Several guys actually had high school experience with football. Stallone put together the offensive line pretty quickly. The leftovers, which included me, were relegated to defense. That was fine with me. I remembered enjoying charging through the line in elementary school. But Stallone had me running after pass receivers. Most were taller than me and left me in the dust. I think that I was about to be benched when one of the defensive line took a break and I stepped up without being invited. At the hike, I squirmed between the two big linemen and found myself diving headfirst at Stallone. My forehead slammed into his thigh as I took him down.

"Damn, kid! You're not suppos'd to kill your own quarterback!" Stallone said as he pushed me off and stood rubbing his thigh. "Watch your head!"

My head! God, was it wrong to hit him with my head? In the States, the football coach on the practice field next to my soccer team used to shout, 'Stick your helmet between his legs and knock his nuts behind his back!' Man! Stallone is going to kill me!

"That was my shoulder! Sorry!"

"Ya sure kid! Now get back in line and you two guys –" looking at his offensive line. "– stop him!" They stopped me most of the time, but I slipped through enough times, by stepping back, -or spinning around, -or using judo to get below their center of gravity, that I found my place on the defensive line.

A weak spot on the team was the center. Robert had climbed off his motorcycle, taken off his glasses, and had the size to stop any of the freshmen. However, his snap wasn't always crisp, and he occasionally let go before Stallone had the ball. Also his deep snaps for a punt occasionally sailed over Stallone's head. One afternoon as practice was breaking up, Stallone came over to me. "Hey kid, you said you knew how to snap the ball."

"Yeah." I said tentatively.

"Can you get it back for a punt?"

Man, it's been years and I was what three feet tall then. "Sure!" I said with a confidence I didn't feel. It took a couple of tries, but I was soon putting nice spirals into Stallone's arms.

He had me run a couple of normal snaps and said he liked the feel but warned me, "It's a different world when someone's comin' on your head." And he was right! The next practice, Robert, our other center, was on my head. At each snap, I got my left arm up quickly, but my right had to stay until Stallone pulled the ball out. By that time, Robert had built up speed and was coming through or over me. He wasn't tricky like me, but he didn't need to be; he relied on brut force and size. My best move was to keep low and slam both forearms into his thighs. This usually brought him down on top of me, but it gave Stallone enough time to make the play. Over and over again I was the last man to stand up from the middle pile-up. *Teach me to volunteer!*

Fortunately, after a single day of practice Stallone put Robert back in and returned me to defense. He liked having a substitute center but liked the security that Robert's size brought. *I wasn't complaining!* Plus, Robert's snaps grew sharper, so Stallone wasn't losing the ball. I like to think I had something to do with that… Stallone did keep me practicing deep snaps for kicks and punts. Robert still hadn't perfected those. But my pleasure was getting through the line!

The last practice before the game Stallone passed out the helmets. They were lightweight white plastic with foam pads, and your ears did stick out the sides. I mentioned that we could wear our ski headbands to protect our ears. That was met with a mixed response. Personally, I had no desire to loose an ear on someone else's helmet, so I wasn't worried about how I looked. As we started to break up, Stallone said, "Okay guys, wur gonna giv'um hell tomorrow. Get ta bed early and no drink'n – especially before the game! Got it?" No one was going to argue with Stallone. We all nodded and headed to the frat house to clean up before dinner.

The game was pitched as our homecoming game – the freshmen against the sophomores. There were several spectators as Stallone led us through a stretch-out routine before the game. Several large water bottles were near the sophomore bench, courtesy of Stallone, I think. There were also several cases of beer hidden in a nearby shed, but Stallone quickly pointed out, "Doze are f'after – Our victory celebration! Got it?"

The game was great fun! We won, of course. We had size, training, and our offense actually had several real plays. However, what the freshmen lacked, they made up for in determination! We knew we were in a battle. I was a regular whirling dervish cutting through their line and, if a tackle was made behind or near the line of scrimmage, I was in the mix – and Stallone wasn't complaining when my helmet slammed into their quarterback's legs! At each kickoff, punt, and extra point kick, I was moved to center. Nothing went over Stallone's head. *Thank God!*

When we retired to the shed for our victory celebration, the beers were gone. It seems this time the spectators were soused and the players left dry! Dragging our sweaty, weary bodies to Le Nord for the beer that had disappeared, I noticed that Kaeti wasn't around. *Had she been there and I missed her? Had I forgotten to tell her?* I was too tired to care – but it would have been nice to have her join our celebration…

Chapter Thirty Six

Spring's Dissolution

Aside from the sporadic spring sports, things took a decided turn for the worse as the spring arrived. There was no skiing, and I saw less and less of Kaeti. No one seemed to be dancing at the Messange any more. My life was back to drinking and playing *zim-zim* – neither of which involved Kaeti. Also, I had been away from the snack bar for so long that I was embarrassed to just show up there... We just didn't seem to have an excuse to be around each other. I began to wonder if she was avoiding me on purpose.

Then when I thought I had reached the depths of the depressing mountain spring, the land gave way under me, and I slid toward the edge. Wilds brought news from the freshman dorm that Dick, the sergeant's son, had committed suicide. He was found dead in his underclothes with his judo belt around his neck and attached to some overhead piping in a bathroom. Apparently his feet were touching the ground, so it was believed that he had to lean into it to finish the job. That sent me into a spiral. *I knew him. He'd joined my family when we first arrived at school. I should've been his friend! He must have needed one. Why was I so selfish? I hadn't thought! God, I hadn't cared!*

I kept this to myself. Perhaps because I was ashamed – perhaps because that was what I thought a man should do. After a long night lying on my balcony staring at the stars I came to grips with the fact that I wasn't to blame but that I could do better – be more aware – in the future. There wasn't anything I could do now. I called my parents the next afternoon to tell them, but they already knew. Millie was taking it hard. I guess she really had liked Dick. Walking back to the frat house after calling, I had an odd thought. *After all the attempted suicides in the girls' dorm last fall, Dick's was the only success – if you can ever call suicide a success...*

The school's response was odd... unlike my boarding school where we had several meetings and discussions when a girl committed suicide, on our mountain, Dick's passing went unrecorded; swept under the rug. As a matter of fact, the following Friday posters were pasted all over the main for a Beer-B-Que a week from Saturday. To give them credit, this may have been an annual tradition likely designed to break the spring doldrums, but it seemed very bad timing. Not that the idea was bad. It was to be a steak and beer blast on the side of the mountain. Madame Linden, my French living teacher, was cooking, and the school promised more beer than we could drink – and given the propensities of the students, that was a lot of beer!

I actually used the party as an excuse to talk to Kaeti. I caught her at the snack bar that evening. "Hey!" I started when I sat on a seat at the front counter.

"Hey, yourself, stranger," she replied with a smile. "What can I get ya?"

"Nothing. I just came to ask... You remember that promise we made..."

"About going to things together, yeah," she cut in, then looked at me challengingly.

"Okay, I'm sorry I haven't been around lately. Did you hear about the Beer-B-Que?"

"Can't miss it. The signs are everywhere."

"Ummm – would you like to go... with me, that is?"

"Sure, sounds like fun! But I'll tell you what. I need to study to get my grades up for the end of the year. I'll meet you up there when they start serving the steaks, okay?"

I smiled and said, "Sounds like a date!" Kaeti looked at me with the glint in her eyes that usually preceded a curt jibe. You could tell that she wanted to say something but thought better of it, then just smiled and went back to work.

I used that as my cue to leave and I headed back to the dorm. I would have liked to have had Kaeti up there the whole time, but I had agreed to take it easy – besides I had never seen her drink a beer, let along all-you-can-drink.

Wilds, Gil, and I headed up early – big mistake! The event was on the bottom of the ski trail, north and up from the base of the telecabine. At least seven wooden kegs of beer were stacked pyramid style awaiting tapping – and one was tapped awaiting us... As with most of Leysin, the natural slope of the mountain made pouring the beer quite easy – even if standing was a little difficult, especially after the slope got wet with spilled beer. Stones were under the downhill side of the kegs to keep them level. As we drew our first litre of beer, we watched some of the kitchen staff go to work on the fire. As with the beer stack, the fire pit was leveled with the grate set on a single layer of stones on the uphill side and at least three layers stacked on the downhill side. The coals were banked to keep them an equal distance under the grate. Meanwhile Madame Linden worked her magic on the steaks. Each was dipped in a batter of mustard, peppercorns, and cognac.

After watching the setup for a few minutes, Wilds, Gil, and I took our beers to a wide area on the slanted field and sat back to enjoy the sun and scenery. The peaked wall of the Chamossaire hung in front of us like a movie backdrop.

"Where's Kaeti?" Wilds asked.

"She's joinin' us for dinner. She has to study. Hey Gil, why're you batch'n it?"

"Don't ask. Seems like the spring put the brakes on dating up here – just the opposite of back home. Can't wait for the summer. What about you guys?"

Wilds agreed, "Yeah, me too."

After thinking for a moment I said, "I'm not sure guys. This mountain is unreal. I think I could live here... but next year I'm back to the real world. Mega studies and a social life tucked in between bouts of homework."

Wilds asked, "You mean your stateside school? What was that called?"

"Earlham, yeah."

"Why not just go to another school?"

"That'd be tough with my parents in Germany. Besides, I kinda feel… like I need to prove I can make it in a real school." That drew laughs from the two. "I'm not kidding guys. This is fun and all but… it's not real."

Later, after about four litres, or a gallon of beer each, the fire was ready and the steaks were grilling. Kaeti showed up as I was finishing my fifth litre. "Hey, Kaeti, looooking great!" I said as I flashed her my best smile. She was looking great in her blue jeans and white turtleneck, her light brown hair pulled back in a long ponytail.

"Wow, Jim! How much have you had to drink?"

"Only a couple beers. Right guys?" Both Wilds and Gil nodded – *although both of them look a little drunk.*

"Maybe you better slow down, okay?"

"Sure." We each grabbed a plate, steaks, utensils, another beer and went back to our spot on the slope. The steaks were unbelievable! Eating from your lap sitting on the side of the mountain was a little challenging, but it was great having Kaeti beside me again. She positively glowed in the sunlight – even if it was a little hard focusing on her. *God, I miss being around her! Spring's really taking its toll on our relationship. When was our last real date – not counting the beerball game, I wondered?*

After finishing my last bites of steak I hiked up to get another beer. When I returned, Kaeti had gone. I looked down the slope and saw her tawny ponytail disappearing around the bend in the dirt road that brought us up here. "What happened?"

Gil shrugged, "She said she had to study and headed down."

"She needs to have a beer!" Wilds said, waving his mug and spilling some beer on his pants. "Oops!"

"You got it!" I said as I slipped on the slope and quickly dropped on my butt. "Oops!" We all started laughing! *Ouch, I think that hurt!*

Wilds said, "DAMN, how'd you do that without spilling a DROP?"

I stared around and found my mug in my hand, upright and ready to drink. "Practice!" I said a little dazed. My right cheek started to sting. *I think I landed on a rock!*

That was just the beginning. After that much beer, I couldn't stop. We watched the party swirling around us. I envied the couples wrestling in a patch of snow shadowed by some trees on the south side of our slanted field. Baby John in bellbottoms and a flowered shirt was playing his guitar and wandering among the groups like a troubadour. Gil, Wilds, and I just sat around, talked – and drank more beer. Sometime in the late afternoon, as dark clouds started rolling over our mountain, I started talking about the end of school and Kaeti.

"You know, guys. Kaeti is going to be someone I'll really miss – and you two as well, of course. But I miss her already. Things seem to be really slowin' down between us."

Wilds said, "Maybe she's just studying. Finals aren't that far away."

Gil added, "Or maybe it's just the end of ski season. There just isn't as much to do up here after the melt…"

"Yeah, but she's soooo cool," I droned on as Wilds and Gil began ignoring me. "I miss her, already. Should I tell her?" No one answered me. Out of the corner of my eye I thought I saw Wilds glance at me and shake his head as he looked behind my back at Gil. *I think I'm drunk.*

After a half dozen more beers, I remember talking about the German beer drinking contests I'd witnessed. "I was at the PISS wall when the WINNER of the beer CHUGGING contest walked in and MADE himself ssSICK so he could GO BACK and drink more." With WHAT was left OF MY inebriated brain THAT seemed a very CLEVER thing to do. "You know GUYS, we won't get a… we won't get HUNGOVER if we BARF it all back UP!" I wandered off into a wooded area to take a leak for the two-hundredth time and stuck my finger down my throat. *I am CLEVER!*

Somewhere after twenty litres, I lost count, the sun disappeared, and someone started a light show. WOW, it was really BIZZARE! Wiggly flashes of lights floated across the sky. I lay on my back on the slope staring at the sky watching the show until my revelry was interrupted with someone pushing my shoulder.

"Jim!" Kaeti said with an edge of annoyance.

"What?" I asked, still staring at the show.

"What the hell are you doing?"

"Kaeti, YOU here? Grreat s' LIGHT show!" I slurred.

"What light show? It's raining, that's lightning! We need to get you off the mountain."

"Why's it allll WEEE-GLY?"

"Could be the water pooling in your eyes."

"REALLY? Cool! Hey, wher's Wil's?" I slurred as I sat up, shook the water off my face, and stared around me. I didn't see anyone, and the light flashes made the earth seem to be sitting at a weird tilt. My head fell slowly over to my shoulder trying to find level. "– or GIL?"

"They're gone. We need to get you home."

A flash of light illuminated Kaeti beside me. She looked like she had just crawled out of a swimming pool after falling in fully dressed. She wasn't standing up straight either – or... the EARTH was tilted! My head fell onto my other shoulder. I put my arm around Kaeti to steady myself as I stood. "Soun's like a GREAT idea! Le's go TOGET'r. My place 'RR yours?"

"Yours – by yourself. I think you need your rest."

"NOT with YOU! I misss-you!" I tried to lean in to get a kiss, but Kaeti turned her head away while bracing me against her side.

"Let's get you back first, okay?"

"SSSS'OoooKAY! Coool show, though!" I said looking up again until my head fell against my back and Kaeti steadied me. I could just feel the raindrops bouncing off my eyeballs and the water pooling in my open mouth...

The walk back took forever. I hit every stone. Kaeti supported me as I nearly fell a dozen times just getting to the dirt road. "DAMN! I think I'm DRUNK! – I misss-you!"

"I know. Let's keep walking."

The lights of a car were visible through the rain. "There'ssa CAR comin'."

"I see it. We'll move off the road."

I was back to tripping over stones again. But the car lights kept getting brighter, like it was coming right at us. "LOOK OUT, Kaeti! The car'ss acomin'!"

"It's okay. We're off the road. We're safe here."

Pushing her to the side. "NO, itss comin'!"

"Hey, careful! It's steep over there." She said pushing me back. "We're safe here! Don't worry!"

"Okay." I said as I tripped again. "I misss-you!" I must have done that two or three more times before the car passed. It seemed to be taking an eternity to get safely by us. Once the car was past, it was forgotten. Actually, one of the times I slipped and admitted that I missed Dick, too. Maybe I hadn't quite come to grips with that yet... The next and last thing I remembered was someone, maybe Kaeti, pulling off my wet boots and clothes, toweling the water from my hair, and lowering me onto my bed. "I misss-you!" *I hope that was Kaeti.* DARKNESS!

The next day I woke with a miserable hangover. The barfing hadn't worked... *Whose idea was that?* I wondered. I took some aspirin and got Wilds to take me to the Parisienne. He and Gil were definitely in better shape than I was. While I was sitting at one of the tables nursing my second cup of hot tea and picking at a croissant, Kaeti showed up.

"Want some company?"

"Yeah... Ah, no... I feel like crap!"

"No wonder! You trying to kill yourself yesterday?"

"No, just stupid, I guess." That admission and the nauseous ache in my stomach almost brought a tear to my eye.

"You said something coming back down to the school about missing me..."

I blinked, shook my head – a painful motion that brought tears to my eyes! – I looked down hiding my face. After a moment I said, "I wondered if I'd said that. I'm sorry!"

"Why? I'm not! I miss us, too."

That brought my head up quickly! An ice pick was plunged into my forehead and immediately removed. "Ahhh... What?" I squeeked out.

"That's what I want to know, Jim. What's going on? We used to have such fun."

I looked at Kaeti as a wave of nausea hit me. "Ugh!" Deep breath. "You want me to think?" I whined. "Ummm... Not sure..." Shaking my head again, more slowly this time. "I think Wilds said something about ski season being over and not having anything to do together."

"Is that really it? We have nothing else in common..."

"Except dancing..." I added with a pitiful smile that caused Kaeti to beam one back as she agreed.

"There is that! – There must be something else this mountain is good for. Scenery... hiking... what about a picnic?"

"Uh! – I don't think that I'm up for that today..." I groaned.

"Next Saturday – I'll get the kitchen to make us sandwiches."

Closing my eyes and lowering my head again as another wave of nausea hit. Then I looked up pleading at Kaeti. "Ask me tomorrow,... I'm sure I'll say 'yes.'" Nodding slightly.

"Get some rest. You look horrible!"

"Gee, thanks! Now, go away!" As Kaeti walked away she added an extra sway to her step, then turned to see if I'd noticed. I gave her as much of a smile as I could muster, but a question came on her face and she turned, walked back, leaned on the table, and looked at me.

"One question," she said. "Didn't you notice the thunder?"

Thunder, what thunder? "Huh?"

Seeing my total lack of comprehension, she just shook her head sadly, turned and walked away – less sway this time. My story of that night was recreated from the story told by Kaeti and my friends over and over again at my expense. Oh, after a while I remembered flashes of the events, like seeing soaked Kaeti standing at a funny slant, not remembering that I was sitting on the side of the mountain. And I distinctly remember the car's headlights. Kaeti later showed me the slope I almost pushed us down trying to avoid them. The descent would have been more falling than tumbling. *Stupid! Stupid! STUPID!*

Chapter Thirty Seven

Old Friends

The hangover actually lasted a couple of more days. I didn't feel normal until Wednesday. By Saturday, I was ready for anything that didn't involve beer... Kaeti and I got together about 10 in the morning and headed for the telecabine. It felt strange hiking to the lift without skis – just tossing sack lunches and an old blanket onto the seat across from us in the lift. When we got out at the top, we hid our lunch and blanket between some rocks and hiked around for a while. The ground was saturated and slick. We slid down the steeper areas in our hiking boots, but it was muddy enough that you didn't want to fall. The cowsheds and the pond had mysteriously reappeared, although the sheds hid large piles of snow on their north side. There were still large patches of snow in many of the other deeply shadowed areas, including the split rock where we had played around the white whale last fall. I told Kaeti about it, and she remembered seeing it, too. She didn't say when or how, and I didn't ask. That was another time and another life.

About noon, we went back up to the top of the Berneuse and retrieved our lunches. We laid the blanket out on top of some flat rocks that were relatively dry and sat in the sun. The wind was chilly, but the sun was baking our backs; the peaks and mountains surrounded us. As we ate, I told Kaeti of my hike to the top of the Tour D'Ai, my harrowing crossing, and the peace I found with the small flower on top of the world. We considered making the trek again, but things were a little wet and slippery this early in the season. We agreed to try it another time. Kaeti's plan for today was to walk down the ski trails. That would be hazardous enough!

While we were looking toward the Chamossaire, a large black rook soared over our heads and then off over the valley. I said, "I often have dreams of flying over these mountains. Especially after watching the Swiss Air Force fly these peaks."

"I didn't know that you wanted to fly airplanes."

"I don't – well that would be fun, but my dreams don't include airplanes. I fly like superman! It's pretty cool! You need to find a large cliff and dive off. Then when you have enough speed, you stretch out your arms, like a swan dive, and catch the wind on your chest. That blows you back up into the air. Then it's kinda like swimming through the air. It's pretty amazing! I'd fly around these peaks and down the valley."

"Sounds fun!"

"You know, in my dreams, I take you by the hand and teach you to fly with me. The first time you stayed holding my hand, but later you flew on your own. We'd fly circles around each other."

"Nice! I never remember my dreams. I'm sure I've had a lot about skiing, but I'm not sure what happens. How do you remember them?"

"Practice. If you have an exceptional dream, stay in bed and review it while you're waking. It stays with you longer. Sometimes, I swear, I can change my dreams. If I crash and wake up, I replay the dream and change the ending – find a way to survive!"

"Really, like nightmares?"

"Sure! Although I rarely have nightmares." Saying that I flashed back to the dream about the crash and burn with the Mini. "I can usually do that... Not always."

To get that out of my mind a crazy thought popped into my head, "Hey, at days like this I feel like I can really do it!" I stood quickly and started running from our level area into the wind down a slight grade, then dove headfirst down the slope. As I hit the peak of the dive, I arched into a swan, then snapped forward landing in a forward roll on the muddy earth.

I heard a yelp coming from Kaeti. She hadn't seen me do gymnastics before, even something this simple. My roll brought me back to my feet, and I turned as she came running up and into me, bowling me over. We went down together, Kaeti on top. "Damn, sometimes you're insane!

I couldn't see you over the top. I... You're nuts!" she shouted as she punched me. We were laughing as we got back up. Unfortunately, I got the worst of it. I had sheltered Kaeti from the soggy ground. There was mud on my hands and down my back from the roll and then up one side from where Kaeti knocked me down.

"You haven't seen me do gymnastics before, have you? I wasn't much on equipment, but my floor ex is pretty good." I threw a round-off but slipped a little before launching a back handspring and ended up sliding on my butt in the mud. "Great!" Wiping the fresh mud off my butt, I said, "I believe that I'll show off in a drier area, okay?"

"Good idea!"

We used the clean side of the blanket to scrape off the bulk of the mud before we started the hike down. The walk was slippery but beautiful. I tried to imagine it covered in snow, but it seemed like a different mountain. We walked hand in hand down the trail. What you could run on skis in minutes took over an hour on foot, but I felt alive and our friendship blossomed again. At first we didn't talk much, just walked and enjoyed. I saw a small bird that I didn't recognize hop between a couple of trees. With a little imagination it looked like the painted bird in the cuckoo clocks, but I didn't hear its call.

Somewhere above the field of moguls where I had taken my fall, Kaeti asked, "Was Dick a friend of yours?"

"Not really. Why do you ask?" I said defensively.

"You said something about missing him the other night on our rainy walk back from the bar-b-que."

"Did I?"

"Yeah."

"I'm not sure I want to talk about that now!"

Kaeti didn't push it, but after walking in silence for a few minutes I opened up about the guilt I felt that I hadn't been a better friend. She just listened and put her arm around me as we walked. I felt better after that walk. You know, there's no magic or mind reading going on at times like this. The secret is just talking and listening – especially listening...

As we hiked down the slope toward the site of the Beer-B-Que, I realized that this area was the last field of moguls before the telecabine, and that the road that I had stumbled down with Kaeti that rainy night was the depression where I almost lost my life! *Man, does this field look different without snow – there aren't even any bumps where the moguls used to be!*

The following weekend it was my turn. I talked to Gil about how to find the waterfall where he and Spyder had picnicked last fall. The one where Spyder fell climbing the rock face. He gave me general directions, but indicated that it was a long walk. The day before the picnic, I went to the *fromager* for some Gruyere cheese and to the general store for a bottle of Yvorne wine. That morning I picked up a fresh demi-loaf of French bread from the Parisienne. I carried the wine, food, and a blanket in a small backpack that I had borrowed from Willie. I met Kaeti at the main at about 9:30 am. I had hoped to get a ride at least part way with Issa, but he wasn't around, as usual. We walked through the village and down the road out of town when a car came buzzing up behind us. Without thinking, I turned and waved. "Allow, Jeem!" someone called from inside an older black Fiat. It was the young guy from the delivery van that took Wilds and me out of Leysin a few months back.

"Hi! Ah…" *What's his name?* "Remember Kaeti?"

"Certainly! I am Claude. Where you go?"

I described our route to the waterfall as best as I could. At first Claude looked confused until I pointed to a general area on the side of the Chamossaire. "Water - Fall! – *Eau - Decende!*" I said with accompanying hand motions.

"Certainly, yes. Vache Pissant! I will take you to path!"

He drove down out of Leysin and a short way up the road toward Gstaad, then pulled into a dirt road that wound up the side of the Chamossaire. Where the road ended he pulled to a halt and showed us the path. We thanked him before he sped away.

"Who was that?" Kaeti asked.

"Not exactly sure, but I think he was the guy at the snack bar on top of the telecabine. He gave Wilds and me a ride the day we picked up the Mini. He seemed to remember you, though!"

"Me how?"

"Aside from your long, beautiful, blonde hair?" I said grinning knowing her reaction in advance.

"Not blonde!" she snapped!

Holding my hands up defensively, I said, "I didn't say it! And I think he was also impressed with your skiing style!"

"A Swiss kid? Now I know you're kidding! What'd he call this place?"

"Don't look at me! Sounded like he said 'cow piss.'"

"Oh, really romantic!" she said with fake disgust. "I have to admit –" She smiled, "– that's what I thought, too!"

"You don't suppose..."

"Nah, we just didn't understand."

Then, turning my attention to the trail, "I've never been to the falls before, but it should be up this trail a little ways. Unlike Spyder, I'm not climbing the rocks to show off for you, though!"

"Darn!" she said with a grin as she took my arm. The trail was steep but nothing we couldn't handle. Without company I probably would have considered jogging it. Never did like walking up hills. After a little while, we spotted a small raucous stream dancing between the trees and down the mountainside.

We heard the falls before we saw them. The roar grew louder, and a heavy mist enveloped us as we entered a thicket of trees. The falls were hidden in a dark area between trees and a cliff face; they were spectacular! They spilled off a rock ledge about fifty feet over our heads then cascaded across scattered stones and ledges before accumulating in a small pool at the base. Actually, they were overwhelming in their intensity. Perhaps the spring thaw was feeding them. Their spray was soaking everything around the base, and the sound was so loud that we couldn't speak to each other. "God!" I yelled over the thunder. "There must be a lot of cows up there today!"

"Jim!" she exclaimed as she smiled disgusted, shook her head, and pushed me.

We were forced to move back down the trail to a drier, quieter area in the trees and stretched out our blanket near the stream. You could just see the Berneuse between the trees, but you couldn't see the main falls from where we settled. A heavy mist was swirling in the area where we had last seen the falls. The gurgling of the nearby stream now dominated the distant roar of the falls, – oh and we now could talk and kiss. The Gruyere cheese was dry and heavy, but it hit the spot with the wine. The crust on the bread was almost impenetrable, but the soft inners were worth the fight. We gouged them out. They added the right texture to mate the wine and cheese. After eating interrupted by gentle kissing and nuzzling, Kaeti looked into my eyes and said, "You know Jim, I don't know whether I've told you this before, but I love kissing you. It's like you enjoy kissing me."

"I do!" Then shaking my head, "But I don't understand."

"Oh, a lot of guys kiss just to get more – you know – but, with you, it's just fun!"

"I love it too. It just feels right. We can talk about 'more' later…" I joked!

We fell back into a kiss for a while until Kaeti asked, "Jim, do you ever wonder what it's like?"

"Sex?"

She nodded.

"Yes, all the time."

"It scares me."

"I didn't think anything scared you Kaeti! – well, except maybe my driving!" We laughed and went back to necking. Then caressing her cheek, "Well you don't have to worry with me."

"I know. That's… that has made this year special!"

"Yes it has."

We were a little damp and chilled as we started the hike back. I put my arm around Kaeti and could feel her shivering. "Hold on!" I said as I dropped my pack and stripped my ski jacket.

"No, Jim, you need that!"

"Hey, I'm not crazy. Wait." I had layered my wool brown and tan plaid Pendleton shirt over my white nylon turtleneck. I figured that I could survive with the turtleneck and jacket, and give my wool shirt to Kaeti. I took off the shirt and gave it to her. "Here, the wool will keep you warm, even when it's damp."

"Thanks!" She gave me a hug and pulled off her jacket, gave it to me, and began putting the shirt on. I rested on a stone while she buttoned it up.

Watching her, my eyes were drawn to the peaks behind her. It was the Berneuse. I was stunned. *I've seen this before! Where? When?* Kaeti reached up and pulled her ponytail out of my shirt and dropped it over her right shoulder onto her chest.

"Hold it!" I shouted! She froze and looked a little startled. I slid off the stone and squatted until I saw Kaeti's head silhouetted in the Berneuse, pines framing either side. "Unbelievable!" She smiled, then looked over her shoulder to see what I was looking at. *It's my dream! She wasn't floating! We were on the opposite mountain looking back at the Berneuse! That's my shirt on Kaeti. Why didn't I recognize it?*

"You're not going to believe this!" I said as I ran over to hold her. "I dreamed about that moment on the way back from the formal on Lac Léman! You were so... you looked so... comfortable in my shirt. Unreal!"

"Really? Is that possible?" she asked as she covered my shirt with her jacket.

"I didn't think it was possible, but it just happened!" I pointed out the mountains behind her, described what I had dreamed and why I didn't believe it could ever come true. I'm not sure that she believed me, but we stood there drinking in the beauty of our mountain from this side of the valley until I felt her shiver again. Without my wool shirt, I soon joined her. We needed to get moving to keep warm.

The hike back to the road up to Leysin went quickly as I described my thoughts about déjà vu. Infrequently I had almost still-life dreams that were so out-of-character given my usual active dreams, and I would try to store those memories until something similar happened. This was the third time I actually remembered the dream. Before that I just went through that déjà vu shock without knowing why. Kaeti was interested but skeptical. I couldn't blame her. A couple of cars passed us on the way back to the village, but the walk was fun and the discussion interesting. We talked about dream symbolism.

Kaeti said, "You talked about flying dreams before. Kathy says they are very sensual."

"Oh yeah! If Kathy thinks those are sexy, she needs to be along for some of my real 'sensual' dreams!"

"Behave!"

"I'll try! Did you ask her what skiing dreams symbolize? Like you, I have those a lot too!" *Especially with you,* I thought. I flashed back to the skiing part of the dream on Saas Fee, then to the other exciting parts!

"In fact, I did!" Kaeti interrupted my fanaticizing and recited. "If they're like practice... certain skills or places you've just been, they're just memories. But if they are like soaring or floating down perfect mountains, they are sensual, too. So you're not the only one with sensual dreams."

I laughed nervously and hugged her to my side as we walked, but she noticed my tension. "What?"

"I won't go there!"

"Where?"

I shook my head. "Uh – Uh." *I am going to get myself into trouble...*

"You have to tell me now!"

"Ahhh... Can I just say that it was a typical guy's fantasy that involved you and... well it was very intense? The strange thing is that I wasn't sure about how I felt about you then. You were still dating Tiny and... we were just friends... This is embarrassing!"

"Don't be! I've had them too. Just not that early! Getting a little ahead of yourself, weren't you?"

"Hey, I've learned from psych class, there's no controlling the subconscious!" We laughed and walked with our arms around each other back to the main. Before Kaeti went up the stairs that afternoon I caught her hand. "I had fun! We need to keep this up! You know, Kaeti, I wouldn't trade your friendship for anything!"

"Me, too! Dancing tonight?"

"Absolutely! Even if we have to wake up Herr Dietrick."

Kaeti almost ran up the stairs, turned, flicked her ponytail over her shoulder and winked, before disappearing into the dorm.

I wish that I could say that the magic lasted until the end of the year, but being the only couple dancing at the Messange soon got boring, and it was tough coming up with new picnic ideas. Kaeti felt the pressure of end-of-year grades, and I... well, I drank and played *zim-zim* more. My grades plunged back to average – but hell, I was passing, right?

Chapter Thirty Eight

Graduation

We struggled through our finals as the mountainside decided to turn green and the mud dried. Soon bells rang throughout the village signaling the cow's return to higher pastures, and graduation followed in rapid succession. For me and, I am sure, most of the sophomores, this wasn't a real graduation; just two years out of a four-year degree, but the school set a pretty opulent stage. The ballroom was booked at the Grand Hotel in the upper village, and the kitchen began preparing a feast fit for an emperor – in case Haile Selassie should desire to see his grandson graduate. In any case, the parents of many of these students were from wealth and would expect nothing less from their tuition. One rumor was going around that a full quarter of our annual food money was being spent for the feast!

My parents and Millie showed up the Thursday before the event with their little travel trailer behind the Buick wagon. I introduced them to my best friends, Kaeti, Wilds, and Gil, and my family adopted them until their folks showed up. Actually Kaeti's weren't coming from the States, so she was permanently taken under their wings. Oh, my mother gave dad a brief questioning smile when Kaeti returned my Pendleton shirt, but didn't ask me about it. *Kaeti had been a best buddy, ski instructor, girlfriend, lover, and now back to best buddies. It'd be a little odd thinking about her as my sister – NAH! Forget sister – a sister to Millie and a new daughter to mom and dad – but a friend to me!* Maybe I shouldn't add mom to that since she had gone in search of Stallone. He had struck her fancy from their first meeting at the hotel across from the main, and somehow she had learned that his parents weren't coming to graduation either. I'm not sure what Stallone thought about having a mother hen looking after him, but he managed to gracefully pass her back as we were standing outside of the main getting ready for the walk to the Grand Hotel.

The faculty handed out the caps and gowns while we stood there. They were bizarre! No clue where they had found the shimmery metallic gray gowns; but according to Willie, they were doctoral robes complete with the doctoral collars. And the caps were unlike anything any of us had ever seen before. They were floppy black berets the size of a large pizza, and each had an inch wide yellow stripe bisecting them. "Goofy" wasn't an adequate word for the caps. We had no clue how to wear them – not that anyone really wanted to be seen in them. *We're going to graduation as clowns! HELP!* While we were standing around griping about the pizza berets, a shout came down from the second floor of the main, where many single teachers lived. I looked up and spotted Mr. Van Vuuren, our South African commando/ art teacher. "Willie," he shouted, "You got me so pissed last night! Now you have to come up here and help me get dressed!" I looked around and spotted Willie. He looked a little green under his gills as he stared up, sent a half-hearted wave, and walked into the main. About fifteen minutes later Willie and Van Vuuren came marching out the front door arm in arm to the laugher and applause of the sophomores.

When we entered the main ballroom, where the graduation was to be held, we noticed that the high schoolers had normal light blue caps and gowns that looked pretty good. *Damn!* I don't remember too much about the speeches. *Who really listens?* Willie's started, "It was the best of times, the worst of times..." and brought a few chuckles as he hit the high and lowlights of the year. The main speaker was Philippe Mottu from the Moral Rearmament World Center. Not sure whose idea that was, but the guy actually caught my attention for a short while. He could have been a Quaker by the way he talked about peace and recovering from the destruction of war. He also talked about communication being the secret to preventing future wars and hoping that our future would be free of conflicts. If I'd had time, I would have liked to talk to him about Vietnam. Maybe he had a clue what we were doing there – or at least a different perspective.

As the diplomas were passed out, the beautiful, if reclusive, Judy Looker was our Magna Cum Laude. Me? I was happy to be graduating, and my grades should get me off academic probation back in the States – or so I thought! Kaeti, Wilds, Gil, Tiny – all of us paraded across the stage to get our diplomas.

We gathered in front of the hotel for pictures and celebrations; then someone lined up an Oompah band while Dean Zagier ushered us into line. I grabbed Kaeti, and Wilds and Tiny grabbed Kaeti's other arm as we lined up four abreast. Willie and three others were ahead of us and led the procession. Well, he was behind our professors, who were behind the band, but he led our class! The high school staff and the seniors followed us. The march down the cobblestone streets to the lower village started to the tune of some polka beat. Baaaroom! – Oompah! Ba Ba Ba BA! Paba Ba Beetledom Oompah! Beetledom Oompah! Beetledom Oompah! We weren't around the first switchback before Willie and his row headed diagonally to the left across the street. Not to be outdone, Kaeti and I dragged our line in the opposite direction. In seconds, every other row of the graduating sophomores linked arms and began marching diagonally across the street in opposite directions and singing along! "Beetledom Oompah!" Dean Zagier had broken loose from the faculty and was having fits as he darted back and forth along our column, futilely trying to stop us. He pleaded for decorum – for a good example for the high schoolers – but to no avail! We danced arm-in-arm and sang down the windy road all the way to the main. "Beetledom Oompah! OOooMPAH!"

When we returned to our dining room, we found the place transformed. There were ice carvings and fountains of champagne. A whole gigantic salmon was resting in ice on a platter near the stage. Bowls of Russian sturgeon roe – caviar – were placed with butter and crackers in strategic spots around the room. Baby triangular sandwiches with strange green stuff inside, like watercress or cucumbers – and no meat or cheese – were stacked on large trays. Wilds and I got together and searched the room for something resembling real food. Neither of us had a desire for a vegetable sandwich. If we had, they were so small it would take twenty each to fill us! After trying the roe, which James Bond may like but it didn't do anything for me, we combined the crackers with some cheeses from the other side of the room to make a palatable snack. Neither of us was into fish, especially a large cold one that was staring at us, but several parents were digging into the facing side. Eventually Wilds found something resembling super-thinly cut cold cuts rolled and pinned with toothpicks and some decent rolls. After unrolling and flattening a couple of dozen pieces of meat and combining them with the cheese, we had decent sandwiches. The champagne was okay, but the stuff was so volatile that each sip seemed to evaporate on your tongue and go up your nose before you could swallow it. Personally, I considered running down the road and picking up a good bottle of Yvorne wine, but we managed to find some Cokes. Even after a couple of makeshift sandwiches, both of us were considering finding Kaeti and asking her to open the snack bar so we could cook up a hamburger and fries. I know, as Wilds said in Paris, "Mayhaps, we no have ah sophistique palate to apprecia zeez meal?" Translation: We ain't got good taste!

After graduation broke up with sporadic handshakes, well wishes, and a solid if a little tearful hug and kiss from Kaeti – well I was tearing anyway – I took the wheel of our Buick and began dragging the trailer off our mountain down the windy road toward the valley and home.

Epilogue

I left the ACS Zoo and the Magic Mountain happy to continue my journey through life. I would miss Kaeti, Wilds, and Gil, but my life as an army brat had held a lot of these departures. My relationship with Kaeti set the pattern for my successful relationships: friends first, then lovers. The few women I would grow to love after her were independent, strong-willed, and enjoyed life. We were partners or teammates, equally capable of taking the lead and following. Cindy, my wife for over twenty years, is a perfect partner, friend, and companion. I have Kaeti to thank for setting me on that right path.

I tried to catch Wilds in Glasgow, Scotland, the summer after school ended. But while I was crossing the channel, I spotted a lovely young lady who I determined to meet. She turned out to be a member of the Bulgarian folk dance team from Sofia. I befriended the team, and they snuck me on their bus. I learned some new dance steps and even had lunch with Rosemarie a couple of afternoons, but the Soviet cultural attaché assigned to the group kept booting me off her bus in the most inconvenient locations, making hitchhiking to catch up nearly impossible, but that's another story.

When I arrived in Glasgow, Wilds and family had left less than a week before. I didn't have his stateside address. A few years back I caught him briefly on the internet, but so much had changed that we couldn't maintain communication. 'Mayhaps' he wanted to forget his time in the zoo. More recently I heard that Gil was a wedding photographer on Santorini, but I never found a way to get in touch. Hopefully my two friends are enjoying their lives, like I am.

Kaeti is another matter. We lost touch for almost forty years, grew up, got... middle aged... and I caught her through none other than Ronnie, her childhood sweetheart, who was looking for classmates to come to their high school's fortieth reunion. My search for her started when I got stuck recalling our relationship. I remembered the high and low points but needed some help putting it back together. She and I remained in constant communication on the internet as I developed the end of the book. I was delighted that she found my memory of her very accurate and insightful! – even more delighted that she remembered me fondly, too!

I have heard more about several of the more famous classmates. Stallone went into spaghetti westerns after leaving college and ended up writing and starring in his own movies, as many of you may have guessed. He never used his given name at ACS, but who can blame him! Who would want to be a nineteen-year-old sharing the name of a cartoon cat? I met him on a shoot in New York City. Some movie about terrorists hijacking a cable car. Hey, as long as it sells! He didn't remember his frat brother and former center on his Swiss football team, but with his lifestyle, who can blame him!

I have heard a variety of tales about Prince Paul after his grandfather, Haile Selassie, was overthrown. He was imprisoned in a castle in Ethiopia with hot and cold running women; he escaped and was in hiding in England with his buddy Prince Charles; and he was working for an internet firm somewhere in California. I have no clue what his true fate is. Many Ethiopians believe that he is still alive, which is more than they can say for most of the rest of his family.

I heard that Issa became a leader of the Arab world – at least he is in Geneva as a representative of some very powerful individuals.

Willie made a fortune in Silicon Valley, spent it, made it again, and is now playing a harmonica and living out of a van somewhere between LA and Boston – although he keeps his hands on his business on the internet. Don't ask him what that business currently is, you may not want to know! He provided unbelievable help in putting together details about the year I had forgotten and in keeping me motivated.

One odd note that Willie brought up – the long-haired Mod – Baby John was seen a few years after graduation playing for a band in Stockholm. He subsequently disappeared and a search by his wealthy girlfriend, Alice-In-Wonderland, could find no record that he or his family ever existed…

Oh, and green-eyed Colleen married Yves and lived happily in Switzerland for decades. They had two fine boys before they grew apart. She currently lives in Montana near her sons. Yves is still in Switzerland, I guess.

Me? I drove a Mini with a small Swiss flag on the grill and an oval EU (Europe United) sticker on the trunk back to my stateside college, determined to prove that I could make it in a real academic institution. I figured that my ACS grades would help my GPA, even if the classes weren't up to Earlham's standards. Unfortunately, Earlham must have been aware of ACS's reputation because my grades were brought back only as pass/fail. My GPA wasn't affected, and I was back on academic probation. It was a rough road, but I eventually graduated with a major in poly sci/ international relations. However, I have never used the training. It is safe to say that my career has been successful, but filled with challenges and plenty of falls! These were met with dogged determination, as Bennie's lesson flashed in my head. "Still learning!"

Skiing? I will always love it… college in Indiana was not the place to do it, but my parents returned from Germany to Colorado. I spent that winter as a ski bum but never returned to racing – I just learned to love other mountains with my skis. My son, a snowboarder, is currently in college and surviving his own adventures – Please!! I pray that he is a little more careful than his old man was.